Italian in 32 Lessons

By Adrienne

French in 32 Lessons
German in 32 Lessons
Spanish in 32 Lessons
Italian in 32 Lessons

The Gimmick Series for the more advanced student

Français parlé
gesprochenes Deutsch
Español hablado
Italiano parlato

The Gimmick Series

Italian in 32 Lessons

Adrienne

adapted by Teresa Powell-Smith Bonvecchiato

W · W · NORTON & COMPANY

NEW YORK   LONDON

Library of Congress Cataloging-in-Publication Data
Adrienne.
    Italian in 32 lessons.
    1. Italian language—Text—books for foreigners.
I. Bonvecchiato, Teresa Powell-Smith. II. Title.
III. Title: Italian in thirty-two lessons
PO1128.A37   1983   458.2´421   82-14146

ISBN 0-393-31346-8

W. W. Norton & Company, Inc., 500 Fifth Avenue, New York, N.Y. 10110
W. W. Norton & Company Ltd., 10 Coptic Street, London WC1A 1PU

  2 3 4 5 6 7 8 9 0

For Carolyn and Jimmy McGown
and their grandfather

Preface

The Gimmicks for the more advanced student have been found so useful by
so many — in French, German, Spanish and English — throughout Europe
and America — that I have prepared a method to meet the needs of students
at an earlier stage of language learning. There is much to criticise in present
methods.

Beginners aren't imbeciles!
The boring repetition of inane exercises in 'modern' methods is an insult to
the intelligence. To repeat, endlessly, structured sentences is a sure way to
kill the discovery of one's own style. Without the freedom to make mistakes,
the student will never learn to 'feel' the language. This is why, after a year or
more of study, the student, often, can barely get a sentence out on his own.
Emphasis on constant structuring discourages creativity, and speaking a
language is a creative process.

Forced feeding
It's no good having perfect grammar if your vocabulary is limited to a few
words. This is THE problem in language learning, for a language IS ITS
VOCABULARY. Grammar and writing exercises over and over should not be
dwelt on ridiculously. It will come automatically if vocabulary is learned
properly. It doesn't matter if the beginner is lost . . . confused. Beginners are
not fragile. They won't break. I don't ask mine to understand. I ask them to
learn . . . hundreds of words. The theorist may need high grammar. Mr and Ms
John Q. Public need words in order to understand and be understood.
Vocabulary should be programmed and progressive — and gobbled up.

Tests
TESTS ARE ABSOLUTELY INDISPENSABLE FOR THOSE WHO WANT
TO LEARN A LANGUAGE IN LESS THEN TEN YEARS! You can be
tested by the teacher or by a friend. Each lesson should be well tested,
written if possible, to make sure the words are 'in the head' and not just in
the book. And, as learning is rarely 'solid' the first time, the same test should
be repeated throughout the year. You must memorize hundreds, thousands
of words. There is no way to communicate without words. I don't care how
perfect your grammar is.

Mistakes are an asset!
Making mistakes is one of the principal ways the student learns a language . . .
when it really sinks in. For verbs there is nothing better. Written resumés are
excellent for this reason, and the student should write them for homework

as of the first lessons: at first a small paragraph about his house, job, family, etc., and then a page summary of a movie, etc. This is the way he will find his style.

Homework
Homework is always a good thing — if only studying for constant vocabulary tests. Written summaries are an excellent way to ensure that verbs and vocabulary are being assimilated.

Pace
A very good class can assimilate one lesson a week (a once- or twice-a-week class). Those with less time might need two to three weeks for each lesson.

Not strictly kosher!
When necessary to facilitate learning, I have sacrificed strict grammatical explanations. The purist may frown on this, but the student will understand more easily. As it is easier to learn a group of words rather than the classic one-to-one translation, the vocabulary is taught by association.

Institut audio-visuel
Those who want to contact me personally should write to: Adrienne, IAV, 40 rue de Berri, 75008 Paris, France.

The ideal lesson
An ideal lesson might include:
— 15 minutes: the students ask each other questions to begin the class — using the verbs and vocabulary they have learned.
— 20 minutes: oral summary of a story, film, etc.
— 15 minutes: test (written and corrected).
— 15 minutes: grammar drills and vocabulary explanation from book, etc.
— 20 minutes: read story or article — they give quick summaries.

Optional
— 10 minutes: dictation.
— 20 minutes: debate.
— 20 minutes: scene playing.

BOXED IN

The 'boxes' are there to concentrate your attention on the vital basic skeleton of language. Read and assimilate each well. Then learn the vocabulary by heart, always testing yourself by writing it down. Next do the exercises, correcting your work with the key at the end of the book. Each lesson represents about one week's work. After years and years of teaching executives, journalists, actors, ministers and diplomats — this method works! This is the best class text or 'self-learner' in town!!

Contents/Indice

Italian in 32 Lessons

LEZIONE 1

E' UNA SEDIA NERA?   Is it a black chair?

Sì, è una sedia nera.   Yes, it's a black chair.
No, non è una sedia nera.   No, it isn't a black chair.

CHE COS'E'?   What is it?

E' una sedia nera.   It's a black chair.

1 = **uno**   2 = **due**   3 = **tre**   4 = **quattro**   5 = **cinque**

translate:

1) Is it a big table?
2) It isn't a black door.
3) See you soon.
4) Is it a little dog?
5) Darn it!
6) It isn't a big black book, but a big blue book.
7) What is it? — It's a watch.
8) Is it a red telephone?
9) It isn't a little chair.
10) Is it a white alarm-clock?

note: — words in Italian are either masculine or feminine — with no logic
to guide you!
— before s (followed by consonant) and z the masculine article
becomes uno: e.g. uno studente (a student), uno zio (an uncle).
— before a vowel una becomes un': e.g. un'aranciata (an orangeade)

ADJECTIVES

un libro **nero**   →   **una** sedia **nera**

note: — adjectives ending in -e remain the same for the feminine: e.g. un
albero verde (a green tree), una foglia verde (a green leaf).
— rosa (pink), blu (blue) are invariable.

give the affirmative and negative answers:

1) E' un gatto piccolo?
2) E' un cane bianco?
3) E' un telefono blu?
4) E' un muro bianco?
5) E' un libro grosso?
6) E' una penna?
7) E' un orologio blu marino?
8) E' una matita nera?
9) E' una sedia?
10) E' una libreria grande?
11) E' un topo bianco?
12) E' una porta?
13) E' una porta verde?
14) E' una sveglia rosa?

The sign ≠ in the following vocabulary section means 'associated opposite'
and refers to the words in the fourth column.

VOCABOLARIO

	traduzione = translation	sinonimo-associato = associated synonym	contrario-associato = associated opposite
1. (un) gatto	cat	(un) topo = mouse	(un) cane = dog
2. (un) tavolo	table ≠ chair		(una) sedia
3. sì	yes		no = no
4. buon giorno	hello ≠ good-bye	ciao, salve	arrivederci, buon giorno
5. ancora una volta	again	di nuovo	
6. (una) penna	pen ≠ pencil		(una) matita, (un) lapis
7. (un) telefono	telephone		
8. (un) muro	wall		
9. (un) orologio	/watch/clock	(una) sveglia = alarm-clock	
10. (una) porta	door	(una) finestra = window, (una) vetrina = shop-window	
11. /e/o	/and/or	ma = but	
12. nero	black		bianco = white
13. accidenti!	darn it!, damn it!	maledizione! porca miseria! = shit!	
14. piccolo	little ≠ big		grande, grosso
15. /il(i) la(le) /un(una)	/the/a		
16. rosso	red	rosa = pink	
17. blu	blue	blu marino = navy blue	
18. (un) libro	book	(una) libreria = bookstore	
19. (un) compito	/homework/task		
20. a più tardi	see you soon		

LEZIONE 2

SONO LIBRI INTERESSANTI?   Are they interesting books?

Sì, sono libri interessanti.   Yes, they're interesting books.
No, non sono libri interessanti.   No, they aren't interesting books.

note: — adjectives are usually placed after the noun.
       — the following adjectives may be shortened if placed before a
         masculine noun:
         buo<u>no</u> = good (un buo<u>n</u> ragazzo = a good boy)
         gran<u>de</u> = big, great (un gra<u>n</u> giardino = a big garden)
         bell<u>o</u> = beautiful (un be<u>l</u> quadro = a beautiful picture).

CHE COSA SONO?   What are they?

Sono sigarette.   They're cigarettes.

translate:
1) How are you? Fine, thank you, and you?
2) Are they cigarettes?
3) Are they black coats?
4) I'm sorry. I apologize.
5) Are they big books?
6) Time's up.
7) What are they? They're pencils.
8) That's it.
9) They're poor kids.
10) Could you repeat it, please?

note: each lesson should begin with a drill of the previous lesson and a quick
      written test.

SINGULAR	→	PLURAL
un libro (a book)	→	**libri/dei libri** (some books)
una lezione (a lesson)	→	**lezioni/delle lezioni** (some lessons)

note: — the plural is usually formed by changing the last vowel into i; some
    irregulars are: men = uomini, fingers = dita, eggs = uova.
  — those feminine nouns and adjectives which end in — a form the
    plural in -e: e.g. una donna bella (a beautiful woman) → donne belle
    (beautiful women).
  — if the noun is plural, the adjective is also plural.
  — nouns ending with a consonant remain the same in the plural:
    e.g. un autobus = a bus → due autobus = two buses.
  — most words ending in /co/go/ca/ga change to /chi/ghi/che/ghe in the
    plural: e.g. albergo = hotel → alberghi, ricco = rich → ricchi.

UN/IL CAPPOTTO BIANCO = A/THE WHITE COAT

un/il — article
cappotto — noun
bianco — adjective

---

6 = **sei**   7 = **sette**   8 = **otto**   9 = **nove**   10 = **dieci**

put in the plural:

un tipo debole	una via larga
una ragazza piccola	una carta spessa
un bimbo forte	una stanza piccola
una donna ricca	un libro rosso
un calzino nero	una chiave grande
un cappotto lungo	una scatola blu
un tipo grosso	un bimbo mite
un uomo vecchio	un fiammifero sottile
un ragazzo giovane	un cappotto leggero
un lapis lungo	un tipo povero
un accendino corto	un'ultima lezione
una vecchia sveglia	un primo bambino
un buon vecchio libro	un tavolo pesante
una notte lunga	un vecchio cane
un buon albergo	un disco italiano

give the affirmative and negative answers; then give the singular form of each question:

1) Sono donne interessanti?
2) Sono uomini forti?
3) Sono bambini poveri?
4) Sono tipi miti?
5) Sono sigarette buone?
6) Sono scarpe nere?
7) Sono pantofole rosse?
8) Sono calzini bianchi?
9) Sono stanze grandi?
10) Sono ragazze giovani?
11) Sono fiammiferi lunghi?
12) Sono bimbi buoni?
13) Sono chiavi vecchie?
14) Sono buche gialle?
15) Sono dischi italiani?
16) Sono alberghi buoni?

IL/I — LA/LE	=	THE
il libro = the book (masculine)	→	**i libri** = the books
la sedia = the chair (feminine)	→	**le sedie** = the chairs

note: — il is replaced by lo before an s followed by a consonant and before z, and by gli in the plural (lo studente = the student, gli studenti = the students).
   — lo and la become l' before a vowel (e.g. l'uomo = the man, l'aranciata = the orangeade).
   — the plural of l' (masculine) is gli (gli uomini = the men).

E'	NERO IL GATTO?	Is the cat black?
	NERA LA GATTA?	
Sì,	il gatto è nero. la gatta è nera.	Yes, the cat is black.
No,	il gatto non è nero. la gatta non è nera.	No, the cat isn't black.

note: il gatto = male cat, la gatta = female cat.

give the singular and plural negative answers:

e.g. E' nero il gatto?

      — No, il gatto non è nero.

      — No, i gatti non sono neri.

1) E' alta la donna?
2) E' debole l'uomo?
3) E' grosso il libro?
4) E' piccola la stanza?
5) E' interessante la lezione?
6) E' pesante il tavolo?
7) E' blu l'impermeabile?
8) E' piccola la scarpa?
9) E' magro il bambino?
10) E' giovane la donna?
11) E' nero il cappello?
12) E' basso il tipo?
13) E' sopra il tavolo la scarpa?
14) E' sopra la sedia il portacenere?
15) E' bianca la prima porta?
16) E' lunga l'ultima lezione?
17) E' sotto la sedia la pantofola?
18) E' ricca la donna?
19) E' larga la via?
20) E' rosso il calzino?
21) E' giovane l'uomo?
22) E' sopra la scatola l'accendino?
23) E' forte il ragazzo?
24) E' grassa la ragazza?
25) E' cattivo il marmocchio?
26) E' buona la sigaretta?

translate and answer in the negative, singular and plural:
e.g. Sono tipi interessanti?
    — Are they interesting guys?
    — No, non sono tipi interessanti.
    — No, non è un tipo interessante.

1) Sono orologi blu?
2) Sono uomini grassi?
3) Sono donne alte?
4) Sono scatole gialle?
5) Sono scarpe grandi?
6) Sono vie corte?
7) Sono bambini belli?
8) Sono impermeabili lunghi?
9) Sono cappelli verdi?
10) Sono stanze grandi?
11) Sono gatti neri?
12) Sono calzini gialli?
13) Sono tipi forti?
14) Sono libri spessi?
15) Sono librerie grandi?
16) Sono lezioni corte?
17) Sono tipi ricchi?
18) Sono cani grossi?
19) Sono scarpe marroni?
20) Sono sigarette cattive?
21) Sono cappotti pesanti?
22) Sono buche rosse?
23) Sono chiavi grandi?
24) Sono stivali neri?
25) Sono topi bianchi?
26) Sono muri bassi?

put in the interrogative, singular and plural:
e.g. E' un orologio.
        — E' un orologio?
        — Sono orologi?

1)   E' una donna giovane.
2)   E' una stanza piccola.
3)   E' una scatola grande.
4)   E' un portacenere giallo.
5)   E' una donna interessante.
6)   E' un bambino mite.
7)   E' un fiammifero lungo.
8)   E' un accendino bello.
9)   E' una via stretta.
10)   E' un cappotto leggero.
11)   E' una donna vecchia.
12)   E' un tipo cattivo.
13)   E' un cane nero.
14)   E' una sveglia verde.
15)   E' un uomo ricco.
16)   E' un muro alto.
17)   E' un libro vecchio.
18)   E' la prima lezione.
19)   E' un giorno lungo.
20)   E' una notte nera.
21)   E' un gatto bianco.
22)   E' un libro sottile.
23)   E' un tavolo pesante.
24)   E' un marmocchio buono?
25)   E' un impermeabile verde.
26)   E' un ragazzo debole.

translate:

1) Would you repeat it, please?
2) The child is under the table.
3) That's not it.
4) The ashtray isn't on the chair.
5) The streets aren't wide.
6) I'm sorry.
7) The woman is big and fat.
8) The guys are poor but interesting.
9) Time's up!
10) Darn it!
11) The letter-box is red.
12) Good-morning. How are you?
13) The books aren't thick.
14) The first lesson is interesting.
15) The girl's thin, me too.
16) The man isn't fat; neither am I.
17) The lighter's old but good.
18) The kids are strong.
19) That's correct. That's it.
20) The hat's little.
21) The first room is small.
22) The shoes are big.
23) The wall is red and blue.
24) The coat is black but the hat is navy blue.
25) A book is on the table.
26) Is a rich girl interesting?
27) A red telephone is on the chair.
28) The yellow socks are under the table.

learn by heart, then ask someone to give you a test:

1) **la ragazza è giovane**   ≠   **vecchia**
   the girl's young   old

2) **la donna è grassa**   ≠   **magra**
   the woman's fat   thin

3) **il tavolo è pesante**   ≠   **leggero**
   the table's heavy   light

4) **la voce è alta**   ≠   **bassa**
   the voice is loud   low

5) **l'uomo è alto**   ≠   **basso**
   the man's tall   short

6) **la via è larga**   ≠   **stretta**
   the street's wide   narrow

7) **Michele è ricco**   ≠   **povero**
   Mike's rich   poor

8) **l'uomo è forte**   ≠   **debole**
   the man's strong   weak

9) **la carta è spessa**   ≠   **sottile**
   the paper's thick   thin

10) **la stanza è grande**   ≠   **piccola**
   the room's big   small

11) **l'uomo è buono**   ≠   **cattivo**
   the man's good   bad

12) **il libro è sopra il tavolo**   ≠   **sotto**
   the book is on the table   under

13) **questa lezione è la prima**   ≠   **ultima**
   this lesson is first   last

VOCABOLARIO

	traduzione	sinonimo-associato	contrario-associato
1. anch'io	me too ≠ me neither		neanch'io
2. Come sta?	How are you? ≠ fine thank you and you?	Come va?	bene, grazie, e Lei?
3. (un) uomo	man ≠ woman	(un) tipo = guy	(una) donna
4. (un) ragazzo	boy ≠ girl		(una) ragazza
5. /(un) bambino /(un) bimbo	/child/kid	(un) marmocchio = brat, (un) lattante = a baby	(un) adulto
6. buon giorno	good morning	salve = hello, ciao = /hello/good-bye	buona sera = good evening
7. (un) giorno	day ≠ night	pomeriggio = afternoon, sera = evening	(una) notte
8. (una) scatola	/box/tin	(una) buca = letterbox	
9. esatto!	that's right ≠ it's wrong	è proprio così, va bene	non è così, non va bene
10. (una) chiave	key	soluzione	
11. /(una) scarpa/ (un) calzino	/shoe/sock	(una) pantofola = slipper, stivali = boots	
12. Può ripetere per favore?	Would you repeat, please?	E'ora = Time's up!	
13. (un) fiammifero	match	(un) accendino = lighter	(un) portacenere = ashtray
14. /verde/marrone	/green/brown	giallo = yellow	
15. corto	short ≠ long		lungo
16. /(un) cappello /(un) cappotto	/hat/coat	impermeabile = raincoat	
17. /mi (di) spiace /chiedo scusa	/I'm sorry /I apologise	mi scusi = excuse me	
18. (un) albergo	hotel	(una) camera = bedroom	
19. /(un) disco /(una) cassetta	/record /cassette	(un) giradischi = record player	

LEZIONE 3

POSSESSIVE ADJECTIVES AND PRONOUNS

il mio, la mia, i miei, le mie	= my/mine
il tuo, la tua, i tuoi, le tue	
il Suo, la Sua, i Suoi, le Sue	= your/yours
il vostro, la vostra, i vostri, le vostre	
il suo, la sua, i suoi, le sue	= his, her, its/ his, hers, its
il nostro, la nostra, i nostri, le nostre	= our/ours
il loro, la loro, i loro, le loro	= their/theirs

note: — this is less complicated than it seems. First you have to find out
what is owned (not *who* owns it) and follow the masculine or
feminine, singular or plural of these words: e.g.
— il mio libro (my book)
— la sua sedia (her or his chair)
— i nostri libri (our books)
— le loro sedie (their chairs)
— the possessives are usually preceded by the article.
No article is used, however, when the possessive adjective precedes a
singular noun denoting relationship, e.g. mia madre (my mother),
mio fratello (my brother); but: i miei fratelli (my brothers).
— IL TUO, LA TUA, I TUOI, LE TUE (when addressing one person
only) and IL VOSTRO, LA VOSTRA, I VOSTRI, LE VOSTRE
(when addressing more than one person) are an added difficulty —
these are special forms for friends and lovers.

E' IL SUO/TUO LIBRO?	Is it your book?
Sì, è il <u>mio</u> libro.	Yes, it's my book.
Sì, è il <u>mio</u>.	Yes, it's mine.

SONO I SUOI/TUOI GUANTI?	Are they your gloves?
Sì, sono <u>i miei</u> guanti.	Yes, they're my gloves.
Sì, sono <u>i miei</u>.	Yes, they're mine.
SONO I SUOI GUANTI?	Are they his/her gloves?
Sì, sono <u>i suoi</u> guanti.	Yes, they are his/her gloves.
Sì, sono <u>i suoi</u>.	Yes, they're his/hers.

DI CHI E' QUESTO LIBRO?	Whose book is it?
E' <u>il Suo</u> libro. E' <u>il Suo</u>.	It's your book. It's yours.
E' <u>il suo</u> libro.	It's her/his book.
E' <u>il suo</u>.	It's hers/his.

11 = **undici**	16 = **sedici**
12 = **dodici**	17 = **diciassette**
13 = **tredici**	18 = **diciotto**
14 = **quattordici**	19 = **diciannove**
15 = **quindici**	20 = **venti**

translate:

1) Is it your scarf? — No, it's hers.
2) Are they his boots? — No, they're hers.
3) What's the matter?
4) Whose bag is it?
5) They aren't my sweaters, they're hers.
6) Thank you. You're welcome.
7) Are your slacks too short?
8) Get it?
9) They aren't your ties, they're mine.
10) It doesn't matter.
11) What's new? — Nothing special.

give the possessive pronouns:
e.g. E' il mio maglione. E' il mio.

1) Sono i Suoi vestiti. Sono . . .
2) E' la mia camicia. E' . . .
3) Sono le loro sigarette. Sono . . .
4) E' la sua gonna. E' . . .
5) Questo accendino rosso è il mio accendino. E' . . .
6) Sono i tuoi guanti. Sono . . .
7) Sono i suoi calzoni. Sono . . .
8) E' la nostra lavagna. E' . . .
9) E' il suo vestito verde. E' . . .
10) E' la nostra camera. E' . . .
11) Sono i loro calzini. Sono . . .
12) Sono i nostri stivali. Sono . . .
13) E' la sua borsetta. E' . . .
14) E' il suo cane. E' . . .
15) E' il tuo cappello. E' . . .
16) E' la Sua cravatta. E' . . .
17) Sono i vostri libri. Sono . . .
18) E' la loro libreria. E' . . .
19) Sono le nostre sciarpe. . . .
20) E' il vostro portacenere. E' . . .

USE OF SOME ADJECTIVES

masculine	feminine	masculine	feminine
bello, bel (beautiful)	→ **bella**	**falso** (false)	→ **falsa**
grande, gran (big, great)	→ **grande**	**pazzo** (crazy)	→ **pazza**
		matto (mad)	→ **matta**
nuovo (new)	→ **nuova**	**sciocco** (silly)	→ **sciocca**
vecchio (old)	→ **vecchia**	**preferito**	→ **preferita**
felice (happy)	→ **felice**	(favourite)	
infelice (unhappy)	→ **infelice**	**schifoso** (shitty)	→ **schifosa**
asciutto (dry)	→ **asciutta**	**facile** (easy)	→ **facile**
gentile (kind)	→ **gentile**	**difficile** (difficult)	→ **difficile**
noioso (boring)	→ **noiosa**	**sensazionale**	→ **sensazionale**
caro (expensive)	→ **cara**	(super)	
sporco (dirty)	→ **sporca**	**amaro** (bitter)	→ **amara**
simpatico (nice)	→ **simpatica**	**intelligente**	→ **intelligente**
		(clever)	

fill in the adjectives:

una cravatta (nuovo) . . .
delle donne (gentile) . . .
il mio amico (preferito) . . .
delle gonne (vecchio) . . .
i suoi vestiti (nuovo) . . .
una camicia (bianco) . . .
una lezione (noioso) . . .
una donna (infelice) . . .
delle scarpe (nuovo) . . .
dei guanti (sporco) . . .
una borsetta (caro) . . .

un compito (difficile) . . .
dei lattanti (asciutto) . . .
la (primo) . . . lezione
dei gatti (nero) . . .
una ragazza (matto) . . .
un uomo (falso) . . .
una donna (grosso) . . .
un marmocchio (sciocco) . . .
un bimbo (felice) . . .
un camera (schifoso) . . .
una cravatta (bianco) . . .

put into the plural:

1) Il nostro bambino è infelice.
2) Il tuo calzino è nero.
3) Il suo disco è sensazionale.
4) Il mio cappello è sopra il tavolo.
5) Questa via non è larga.
6) La loro camera è grande.
7) Questo tavolo è pesante.
8) La sua camicia è sporca.
9) Anche la mia cravatta è verde e gialla.
10) Questo albergo è caro.
11) E' il mio colore preferito.
12) E' una ragazza sciocca.

translate and put into the negative:

1) His gloves are small.
2) Her book is on the table.
3) My homework is easy.
4) Your new boots are dirty.
5) Her guy is crazy.
6) Their clothes are old.
7) Our sweaters are new.
8) This lesson's boring.
9) His new suit is black.
10) Our new shirts are beautiful.
11) Her blue skirt is expensive.
12) My slacks are dry.
13) Our blackboard is wide.
14) Their children are kind.
15) His vest is dirty.
16) Our slippers are red.

VOCABOLARIO

	traduzione	sinonimo-associato	contrario-associato
1. (un) vestito	/dress/suit	(una) gonna = skirt (una) camicetta = blouse	
2. /(una) camicia /(una) cravatta	/shirt/tie	(un) gilé = vest (una) giacca = jacket	
3. (dei) calzoni, (dei) pantaloni	slacks, trousers		
4. /(una) borsetta /(un,dei) guanti /(una) sciarpa	/handbag/gloves/ scarf	(un) portafoglio = wallet	
5. Come si chiama?	What's your name?	Come ti chiami?	Mi chiamo . . . = My name is . . .
6. (un) maglione	sweater	(una) maglietta = teeshirt	
7. Che colore è?	What colour is it?	Di che colore è . . . ? = What's the colour of . . . ?	
8. Grazie mille	many thanks ≠ you're welcome	per favore = please	prego
9. (un, dei) vestiti	clothes, clothing		
10. guardare	to watch, look at		
11. (una) lavagna	blackboard	(un) gesso = chalk	
12. Che (cosa) c'è?	What's the matter?	Che cosa non va?	Va bene = It's OK
13. Non importa	it doesn't matter	non fa niente = never mind	
14. è tutto qui	that's all		
15. Capisce?	Do you understand? ≠ I don't understand	capito? = get it?	Non capisco
16. Che c'è di nuovo?	What's new? ≠ Nothing special		Niente di speciale
17. anche	also ≠ neither		neanche, neppure

LEZIONE 4

POSSESSION

L'ombrello di Giovanna.	Jane's umbrella
Gli ombrelli di Giovanna	Jane's umbrellas
Le macchine dei ragazzi	The boys' cars

note: − at last something easier in Italian than in English!
− the Italians say: 'the umbrella of Jane', not 'Jane's umbrella'.

OF THE

di + il → del	**Il libro del ragazzo** = the boy's book
di + i → dei	**I libri dei ragazzi** = the boys' books
di + la → della	**La macchina della ragazza** = the girl's car.
di + le → delle	**Le macchine delle ragazze** = the girls' cars.

note: − di + lo → dello (dello studente); plural: degli (degli studenti).
− before a vowel: dell' (e.g. dell'albergo).

translate:

1) Peter's eyes are green.
2) How do you spell it?
3) The girl's mouth is large.
4) The woman's teeth are white.
5) Wait a minute!
6) Jane's face is beautiful.
7) The girl's legs are thin.
8) The man's hands are behind me.
9) The guy's car is green.
10) Jane's uncle's umbrella is black.

Fill in the blank spaces, chosing from **del, dell', dello, dei, degli, della, delle.**

il libro . . . studente
le gonne . . . donne
i giorni . . . settimana
i libri . . . studenti
gli occhi . . . bambini
la bocca . . . donna
il piede . . . uomo
i mesi . . . anno
la testa . . . ragazzo
le mani . . . ragazza
il braccio . . . bambino
gli ombrelli . . . ragazze
le gambe . . . marmocchi

il naso . . . Giovanna
le dita . . . mano
le unghie . . . piede
gli anni . . . secoli
la finestra . . . stanza
le vetrine . . . vie
gli orecchi . . . cane
gli stivali . . . uomini
la camicia . . . ragazzo
il prezzo . . . giacca
la lezione . . . bambini
la macchina . . . tipo
la pioggia . . . pomeriggio

```
QUALE? QUALI? = WHICH? — (WHAT?)

masculine                          feminine
Quale tipo? = Which guy?           Quale donna? = Which woman?
Quali tipi? = Which guys?          Quali donne? = Which women?
```

note: which one? = quale?

use the correct form of **quale**:

. . . uomo   . . . sedie
. . . libro   . . . orologio
. . . naso   . . . macchine
. . . secolo   . . . stivali
. . . donne   . . . borsetta
. . . ragazzo   . . . gonne
. . . occhi   . . . cappotti
. . . gatto   . . . vestiti
. . . finestre   . . . orecchi
. . . tipi   . . . gambe
. . . anni   . . . unghie
. . . mesi   . . . settimana
. . . ombrello   . . . sigarette
. . . cane   . . . accendino
. . . martedì   . . . giacche
. . . mani   . . . piedi
. . . studenti   . . . lezione

learn to say the alphabet:

A-B-C-D-E-F-G-H-I-L-M-N-O-P-Q-R-S-T-U-V-Z.

note: 21 letters only!

THIS = **QUESTO/QUESTA**	→	THESE = **QUESTI/QUESTE**
this boy = **questo ragazzo**	→	these boys = **questi ragazzi**
this girl = **questa ragazza**	→	these girls = **queste ragazze**

THAT = **QUEL/QUELLA**	→	THOSE = **QUEI/QUELLE**
that boy = **quel ragazzo**	→	those boys = **quei ragazzi**
that girl = **quella ragazza**	→	those girls = **quelle ragazze**

note: — before s followed by a consonant and before z, quel → quello:
      e.g. quello student = that student.
    — before a vowel → quell' (e.g. quell'albergo = that hotel).
    — the plural of both quello and quell' is quegli: quegli studenti = those students, quegli alberghi = those hotels.

put in the singular:
e.g. Questi libri sono i miei.
   – Questo libro è il mio.

1) Queste borsette sono sopra il tavolo.
2) Quelle gonne sono sotto le mie.
3) Questi vestiti sono piccoli per quei tipi.
4) Quei vestiti sono provocanti.
5) Questi orologi sono i miei e quelli sono i vostri.
6) Queste camicie sono le mie e quelle sono le vostre.
7) Quei libri sono lontani da Giovanna, ma questi sono vicini.
8) Quelle macchine sono nuove e care.
9) Quelle gatte sono dietro la porta, ma queste sono sotto il tavolo.
10) Quelle donne sono laggiù.
11) Questi tipi sono ricchi e quelli sono poveri.
12) Queste prime lezioni sono noiose e le ultime lezioni corte.
13) Quei visi sono belli.
14) Questi stivali sono nuovi e gli altri sono vecchi.

translate:

1) Those guys are weak.
2) Those gloves are new, but these are old.
3) This man is rich, the other is poor but good.
4) This chair isn't in that room.
5) This bag is behind the table.
6) This book is yours, that one is mine.
7) These cars are behind the hotel, but those are over there.
8) This woman is crazy but interesting.
9) Is that guy boring? – This one isn't.
10) Are those women rich? – These aren't.
11) That car is big, but this one isn't.
12) Which lessons are interesting? – Those.
13) Which kid is yours? – This one.

VOCABOLARIO

	traduzione	sinonimo-associato	contrario-associato
1. Vada avanti!	go on ≠ wait a minute	Continui!	Aspetti un momento!
2. (un) prezzo	price		
3. Quanto costa?	How much is it?	Quant'è?	
4. (un) ombrello	umbrella	(la) pioggia = rain	
5. (un) giorno	day ≠ night	(una) settimana = week	(una) notte
6. /(un)anno/ /(un) mese	/year/month	(un) secolo = century	
7. domenica	Sunday	lunedì, martedì, mercoledì, giovedì, venerdì, sabato	
8. /dove/con/in /quando	/where/with/in /when		
9. qui	here ≠ there	qui vicino = near by	là, laggiù = over there
10. vicino (a)	near ≠ far from		lontano (da)
11. davanti a	in front of ≠ behind	di fronte a	dietro
12. su	on ≠ under	sopra	sotto
13. a fianco di	next to		
14. /(una) testa /(un) braccio	/head/arm	viso = faccia = face, muso = kisser	
15. /(un) occhio, (gli) occhi /(un) naso	/eye(s)/nose	vedere = to see	
16. (un) orecchio	ear	sentire = to hear	
17. (una) mano	hand	toccare = to touch	(un) piede = foot, (una) gamba = leg
18. (una) bocca	mouth	baciare = to kiss	
19. (un) dente	tooth	(la) lingua = tongue	
20. (un) dito	finger ≠ toe	(un') unghia = nail	(un) dito del piede
21. Come si scrive?	How do you spell it?		

LEZIONE 5

CHE ORA E'?	What time is it?
E' l'una.	It's one o'clock.
Sono le dieci.	It's ten o'clock.
Sono le dieci meno un quarto.	It's a quarter to ten.
Sono le dieci e un quarto.	It's a quarter past ten.
Sono le dieci e mezzo.	It's ten thirty.

C'E' = THERE IS	
C'E' UN UOMO QUI?	Is there a man here?
Sì, c'è un uomo qui.	Yes, there's a man here.
Sì, ce n'è uno.	Yes, there is (one).

CI SONO = THERE ARE	
CI SONO UOMINI QUI?	Are there men here?
Sì, ci sono uomini qui.	Yes, there are men here.
Sì, ce ne sono.	Yes, there are (some).
No, non ci sono uomini qui.	No, there aren't any men here.
No, non ce ne sono.	No, there aren't.

note: — ci (= there) becomes ce when followed by ne (= one, some).
       — ci and ne become c' and n' when followed by a vowel.

CHE?		=	WHAT? (WHICH?)	
	libro?			book?
Che	libri?		What	books?
	macchina?		(Which)	car?
	macchine?			cars?

note: che can be used instead of quale.

20 = venti	40 = quaranta
21 = ventuno	50 = cinquanta
22 = ventidue	60 = sessanta
23 = ventitrè	70 = settanta
24 = ventiquattro	80 = ottanta
25 = venticinque	90 = novanta
26 = ventisei	100 = cento
27 = ventisette	101 = centouno
28 = ventotto	200 = duecento
29 = ventinove	1000 = mille
30 = trenta	2000 = duemila
31 = trentuno	10000 = diecimila
32 = trentadue	1000000 = un milione
38 = trentotto	2000000 = due milioni

note: venti, trenta, quaranta . . . drop the final vowel in combining with uno or or otto.

```
┌─────────────────────────────────────────────────────────────────────┐
│  THIS ONE? =              →    THAT ONE? =                            │
│  QUESTO?/QUESTA?               QUELLO?/QUELLA?                         │
│                                                                       │
│                  ⟨this one?                        ⟨questo?           │
│  — which man?     that one?    →  quale uomo?       quello?           │
│                                                                       │
│                    ⟨this one?                       ⟨questa?          │
│  — which woman?     that one?  →  quale donna?       quella?          │
└─────────────────────────────────────────────────────────────────────┘
```

translate:

1) Are there thirty hours in a day?
2) It's three-thirty.
3) Are these roads dangerous? Which ones are?
4) It's a quarter to twelve.
5) Are there taxis or buses in the evening? No, there aren't.
6) It's all the same to me.
7) Which ceiling is high? — This one.
8) Which bottle's full? — That one.
9) His bike's fast.
10) That road's dangerous.
11) Are there empty bottles on the table?
12) Are there bikes in this road?
13) There are three false teeth. Which are they?
14) It's a quarter past four.
15) Of course not!
16) What time is it? — It's ten o'clock.
17) Two guys are stupid. Which ones?
18) Is the candy sweet or sour?
19) What's your name? — My name's Peter.
20) This room is dirty but that one is clean.
21) Are today's lessons easy or difficult?
22) Is his girl pretty or ugly? — Which girl?
23) Are there safe planes in winter?
24) What kind of kids are they?
25) Are there twelve months in a year?
26) There are three pretty cars in this road. Which ones?
27) There is a full bottle under the table.
28) There's a boring lesson in this book. Which one?

CONTRARI (OPPOSITES) 2

1) **il gatto è <u>carino</u>/<u>bello</u>** ≠ **<u>brutto</u>**
   the cat's pretty   ugly

2) **il cappotto è <u>sporco</u>** ≠ **<u>pulito</u>**
   the coat's dirty   clean

3) **quell'uomo è <u>intelligente</u>** ≠ **<u>stupido</u>/<u>incapace</u>**
   that man's bright   stupid

4) **la strada è <u>pericolosa</u>** ≠ **<u>sicura</u>**
   the road's dangerous   safe

5) **le lezioni sono <u>facili</u>** ≠ **<u>difficili</u>**
   the lessons are easy   difficult

6) **la riga è <u>lunga</u>** ≠ **<u>corta</u>**
   the ruler's long   short

7) **la mia bicicletta è <u>veloce</u>** ≠ **<u>lenta</u>**
   my bike's fast   slow

8) **la stanza è <u>fredda</u>** ≠ **<u>calda</u>**
   the room's cold   hot

9) **la bottiglia è <u>vuota</u>** ≠ **<u>piena</u>**
   the bottle's empty   full

10) **la caramella è <u>dolce</u>** ≠ **<u>acida</u>/<u>amara</u>**
    the candy's sweet   sour/bitter

11) **il soffitto è <u>alto</u>** ≠ **<u>basso</u>**
    the ceiling's high   low

12) **la nostra lezione è <u>interessante</u>** ≠ **<u>noiosa</u>/<u>barbosa</u>**
    our lesson is interesting   boring/dull

VOCABOLARIO

	traduzione	sinonimo-associato	contrario-associato
1. a mezzogiorno	at noon ≠ at midnight		a mezzanotte
2. di mattina	in the morning ≠ at night	di pomeriggio = in the afternoon	di sera = in the evening
3. /(un') estate/ /(una) primavera /(una) stagione	/summer/spring /season	(un) inverno = winter, (un) autunno = fall	
4. Quanti(e)?	How many?		
5. /(un) genere /(un) modo	/kind/way	(una) specie = sort	
6. oggi	today	domani = tomorrow	ieri = yesterday
7. per me fa lo stesso	I don't care, it's all the same to me		
8. andare	to go ≠ to come	andarsene = to go away, partire = to leave, uscire = to go out	venire, restare = to stay
9. (un') ora	hour	(una) mezz'ora = half an hour	
10. (un) secondo	second	(un) minuto = minute	un momento = a while
11. gennaio	January, etc.	febbraio, marzo, aprile, maggio, giugno, luglio, agosto, settembre, ottobre, novembre, dicembre	
12. /(una) macchina /(un) aereo/(un) battello/(un) treno/(un) tassì	/car/plane/boat /train/taxi	(un) autobus = bus, (una) metropolitana = subway, (una) stazione = station	
13. domandare	to ask ≠ to answer	fare una domanda = to ask a question	rispondere, (una) risposta = answer
14. va bene	all right		non va bene
15. senz'altro	of course ≠ of course not	certo	nemmeno per sogno
16. matto	crazy, mad	stravagante, strano, pazzo	

LEZIONE 6

ESSERE = TO BE

(io) **sono**	I am	**non sono**	I'm not
(tu) **sei**	you are	**non sei**	you aren't
(egli) (ella) **è** { he she is you are		**non è** { he she isn't you aren't	
(noi) **siamo**	we are	**non siamo**	we aren't
(voi) **siete**	you are	**non siete**	you aren't
(essi) (esse) **sono** { they are you are		**non sono** { they aren't you aren't	

note: — the subject pronouns are usually left out in conversation unless
       emphasis is desired.
     — tu is for friends and lovers.
     — the plural of tu is voi.
     — you always write Lei and Loro with capitals.
     — the present in Italian can also translate our present perfect, e.g. I've
       been here for two years = sono qui da due anni.

E' AMERICANO?	Are you American?
Sì, sono americano.	Yes, I'm American.
No, non sono americano.	No, I'm not American.

translate:

1) I'm not dirty. Are you?
2) That man's a doctor.
3) What does it mean?
4) The businessman's rich and fat.
5) Do you think so?
6) He isn't French, but you are.
7) We aren't happy.
8) Either one.

put in the negative:
e.g. Sono troppo gentile.
    — Non sono troppo gentile.

1) E' uno sporco poliziotto.
2) Giovanni è un padrone abbastanza gentile.
3) Siete studenti molto interessanti.
4) Gli uomini d'affari sono troppo ricchi.
5) Il problema è troppo difficile.
6) Questo lavoro è molto lungo.
7) Il mio lavoro è noioso.
8) L'avvocato è americano.
9) E' molto violenta.
10) I professori di quest'anno sono barbosi.
11) I giorni in dicembre sono corti.
12) Peccato!
13) I battelli sono veloci.
14) La bottiglia è vuota.
15) La stanza è sporca.
16) Siamo interessanti.
17) Il film è amaro.
18) E' brutta.
19) E' dietro la porta.
20) Sono la segretaria del direttore.

ANCHE – NEANCHE	=	TOO, ALSO – EITHER, NEITHER

E' carina, anch'io.   She's pretty and <u>I am too.</u>
Non è carina, neanch'io.   She isn't pretty and <u>I'm not either.</u>

E' ricca, **anch'io**   (me too)
         anche tu   (you too)
         anche lui   (he too)
         anche lei   (she too)
         anche Lei   (you too)
         anche noi   (we too)
         anche voi   (you too)
         anche loro   (they too)
         anche Loro   (you too)

translate, then put in the negative:
e.g. I'm Italian and he is too.
     — Sono italiano, anche lui.
     — Non sono italiano, neanche lui.

1)   The boss is nice and I am too.
2)   The student is boring and you are too.
3)   The businessman is rich and you are too.
4)   The secretary is bright and her guy is too.
5)   I'm kind and so are you.
6)   The office is far away and the subway is too.
7)   My boss is big and his secretary is too.
8)   The hospital is near and the school is too.
9)   They're businesswomen and so are we.
10)   You're students and we are too.
11)   You're shitty and so are they.
12)   Your problems are easy and so are mine.
13)   Her bottle is empty and mine is too.
14)   Your cat's pretty and so is ours.
15)   This room is dirty and so is that one.
16)   His bike is fast and so is mine.
17)   Winter is cold and autumn is too.
18)   The teacher's boring and you are too.
19)   My guy's ugly and so is yours.
20)   I'm strong and so are they.

```
FA = IT'S

fa bel tempo     = it's nice out
fa freddo/caldo  = it's cold/hot

FA BEL TEMPO?

Sì, fa bel tempo.
No, non fa bel tempo.
```

note: <u>fa</u> for weather.

```
E' = IT'S

E' interessante            it's interesting
E' noioso                  it's boring
E' simpatico               it's nice
E' presto/tardi            it's early/late
E' caro/a buon mercato     it's expensive/cheap
E' certo che               it's certain that
E' necessario              it's necessary, a must
E' facile/difficile        it's easy/difficult
E' vero                    it's true
```

translate:

1) It's nice out today.
2) It's too late to go.
3) It's boring.
4) It's cold.
5) It's too early.
6) It's nice.
7) It's very expensive.
8) It's interesting.
9) It's hot.
10) It's cheap.

VOCABOLARIO

	traduzione	sinonimo-associato	contrario-associato
1. Mi piacerebbe presentarLe ...	I'd like you to meet ...		piacere = pleased to meet you
2. /chi?/quale?	/who?/which?	che = that, who	
3. /(un) dottore /(un) avvocato /(un) testimone	/doctor/lawyer /witness	ospedale = hospital infermiera = nurse	
4. /(un) uomo d'affari/gli affari	/businessman /business	(una) donna d'affari = businesswoman	
5. /(uno) studente, /(una) studentessa /(una) scuola	/student/school	(un) alunno, (un') alunna = pupil	(un) professore, (una) professoressa = teacher
6. (un) poliziotto	cop, policeman	(un) vigile = traffic policeman	
7. /(un) capufficio /(un) ufficio	/boss/office	(un) padrone = employer, (un) capo = chief, (un) direttore = director	
8. troppo	too much ≠ not enough	abbastanza = enough	poco
9. soprattutto	above all		
10. (un) problema	problem	(delle) preoccupazioni = worries	
11. (un) lavoro	work	(un') occupazione, (un) posto = job	
12. /Io la penso così /penso di sì	/that's what I think /I think so	Spero bene = I would hope so	Lei trova? = Do you think so?
13. o l'uno o l'altro	either (one) ≠ neither (one)		né l'uno né l'altro
14. che significa?	what does it mean?	(un) significato = meaning	
15. (un) cinema	cinema (movies)	(un) film = film	
16. (un, una) segretario(a)	secretary	(un, una) dattilografo(a) = typist	
17. peccato!	it's a pity! ≠ thank heaven!		grazie al cielo!

LEZIONE 7

AVERE = TO HAVE

ho	I have	**non ho**	I don't have
hai	you have	**non hai**	you don't have
ha	{ he she } has you have	**non ha**	{ he she } doesn't have you don't have
abbiamo	we have	**non abbiamo**	we don't have
avete	you have	**non avete**	you don't have
hanno	{ they have you have	**non hanno**	{ they don't have you don't have

note: remember the Italian present can also be our present perfect
e.g. I've had my car for five years = ho la macchina da cinque anni.

HA UNA SIGARETTA?   Do you have a cigarette?

Sì, ho una sigaretta.   Yes, I have a cigarette.
No, non ho una sigaretta.   No, I don't have a cigarette.

```
SPECIAL NEGATIVES
NON . . . NIENTE        =    NOTHING, ANYTHING
Non ho niente.               I have nothing/I don't have anything.

NON . . . PIU'          =    NOT ANY MORE, NOT ANY LONGER
Non ha più la macchina.      He(she) doesn't have a car any more.

NON . . . NESSUNO       =    NOT ANYONE, ANYBODY, NOBODY
Non c'è nessuno.             There isn't anyone.

NON . . . MAI           =    NEVER, NOT EVER
Non è mai qui.               He(she) isn't ever here/He(she) is never
                             here.

NON . . . ANCORA        =    NOT YET
Non è ancora giugno          It isn't June yet.
```

note: — these special negatives are rather tricky but extremely important
in the spoken language (they can be used with any verb).

— He is still here = è $\frac{ancora}{sempre}$ qui.

translate and then put in the interrogative:

1) Soprattutto non abbiamo tempo oggi.
2) Non è più qui da due mesi.
3) Non avete mai molto denaro.
4) Non c'è nessuno nella stanza.
5) Non ha niente d'interessante.
6) Non sono ancora qui.
7) Non abbiamo ancora due macchine.
8) Non abbiamo mai problemi.
9) Non ho più niente.
10) Non è mai in ufficio.

translate:

1) She's still in Rome./She isn't in Rome any more.
2) We still have a lot of time./We don't have a lot of time any more.
3) The boss still has a secretary./The boss doesn't have a secretary any more.
4) He still hasn't anything./He doesn't have anything any more.
5) They are still young./They aren't young any more.

translate, then put in the interrogative:

1) He hasn't any more work this month.
2) There isn't anyone in the room.
3) She has only two skirts.
4) He is never here on Sundays.
5) We don't have anything interesting.
6) She isn't here yet.
7) She's still in Italy.
8) We don't have the time any more.
9) We still have a lot of work.
10) You only have one car.
11) He's already the boss.
12) His film is more or less shitty.
13) They aren't usually here early.
14) We've had our car for a year.
15) They have only two kids.
16) He never has a job.
17) We have only one teacher.
18) The kids are never at home in the afternoon.
19) I have only two cigarettes.
20) There isn't anybody.

AVERE		TO BE
avere fame	=	to be hungry
avere sete	=	to be thirsty
avere . . . anni	=	to be . . . years old
avere sono	=	to be sleepy
avere freddo	=	to be cold
avere caldo	=	to be hot
avere paura	=	to be afraid
avere torto	=	to be wrong
avere ragione	=	to be right
avere successo	=	to be successful
avere bisogno di	=	to be in need of
avere fretta	=	to be in a hurry
avere vergogna	=	to be ashamed

translate:

1) The teacher isn't always right.
2) The businessman is already successful.
3) I'm not hungry but I'm thirsty.
4) In any case, I'm afraid.
5) You aren't right.
6) We never have any money.
7) She's fifteen years old.
8) I'm often cold in the winter and hot in the summer.
9) She's rarely sleepy.
10) The boss's secretary is never wrong.
11) I'm never in a hurry.
12) They are ashamed of their house.

AVVERBI E LOCUZIONI (ADVERBS AND PHRASES) 1

1. **a causa di**	because of	17. **almeno**	at least
2. **di rado**	rarely	18. **.... fa**	... ago
3. **spesso**	often	19. **– una volta**	– once
4. **quasi**	– almost – nearly	**– una volta** **alla settimana**	– once a week
5. **in ogni modo**	– at any rate – in any case	20. **già**	already
6. **appena**	– scarcely – hardly	21. **non ... più**	not ... any more
		22. **senza**	without
7. **fino a**	until, till	23. **tranne**	except
8. **di solito**	usually	24. **tutti e due,**	both
9. **il giorno in cui**	the day when	**tutte e due**	
10. **mai**	never, ever	25. **insieme,** **assieme,**	together
11. **sempre**	always	26. **– solo**	only
12. **più o meno**	more or less	**– solamente**	
13. **in punto**	on the dot (time)	27. **contemporanea-** **mente**	at the same time
14. **molto** **≠ un poco**	much, very – a little, a bit	28. **– dove?** **–da dove?**	– where? – where from?
15. **abbastanza**	enough	29. **– ancora una** **volta**	– once more
16. **nel caso in cui**	in case	**– un'altra volta**	– again

VOCABOLARIO

	traduzione	sinonimo-associato	contrario-associato
1. e Lei?	what about you?		
2. /piovere/(una) pioggia	/to rain/rain	piovere a scrosci = to pour	
3. nevicare	to snow	(una) neve = snow	
4. il tempo	the weather	note: non ho tempo = I don't have the time	
5. una volta	once	due volte = twice	
6. studiare	to study	imparare = to learn	
7. /(il) sole/(la) luna	/sun/moon	c'è il sole = it's sunny	(un') ombra = shade, (una) nuvola = cloud
8. molto	much ≠ a little, a bit	un mucchio di, la maggior parte di = most of	un pochino
9. /(un) temporale /(un) vento	/storm/wind		fa bel tempo = it's nice out
10. /vestirsi/lavarsi	/to get dressed /to get washed		svestirsi = to get undressed
11. andare a letto	to go to bed ≠ to get up		alzarsi, svegliarsi = to wake up
12. (una) cosa	thing	(la) roba = stuff	
13. ho fretta	I'm in a hurry ≠ not in a hurry	to run = correre	ho tempo
14. fumare	to smoke		
15. /mangiare/bere	/to eat/to drink	una bibita, una bevanda = a drink	
16. fare spese	tò go shopping	(delle) commissioni = errands	
17. /a scuola/al lavoro/a casa/all'albergo /alle otto di sera/a Roma/alla stazione /all'aeroporto	/at school/at work/at home/at the hotel /at 8 p.m./in Rome/at the station /at the airport		
18. /qualcuno /qualche cosa	/somebody, anybody ≠ nobody/something, anything ≠ nothing		nessuno = nobody, niente = nothing

LEZIONE 8

There are three groups of verbs in Italian: '-ARE', '-ERE', '-IRE'.

PRESENT VERBS IN '-ARE': PARLARE

parlo	I speak/am speaking	**non parlo**	I don't speak/ I'm not speaking
parli	you speak	**non parli**	you don't speak
parla	he speaks she speaks you speak	**non parla**	{ he she doesn't speak you don't speak
parliamo	we speak	**non parliamo**	we don't speak
parlate	you speak	**non parlate**	you don't speak
parlano	they you speak	**non parlano**	{ they you don't speak

---

note: — the above endings are added to the stem of the verb.
 — the Italian present is for: 1) an action one is doing now:
   parlo ora = I'm speaking now.
  2) a repeated action:
   parla spesso = he(she) often speaks.
  3) an action started in the past that still
   goes on (our present perfect): parlate
   da un'ora = you have been speaking
   for an hour.
 — the use of si with the third person (singular or plural) is extremely
   frequent. It can be translated by one, we, you or they e.g. si parla
   italiano = we speak Italian (Italian spoken).

PARLA SPESSO INGLESE?	Do you often speak English?
Sì, parlo spesso inglese. **No, non parlo spesso inglese.**	Yes, I often speak English. No, I don't often speak English.

42

SOME REGULAR '-ARE' VERBS

aspettare = to wait (for)
chiamare = to call
cominciare = to begin
comprare = to buy
consegnare = to hand
contare = to count
firmare = to sign
fumare = to smoke
gettare = to throw
giocare = to play (a game)
imbucare = to post

incontrare = to meet
lavorare = to work
mandare (a) = to send (to)
mangiare = to eat
pensare (a) = to think (of)
portare = to bring, to carry
progettare = to plan
riposare = to rest
sperare (di) = to hope
suonare = to play (an instrument)
trovare = to find

SOME IRREGULAR VERBS = VERBI IRREGOLARI

andare = to go	**dare** = to give	**stare** = to stay, to be, to live	**fare** = to do, to make
vado = I go	do = I give	sto = I stay	faccio = I do
vai	dai	stai	fai
va	dà	sta	fa
andiamo	diamo	stiamo	facciamo
andate	date	state	fate
vanno	danno	stanno	fanno

translate:

1) We don't often speak Italian.
2) Does she usually go to the movies on Sundays?
3) Do they often work together with the boss?
4) Whose turn is it?
5) We're eating.
6) He doesn't listen to John any more.
7) You've been speaking for an hour.
8) I'm at last beginning this work.

put in the negative:

1) Mi piace molto la tua gonna.
2) Lavoriamo spesso molto il lunedì.
3) Compri un vestito nuovo.
4) Lavori presto la mattina.
5) Ascoltate più o meno il professore.
6) Gli studenti fanno domande stupide.
7) Quel bambino gioca senza parlare.
8) Cominciamo in orario oggi.
9) Mostrate il compito al professore.
10) Vanno in ufficio tutti i giorni.
11) Giovanni dà una penna a Maria.
12) Stiamo tutti bene.
13) Sgobbiamo anche la domenica.
14) Aiuta spesso suo fratello a fare il compito.
15) Studiate da un'ora.
16) Oggi lavoriamo.
17) Sgobbo a Roma da un anno.
18) Ascoltate il professore.
19) Si spera di venire presto.
20) La macchina va bene.
21) Il capufficio chiama la sua segretaria e poi firma.
22) Speriamo di incontrare il direttore.

non . . . più	non parla più	= he doesn't speak any more
non . . . mai	non parla mai	= he never speaks
non . . . ancora	non è ancora qui	= he isn't here yet
ancora, sempre	parla ancora/sempre	= he's still speaking
non . . . niente	non mi dà niente	= he doesn't give me anything
non . . . nessuno	non parla a nessuno	= he isn't speaking to anyone
non . . . affatto	non parla affatto	= he doesn't speak at all

translate:

1) We still work early in the morning.
2) The bastard doesn't speak to anyone.
3) He never listens to John.
4) You're eating too much.
5) You've been eating for an hour.
6) She only speaks English.
7) We wish to go with Mary.
8) You've been smoking for an hour.
9) They're working with the boss.
10) He's still studying Italian.
11) He's been studying Italian for three years.
12) I adore my guy.
13) We never go to the movies at night.
14) They only go to the movies once a month.
15) I often go for a walk in the evening.
16) I'm sending the money today.
17) He doesn't smoke at all.
18) She's still eating.
19) They hope to go with John.
20) We're thinking of you.
21) I love Mary.
22) She only buys green sweaters.

CHI? = WHO? − (WHOM?)	**CHE?** − CHE COSA? = WHAT?
Chi parla? = Who's speaking	**Che mangia?** = What are you eating?
Chi aspetta? = Who are you waiting for?	**Che fa?** = What are you doing?

translate:

1) What are you smoking?
2) Who's working?
3) What is she buying?
4) What do you hope to do?
5) Who's talking with your sister?
6) Who do you love?
7) What are you waiting for?

A + . . . = TO

a + il = al	**Parlo al ragazzo**	= I speak/am speaking to the boy.
a + i = ai	**Parlo ai ragazzi**	= I speak/am speaking to the boys.
a + la = alla	**Parlo alla ragazza**	= I'm speaking to the girl.
a + le = alle	**Parlo alle ragazze**	= I'm speaking to the girls.

note: − a + lo = allo (allo students), a + l' = all' (all'amico), a + gli = agli (agli studenti).
   − careful: with verbs of movement you use da when one goes to someone's, e.g. vado da mio padre = I'm going to my father's.

fill in:

1) Il professore parla . . . alunni.
2) Io penso . . . voi.
3) Mostriamo la neve . . . bambini.
4) Manda un libro . . . segretaria del capufficio.
5) Giovanna dà un ombrello . . . ragazze.

VOCABOLARIO

	traduzione	sinonimo-associato	contrario-associato
1. ogni (giorno)	every(day), each	tutti i giorni, ognuno = everyone	all = tutto, tutti
2. /nel mio ufficio /nella mia stanza	/in my office /in my room	tra un'ora = in an hour	
3. certo	certain, sure	sicuro	dubbio = doubtful
4. forse	perhaps, may be	chissà	
5. volere	to want	desiderare, augurare = to wish	
6. amare	to love ≠ to hate	adorare = to adore, andare pazzo per = to be crazy about	odiare, non sopporto = I can't stand
7. mi piace	I like ≠ I don't like		non mi piace
8. mi dispiace	I'm sorry	excuse me	
9. mostrare a	to show to	(una) mostra = show, display	
10. ascoltare	to listen to		
11. telefonare a	to call (phone)		
12. aspettare	to wait for	L'aspetto = I'm waiting for you	
13. lavorare	to work	sgobbare = to work hard	non far niente = to do nothing
14. il dolce far niente!	it's a good life!		
15. in orario	on time ≠ late	presto = early	in ritardo, tardi
16. felice	happy ≠ sad	contento = glad	infelice, triste
17. mascalzone	bastard ≠ bitch		vacca
18. la fine	the end ≠ the beginning		il principio
19. interessante	interesting ≠ boring	appassionante	noioso, barboso
20. a chi tocca?	Whose turn is it?		
21. aiutare	to help	aiuto! = help!	
22. camminare	to walk	andare a passeggio = to go for a walk	
23. prima (di)	before ≠ after		poi, dopo (di)

LEZIONE 9

PRESENT VERBS IN **'-ERE'** : **VENDERE**

vend<u>o</u>	I sell/am selling	**non vend<u>o</u>**	I don't sell/ am not selling
vend<u>i</u>	you sell	**non vend<u>i</u>**	you don't sell
vend<u>e</u>	{ he sells she sells you sell	**non vend<u>e</u>**	{ he she doesn't sell you don't sell
vend<u>iamo</u>	we sell	**non vend<u>iamo</u>**	we don't sell
vend<u>ete</u>	you sell	**non vend<u>ete</u>**	you don't sell
vend<u>ono</u>	{ they you sell	**non vend<u>ono</u>**	{ they you don't sell

note: remember: the Italian present is also for a past action which still goes on, e.g. I've been selling cars for ten years = vendo macchine da dieci anni.

SCRIVE SPESSO LETTERE? Do you write letters often?

Sì, <u>scrivo</u> spesso lettere. Yes, I write letters often.
No, <u>non scrivo</u> spesso lettere. No, I don't write letters often.

translate:

1) Are you writing a letter?
2) He's reading a book.
3) What are you seeing at the movies?
4) Do you take some bread and butter?
5) Are you laughing or not?
6) He's answering the telephone.

SOME REGULAR 'ERE' VERBS

ammettere = to admit
battere = to beat
chiudere = to close
correre = to run
credere = to believe
insistere = to insist
leggere = to read
mettere = to put
prendere = to take

ricevere = to receive
ridere (di) = to laugh (at)
ripetere = to repeat
rispondere (a) = to answer
scrivere = to write
temere = to fear
vedere = to see
vendere = to sell
vivere = to live

SOME IRREGULAR VERBS

bere = to drink	dovere = must	tenere = to keep	ottenere = to get	piacere = to please
bevo	devo	tengo	ottengo	piaccio
bevi	devi	tieni	ottieni	piaci
beve	deve	tiene	ottiene	piace
beviamo	dobbiamo	teniamo	otteniamo	piacciamo
bevete	dovete	tenete	ottenete	piacete
bevono	devono	tengono	ottengono	piacciono

potere = can	proporre = to suggest	raccogliere = to collect	rimanere = to remain	scegliere = to choose
posso	propongo	raccolgo	rimango	scelgo
puoi	proponi	raccogli	rimani	scegli
può	propone	raccoglie	rimane	sceglie
possiamo	proponiamo	raccogliamo	rimaniamo	scegliamo
potete	proponete	raccogliete	rimanete	scegliete
possono	propongono	raccolgono	rimangono	scelgono

seder(si) = to sit down	sapere = to know (how to)	tacere = to keep silent	valere = to be worth	volere = to want
mi siedo	so	taccio	valgo	voglio
ti siedi	sai	taci	vali	vuoi
si siede	sa	tace	vale	vuole
ci sediamo	sappiamo	tacciamo	valiamo	vogliamo
vi sedete	sapete	tacete	valete	volete
si siedono	sanno	tacciono	valgono	vogliono

RELATIVE PRONOUN

CHE = who, who(m), which, that

l'uomo che è là =
the man who's there

l'uomo che vedo =
the man I see

la macchina che è nella strada =
the car which is in the road

il libro che leggete =
the book (which) you're reading

il prezzo che paghiamo =
the price (that) we pay

il prezzo che vogliono =
the price (that) they want

translate:

1) It's only worth a little.
2) I see only one man who's eating.
3) We never do interesting work.
4) They don't live in New York any more.
5) She isn't buying anything.
6) We've been eating for an hour.
7) We're having [taking] a steak today.
8) She's been reading the book for a week.
9) He doesn't drink any more.
10) We're taking Italian lessons this year.
11) He only sells cars.
12) He's been selling cars for five years.
13) A cup of coffee, please!
14) Men who work too much are unhappy.
15) The car which you're buying is too expensive.

---

revision/ripetizione

I don't live there any more.	Non vivo più là.
I don't sell anything.	Non vendo niente.
I only sell cars.	Vendo solo macchine.
We never live together.	Non viviamo mai assieme.
I don't see anybody.	Non vedo nessuno.

SI PUO' IMPARARE PRESTO L'ITALIANO?
Can one learn Italian quickly?

Sì, si può imparare presto. Yes, you can learn it quickly.
No, non si può imparare presto. No, you can't learn it quickly.

SI POSSONO VEDERE FILM AMERICANI IN ITALIA?
Can one see American films in Italy?

Sì, si possono vedere. Yes, you can.
No, non si possono vedere. No, you can't.

---

note: — don't forget the importance of si with the third person of a verb,
singular or plural. It can be translated by one, we, you or they.
— in negative sentences non is placed before si.

translate:

1) Non si vede niente.
2) Non si vendono più.panini qui.
3) Non si mangiano patate in Italia.
4) Non voglio più rispondere a questa domanda.
5) Il cameriere non vuole più lavorare.
6) Voglio solo un caffè.
7) Non ottengo mai niente.
8) Non vedo nessuno.

BISOGNA MANGIARE!	It's necessary to You must ⟩eat! You have to

DOVERE = TO HAVE TO, MUST

devo	I have to/must	**dobbiamo**	we have to/must
devi	you have to/must	**dovete**	you have to/must
deve	{ he she has to/must you have to/must	**devono**	{ they have to/must you have to/must

translate:

1) Devi riposare un poco!
2) Dobbiamo andare ora.
3) Deve mangiare qualche cosa!
4) Dovete scrivere al direttore.
5) Devono prendere il treno delle sette e un quarto.
6) Bisogna bere acqua ogni giorno.
7) Bisogna telefonare al signor Bianchi tra un'ora.
8) We have to see that movie.
9) They have to eat in the restaurant in spite of the price.
10) I must ask a question.
11) Do you have to go now?
12) You don't have to speak to Mary.
13) Is the cooking good in this restaurant?
14) Can I have the menu, please?
15) Instead of a meal, I'm eating a sandwich.
16) They never take the underground (subway) on Saturdays.

VOCABOLARIO

	traduzione	sinonimo-associato	contrario-associato
1. caro	expensive ≠ cheap	di valore = valuable	a buon mercato
2. parlare a	to speak to		
3. /-a piedi/-in vacanza/-alla radio	/-on foot/-on vacation /-on the radio	con la metropolitana = by underground (US subway)	
4. ora	now, at present	in questo momento, al momento = for the time being	ora no = not now, subito = at once
5. per	for, to		
6. (un) pasto	meal	(un) panino = sandwich	
7. /(una) prima colazione,/(una) colazione, (un) pranzo	/breakfast/lunch	l'ora di colazione, l'ora di pranzo = = lunchtime, cena = dinner	
8. assaggiare	to taste	si serva = help yourself	
9. /(un) coltello /(una) forchetta /(un) cucchiaio /(un) tovagliolo	/knife/fork/spoon /napkin	(un) cucchiaino da caffè = coffee spoon	
10. bisogna che io . . .	I have to . . .	devo = I must	
11. dire	to say	raccontare = to tell	
12. (un) ristorante	restaurant	(una) lista del giorno = menu	
13. /comandare /(un) cameriere	/to order/waiter	(una) cameriera = waitress	
14. /(una) tazza/(un) bicchiere/l'acqua /(una) brocca d'acqua	/cup/glass/water /a jug of water	acqua del rubinetto = tap water, (un) piattino = saucer, (una) bottiglia = bottle	
15. /pane/burro	/(some) bread/butter	pane tostato = toast	
16. (una) carne	meat	(una) bistecca = steak	
17. (un) piatto	plate, dish		
18. Is the cooking good?	Si mangia bene?		

LEZIONE 10

PRESENT VERBS IN '-IRE': PARTIRE

parto	I leave/am leaving	**non parto**	I don't leave/ am not leaving
parti	you leave	**non parti**	you don't leave
parte	he she leaves you leave	**non parte**	he she doesn't leave you don't leave
partiamo	we leave	**non partiamo**	we don't leave
partite	you leave	**non partite**	you don't leave
partono	they you leave	**non partono**	they you don't leave

note: remember the use of the Italian present for an action started in the past and still going on, e.g. dorme da ieri sera = he's been sleeping since last night.

DORME MOLTO?	Do you sleep a lot?
Sì, dormo molto.	Yes, I sleep a lot.
No, non dormo molto.	No, I don't sleep a lot.

SOME REGULAR 'IRE' VERBS

aprire = to open
avvertire = to warn
coprire = to cover
divertir (si) = to amuse (oneself)
dormire = to sleep
fuggire = to run away
mentire = to lie

offrire = to offer
punire = to punish
scoprire = to discover
seguire = to follow
sentire = to hear
servire = to serve
vestir(si) = to get dressed

IRREGULAR VERBS WHICH ADD 'ISC'
(except for <u>noi</u> and <u>voi</u>)

FINIRE			
fin<u>isc</u>o	I finish/am finishing	**non fin<u>isc</u>o**	I don't finish/ am not finishing
fin<u>isc</u>i	you finish	**non fin<u>isc</u>i**	you don't finish
fin<u>isc</u>e	{ he / she finishes / you finish	**non fin<u>isc</u>e**	{ he / she doesn't finish / you don't finish
fin<u>ia</u>mo	we finish	**non fin<u>ia</u>mo**	we don't finish
fin<u>ite</u>	you finish	**non fin<u>ite</u>**	you don't finish
<u>fin<u>isc</u>ono</u>	{ they / you finish	**non fin<u>isc</u>ono**	{ they / you don't finish

note: same thing for:
 <u>capire</u> = to understand; <u>preferire</u> = to prefer; <u>ubbidire</u> = to obey,
 <u>pulire</u> = to clean; <u>costruire</u> = to build; <u>proibire</u> = to forbid;
 <u>spedire</u> = to send; <u>punire</u> = to punish.

SI FINISCE TARDI OGNI GIORNO? Do you finish late every day?

Sì, <u>si finisce</u> tardi ogni giorno.   Yes, we finish late every day.
No, <u>non si finisce</u> tardi ogni giorno.   No, we don't finish late every day.

OTHER IRREGULAR VERBS

dire = to say	salire = to go up	uscire = to go out	venire to come
dico	salgo	esco	vengo
dici	sali	esci	vieni
dice	sale	esce	viene
diciamo	saliamo	usciamo	veniamo
dite	salite	uscite	venite
dicono	salgono	escono	vengono

VERBS OF MOVEMENT + DA

DA + . . . = FROM/TO

da + il = <u>dal</u>   **Vengo <u>dal</u> ristorante** = I'm coming from the restaurant.

da + i = <u>dai</u>   **Andiamo <u>dai</u> vicini** = We're going to the neighbours.

da + la = <u>dalla</u> **Viene <u>dalla</u> Francia** = It comes from France.

da + le = <u>dalle</u> **Vanno <u>dalle</u> zie**   = They're going to see their aunts.

note: da + lo = <u>dallo</u> (dallo studente), da + l' = <u>dall'</u> (dall'amico),
da + gli = <u>dagli</u> (dagli amici).

translate:

1) Do you hear anyone?
2) Why aren't you saying anything?
3) I sleep from time to time in the afternoon.
4) The children aren't sleeping yet.
5) She never understands the first time.
6) He never comes.
7) She's choosing from the menu.
8) I prefer wine, do you?
9) They don't understand anything.
10) Before going out we have to pay the bill.
11) We're coming from the station.
12) Do we have to leave?
13) They're building new houses near Rome.
14) I'm working a lot in order to finish early.

AVVERBI E LOCUZIONI (ADVERBS AND PHRASES) 2

1. **solo, sola, soli, sole**	alone	16. **– sul punto di** **– in procinto di**	– about to
2. **circa**	about, around	17. **anche prima**	even before
3. **tra**	– between – in (time)	18. **improvvisamente**	– all of a sudden – suddenly
4. **finalmente**	at last	19. **d'altra parte**	on the other hand
5. **nel frattempo**	in the meantime	20. **– subito** **– immediata-** **mente**	– at once – immediately
6. **forse**	perhaps		
7. **malgrado**	in spite of	21. **altrimenti**	otherwise
8. **invece di**	instead of	22. **verso**	towards
9. **di quando in quando**	from time to time	23. **– affinchè** **– perchè**	so that
10. **– a tempo** **– in orario**	on time	24. **– per prima cosa** **– dapprima**	at first
11. **– così** **– allora** **– e poi**	– thus – so – therefore	25. **– non ancora** **– già**	– not yet – already
12. **tuttavia**	however	26. **al più presto possibile**	as soon as possible
13. **– benchè** **– sebbene**	– although	27. **in qualche modo**	in some way
14. **esattamente**	exactly	28. **la prima volta**	the first time
15. **– per** **– al fine di**	– to – in order to		

VOCABOLARIO

	traduzione	sinonimo-associato	contrario-associato
1. scoppio	I've had enough ≠ I'm hungry	sono pieno = I'm full	ho fame, sono affamato, muoio di fame = starving
2. (il) sale	salt	(una, delle) spezie = spices	(il) pepe = pepper
3. /(un) pollo /(un) vitello	/chicken/veal		
4. al sangue	rare ≠ well done	molto al sangue = very rare	ben cotto, cotto a puntino = medium
5. /(un) agnello /(un) pesce	/lamb/fish	frutti di mare = seafood	
6. (una) patata	potato	(delle) patatine fritte = French fries	
7. (una) minestra	soup	(una) zuppa	
8. /(una) lattuga /(un) pomodoro	/lettuce/tomato	(un') insalata = salad	
9. Quant'è? /(il) prezzo	/How much is it? /price	Quanto costa?	gratuito = free
10. /(un) dolce /(la) frutta	/cake/dessert	(un) gelato = ice cream, (un) aroma = flavour	
11. /(un) conto /(una) mancia	/bill/tip	servizio compreso = tip included	
12. /(il) tè /(il) caffè	/tea/coffee	(il) latte = milk, (il) cappuccino = coffee with milk, (lo) zucchero = sugar	
13. (delle) uova con pancetta	eggs and bacon	(il) prosciutto = ham	
14. (un) formaggio	cheese	(il) vino = wine	
15. /(la) verdura /(un, dei) piselli	vegetables/peas	(una, delle) carote = carrots, dei fagiolini = runner (US string) beans	
16. Che cosa Le piacerebbe?	What would you care for?	Di che cosa ha voglia?	ho voglia di un caffè = I feel like a coffee
17. scegliere (da)	to choose (from)	(una) scelta = choice	
18. con ghiaccio	with ice ≠ straight		liscio

LEZIONE 11

DIRECT OBJECT PRONOUNS

subject		object
(io) I	→	**mi** me
(tu) you	→	**ti** you
(egli, lui, esso) he, it	→	**lo** him, it This answers the question:
(ella, lei, essa) she, it	→	**la** her, it WHO(M)? = **CHI?** WHAT? = **CHE COSA?**
(Lei) you	→	**La** you
si one, we, you, they		
(noi) we	→	**ci** us
(voi) you	→	**vi** you
(essi, loro, Loro) they	→	**li, Li** them, you (masculine plural)
(esse, loro, Loro) they	→	**Le, Le** them, you (feminine plural)

note: — lo, la, La become l' and L' before a vowel or h: e.g. l'amo = I love
him/her, L'aspetto qui = I'm waiting here for you.
       — you always write with capitals Lei, La, Loro, Li, Le.

MI VEDE?	Do you see me?
Sì, La vedo. **No, non La vedo.**	Yes, I see you. No, I don't see you.

He sees me.	**mi vede.**
I see you.	**ti/vi/La vedo, etc.**
I see him/it.	**lo vedo.**
I see her/it.	**la vedo.**
He sees us.	**ci vede.**
I see them.	**li/le vedo.**

note: one sees her = la si vede: si is always placed immediately before the
verb.

NEGATIVE

Non mi vede.	He doesn't see me.
Non ti vedo.	I don't see you.
Non lo vedo.	I don't see him.
Non la vedo.	I don't see her.
Non La vedo.	I don't see you.
Non ci vede.	He doesn't see us.
Non vi vedo.	I don't see you.
Non li/le vedo.	I don't see them.

note: non lo si vede = one doesn't see him, etc.

translate:

1) I see them.
2) She wants it.
3) We're listening to you.
4) We're eating it.
5) The lessons are too difficult and we don't understand them.
6) I'm taking the underground (US: subway). Are you?
7) Do you beat your wife from time to time? No, I never beat her.
8) The teacher is boring and we don't often listen to him.

Vanno a veder<u>lo</u>.   They're going to see him.
Vogliono ascoltar<u>li</u>.   They want to listen to them.

note: when the pronoun is the object of an infinitive, it follows and is attached to the verb.

put the correct pronoun instead of the noun:
e.g. Vedo <u>questo cane</u>.
         — <u>Lo</u> vedo.

1) Non capisco <u>questa lezione</u>.
2) Mettono <u>questo tappeto</u> nel loro appartamento.
3) Non possiamo comprare <u>questa vecchia poltrona</u>.
4) Mangio <u>formaggio</u> tutti i giorni.
5) Fanno entrare <u>questa signora</u> nel mio ufficio.
6) Prende a prestito di quando in quando <u>il mio cappotto</u>.
7) Compra <u>una macchina</u> la settimana prossima.
8) Prendiamo <u>l'aereo</u> alle otto di sera.
9) Aprono <u>la porta</u> ogni dieci minuti.
10) Fanno bene <u>il loro lavoro</u>.
11) Non riconosco <u>la donna</u>.
12) Mettete <u>sei libri</u> sulla tavola.
13) So <u>la risposta</u>.
14) Beviamo <u>del buon caffè</u>.
15) Posso vedere il <u>mio professore</u> per un'ora.
16) Impariamo <u>i verbi</u>.
17) Cominciamo <u>la lezione</u> con un controllo.
18) Non vediamo spesso <u>i film di quel tipo</u>.
19) Maria aspetta spesso <u>Pietro e me</u> dopo la lezione.
20) Vedo spesso <u>vostro fratello</u> e voi al cinema.

translate:

1) I don't like this hard cake and I don't want it.
2) I can see them with the director.
3) We can't hear you.
4) I'm not sending it.
5) He must make his bed.
6) You have to go upstairs to find it.
7) This diamond is expensive but I really like it.
8) It's the same as mine.
9) This lesson is difficult and I don't understand it.
10) You can see them often.
11) I don't like this woman.
12) Do you recognize them?
13) Do you want it for Monday?
14) The rooms upstairs are small.
15) I know many interesting things.
16) We only eat two meals a day.
17) The lesson's beginning. Do you find it difficult?
18) The word is difficult. I can't write it.
19) The work is rather long. I don't want to do it.
20) I'm playing a wonderful game. Do you know it?
21) She's a fabulous gal. Do you know her?
22) I need some cigarettes and must buy them.
23) The book's difficult but I must finish it.
24) They're calling us.
25) Can you see those women? — Yes, I can see them.
26) Do you love your parents, Johnny? — Yes, I love them.
27) Does she really want it? She can have [take] it.
28) If you want to borrow my yellow raincoat, you can have [take] it.

CONTRARI (OPPOSITES) 3

1) **Sono felice** ≠ **triste**
   I'm happy / sad

2) **Enrico è grande** ≠ **piccolo**
   Harry's tall / small

3) **E' come il mio** ≠ **diverso da**
   It's the same as mine / different from

4) **Il dolce è duro** ≠ **molle**
   The cake's hard / soft

5) **La biancheria è asciutta** ≠ **bagnata**
   The laundry's dry / wet

6) **E' venuto prima** ≠ **dopo**
   He came before / after

7) **Un cappotto di pelliccia è caro** ≠ **a buon mercato**
   A fur coat is expensive / cheap

8) **L'acqua è profonda** ≠ **bassa**
   The water's deep / shallow

9) **Le stanze in alto** ≠ **in basso, a pianterreno**
   The rooms upstairs / downstairs

10) **La mia macchina è vecchia** ≠ **nuova**
    My car's old / new

11) **La risposta è buona/giusta** ≠ **sbagliata**
    The answer's true/so / false

12) **Il mio diamante è vero** ≠ **falso/una bidonata**
    My diamond's real / fake/phony

13) **Lavoro a orario ridotto** ≠ **a orario completo**
    I work part-time / full-time

14) **Veste da città/elegante** ≠ **sportivo**
    He wears formal clothes / casual

15) **Il ricevimento à in abito da sera** ≠ **alla buona**
    The party is formal / informal

16) **Non sia grossolano/maleducato**   ≠   **educato**
    Don't be rude   polite

17) **Il suo lavoro è accurato**   ≠   **trascurato**
    His work is careful   careless

18) **Mio fratello è gentile/cortese**   ≠   **scortese/cattivo**
    My brother's kind   mean

19) **Il cinema è pieno/affollato**   ≠   **vuoto/non un'anima viva**
    The movie is crowded   empty/not a soul

20) **Intelligente**   ≠   **stupido/sciocco**
    Bright/intelligent   stupid/dumb

21) **La mia camera è in disordine**   ≠   **in ordine**
    My room's sloppy   neat

22) **Cominciare/iniziare**   ≠   **finire/fermare**
    To start/to begin   to finish/to stop

23) **Insegnare**   ≠   **imparare**
    To teach   to learn

24) **Prendere a prestito**   ≠   **imprestare/dare a prestito**
    To borrow   to lend

25) **Chiudere**   ≠   **aprire**
    To close/to shut   to open

26) **Dare**   ≠   **prendere**
    To give   to take

27) **E' agiato/benestante**   ≠   **è senza un soldo/al verde**
    He's well off   broke

28) **Quest' uomo è coraggioso**   ≠   **vigliacco**
    This man is brave   cowardly

VOCABOLARIO

	traduzione	sinonimo-associato	contrario-associato
1. (una) camera	bedroom	fare il proprio letto = to make one's bed	
2. /(un) soggiorno /(una) sala da pranzo	/living room /dining room	(un) salotto = drawing room, (una) stanza = room	
3. (una) cucina	kitchen	(una) padella = pan, (una) pentola = pot	
4. /(una) stanza da bagno/(un) acquaio/(un) lavandino	/bathroom/sink /washbasin	quel posticino = the John = (il) gabinetto, (la) latrina	
5. /(una) moquette /(una, delle) tende	/fitted carpet /curtains	(un) tappeto = carpet	
6. di sotto	downstairs ≠ upstairs		di sopra
7. /(un) apparta-mento/(una) casa	/apartment or flat /house	(uno, dei) mobili = furniture	
8. (una) lampada		(una) lampadina = bulb, (una) luce = light	
9. —sto bene —trovo che Lei ha torto	—I feel good —I feel you're wrong		
10. (una) via	street	(una) strada = road	
11. (un) ascensore	lift, elevator	(le) scale = stairs	
12. comodo	comfortable		scomodo = uncomfortable
13. (un) piano	floor	in terra, sul pavimento = on the floor, (il) suolo = ground	(il) soffitto = the ceiling
14. dipende da Lei	it depends on you		
15. faccia presto!	Hurry up!		faccia con calma!
16. (un) armadio	cupboard	(uno) scaffale = shelf	

LEZIONE 12

INDIRECT OBJECT PRONOUNS

direct object			indirect object	
mi	me	→	(a) **me, mi**	(to) me
ti	you	→	(a) **te, ti**	(to) you
lo	him, it	→	(a) **lui, gli**	(to) him, (to) it
la	her, it	→	(a) **lei, le**	(to) her, (to) it
La	you	→	(a) **Lei, Le**	(to) you
ci	us	→	(a) **noi, ci**	(to) us
vi	you	→	(a) **voi, vi**	(to) you
li, le	them	→	(a) **loro, loro**	(to) them

note: — these indirect pronouns don't exist in English and are a true problem.
— whenever 'to' is said or implied in English, you must use these in Italian.
— me, te, lui, lei, Lei, noi, voi, loro are used for stress, after prepositions and in comparisons: e.g. guarda me, non te = it's me that he's looking at, preferisco andare con lui = I prefer to go with him, è più alto di me = he's taller than me.

GLI PARLA SPESSO?	Do you often speak to him?
Sì, gli parlo spesso.	Yes, I often speak to him.
No, non gli parlo spesso.	No, I don't often speak to him.

Mi parla	He's speaking <u>to me.</u>
Ti parlo	I'm speaking to you.
Gli parlo	I'm speaking <u>to him.</u>
Le parlo	I'm speaking <u>to her.</u>
Le parlo	I'm speaking <u>to you.</u>
Ci parla	He's speaking <u>to us.</u>
Vi parlo	I'm speaking <u>to you.</u>
Parlo **loro**	I'm speaking <u>to them.</u>

note: — parlo <u>a me</u> = I'm speaking to myself.
       — <u>loro</u> is always placed after the verb.

NEGATIVE

Non mi parla.	He's not speaking <u>to me.</u>
Non ti parlo.	I'm not speaking <u>to you.</u>
Non gli parlo.	I'm not speaking <u>to him.</u>
Non le parlo.	I'm not speaking <u>to her.</u>
Non Le parlo.	I'm not speaking <u>to you.</u>
Non ci parla.	He's not speaking <u>to us.</u>
Non vi parlo.	I'm not speaking <u>to you.</u>
Non parlo loro.	I'm not speaking <u>to them.</u>

translate:

1) I often speak to her but not to him.
2) These books don't belong to the boss, they belong to me,
3) My mother-in-law doesn't write to us often.
4) I love my parents and I often think of them.
5) He's giving me his last book.
6) They're always telling us their problems.
7) I never speak to him.
8) We're sending the books to you today.

DIRECT AND INDIRECT PRONOUNS TOGETHER

Me lo mandi?   Do you send it to me?
Te lo do.   I give it to you.
Glielo do.   I give it to him/her/you.

note: — when two pronouns are used with the same verb, the indirect object
       precedes the direct object, contrary to English usage.
      — mi, ti, ci, vi become me, te, ce, ve when followed by lo, la, le, li, ne
       (= of it). e.g. ve lo do = I give it to you.
      — gli and le/Le become glielo, gliela, glieli, gliele and gliene when
       followed by the same pronouns. e.g. glieli porto = I bring them to
       you.

REMEMBER!!
   when the pronoun is the object of an infinitive, it follows and is attached
   to the verb.

ATTACHED PRONOUNS

Voglio mandarglielo.   I want to send it to him/her/you.
Preferisco portartelo.   I prefer to bring it to you.
Non vogliono dirmi la verità. They don't want to tell me the truth.
Non vogliono dirmela.   They don't want to tell it to me.

note: the direct and indirect object are attached to the infinitive.

68

VERBS FOLLOWED BY A

appartenere a	to belong to
dare a	to give to
dire a	to say to, to tell to
mandare a	to send to
mostrare a	to show to
pensare a	to think of
portare a	to bring to
raccontare a	to tell to
scrivere a	to write to
spiegare a	to explain to

gli scrivo	I'm writing to him.
le scrivo	I'm writing to her.
Le scrivo	I'm writing to you.
ti spiego il problema	I'm explaining the problem to you.
mi spiegano il problema	they're explaining the problem to me.
le dà tutto	he/she gives her anything.
non ci scrivete spesso	you don't write often to us.

translate:

1) Gli scrivo di quando in quando.
2) Ti dico di farlo!
3) Le date il tempo di lavorare.
4) Ci spiegano il problema.
5) Pensiamo molto a te.
6) Lo trovo facile.
7) Tua sorella gli dà tutto.
8) Mio zio vi dice cose stupide.
9) Suo padre le insegna l'italiano.
10) Vado a mostrarglielo.

insert the correct pronoun:

1) Posso veder(lo, gli) solo una volta alla settimana.
2) Dovete dir(essi, loro) tutto.
3) Tuo padre vuole offrir(tu, ti, te) un lavoro.
4) Devo lasciar(la, le) sola questa sera.
5) Che cosa (Le, La, Lei) porto, signore?
6) Potete scriver(io, mi, me) subito?
7) Tu (la, le, lei) conosci forse.
8) La suocera di (la, le, lei) è ancora una bella donna.
9) I genitori di (lo, gli, lui) abitano a Roma.
10) Il marito della mia segretaria non (la, le, lei) dà mai denaro.
11) I nonni della mia fidanzata non (la, le, lei) vedono da due anni.
12) I suoi nonni abitano in Italia e non (essi, li, loro) vede da due anni.
13) Può imprestar (io, mi, me) del denaro? — Mi dispiace, non posso imprestar (glielo, gliela, glieli, gliele).
14) Mia moglie vuole una donna ad ore per fare i lavori di casa, ma non (la, le, lei) trova.

translate:

1) I know his mother. Do you?
2) Fortunately, the maid does the housework.
3) The car belongs to me.
4) She tells them all her problems.
5) He's giving her a nice sweater. What are you giving her?
6) I've been working for a long time. Are you still working?
7) He often thinks of his wife.
8) Do you often speak to her? — I hardly ever speak to her.
9) Who does that house belong to?
10) I see him every day.
11) Do you often see them? — No, I rarely see them.
12) Can I borrow your pencil? — Yes, you can borrow it.

VOCABOLARIO

	traduzione	sinonimo-associato	contrario-associato
1. perfino	even	perfino io = even me	
2. se	if	se sì o no = whether or not	
3. (una) madre	mother		(un) padre = father
4. (una) sorella	sister		(un) fratello = brother
5. (una) suocera	mother-in-law	(i) suoceri = in-laws	(un) suocero = father-in-law
6. (una) nipote	niece	(una) zia = aunt, (uno) zio = uncle	(un) nipote = nephew
7. /(un) nonno/(un, una) nipotino(a)	/grandfather /grandchild		(una) nonna = grandmother
8. (un) marito	husband		(una) moglie = wife
9. (un) figlio	son ≠ daughter	(i)genitori = parents	(una) figlia
10. celibe	bachelor man ≠ married	nubile = single woman fidanzato = fiancé	sposato
11. (una) famiglia	family	(i) parenti = relatives	
12. (una) persona	person	la gente = people	
13. ad esempio	for instance		
14. gentile	nice ≠ mean	giusto = fair	sgarbato
15. fare i lavori di casa	to do the housework	(una) casalinga = housewife	
16. per	for	durante = during	fino a = until
17. strano	strange, bizarre	curioso, bizzarro	normale
18. fortunatamente	fortunately ≠ unfortunately	per fortuna = luckily	sfortunatamente
19. (una) domestica	maid	(una) donna ad ore	
20. pazienza!	too bad, never mind ≠ all the better		tanto meglio!

LEZIONE 13

SU + . . . = ON THE

su + il = **sul**	**Il giornale è sul letto.** = The newspaper's on the bed.
su + i = **sui**	**I tovaglioli sono sui piatti.** = The napkins are on the plates.
su + la = **sulla**	**La Sua camicia è sulla sedia.** = Your shirt's on the chair.
su + le = **sulle**	**Ci sono francobolli sulle lettere?** = Are there any stamps on the letters?

note: — su + lo = **sullo** (sullo specchio = on the mirror), su + l' = **sull'** (sull'albero = on the tree), su + gli = **sugli** (sugli alberi = on the trees).
— remember: you can say 'sopra' instead of 'su', e.g. sul letto = sopra il letto = on the bed, sulla sedia = sopra la sedia = on the chair.

IN + . . . = IN THE

in + il = **nel**	**Siamo nel giardino.** = We're in the garden.
in + i = **nei**	**C'è molta frutta nei negozi.** = There is a lot of fruit in the shops.
in + la = **nella**	**Ci sono topi nella casa?** = Are there mice in the house?
in + le = **nelle**	**A Venezia non ci sono veicoli nella vie.** = In Venice there aren't vehicles in the streets.

note: in + lo = **nello** (nello stivale = in the boot), in + l' = **nell'** (nell'albero = in the tree), in + gli = **negli** (negli stivali = in the boots).

NE = SOME, ANY

HA DENARO?   Have you (some) money?

Sì, ne ho.   Yes, I have (some).
No, non ne ho.   No, I don't have any.

note: NE is often used in Italian as a pronoun: He has some books = ha dei
      libri. He has some = ne ha.

translate:

1) E' sulla tavola la scarpa?
2) E' sulla sedia il portacenere?
3) E' sul letto la Sua penna?
4) E' sul libro la matita?
5) E' sul piatto il formaggio?
6) Sono nel giardino i Suoi suoceri?
7) Vuole una sigaretta? — No, grazie, ne ho.
8) La segretaria è nell'ufficio del direttore.
9) C'è una macchina rossa nella via.
10) C'è burro sul pane?
11) Is there a carpet in the room?
12) Are there bikes in the underground?
13) There is a boring lesson in the book. Which one?
14) Are there boring teachers in the room?
15) You can see them in the road.
16) Are there mice in the kitchen?
17) Is there wine in the bottles?
18) Is there water in the glasses?
19) Is there some coffee in the cups?
20) I don't have any newspapers. Do you have any?

POCO	=	FEW, LITTLE
Ho **poco** denaro.	=	I have little money.
Ho **pochi** libri.	=	I have few books.
Ho **poca** pazienza.	=	I have little patience.
Ho **poche** matite.	=	I have few pencils.

MOLTO	=	A LOT OF, MUCH, MANY
Ho **molto** denaro.	=	I have a lot of money.
Ho **molti** libri.	=	I have a lot of/many books.
Ho **molta** pazienza.	=	I have a lot of/much patience.
Ho **molte** matite.	=	I have a lot of/many pencils.

note: — molto and poco when used as adjectives agree with the noun in number and gender.
— remember: molto and poco when used as adverbs are invariable: e.g. una ragazza molto bella = a very beautiful girl, sono tipi poco intelligenti = they're guys of little intelligence.

UN PO'	=	A LITTLE
Ho **un po'** di denaro.	=	I have a little money.
Denaro? **Ne** ho **un po'**.	=	Money? I have a little (of it).

QUALCHE	=	SOME, ANY
Ha qualche libro?	=	Do you have some/any books?
Sì, ho qualche libro.	=	Yes, I have some books.
Sì, ne ho.	=	Yes, I have some.

note: CAREFUL! 'qualche' is invariable and it always precedes a singular
      noun: (Are there any girls? = C'è qualche ragazza?).

ESSERE ABITUATO A	=	TO BE USED TO
E' ABITUATO A BERE VINO?	=	Are you used to drinking wine?
Sì, sono abituato a bere vino.	=	Yes, I'm used to drinking wine.
No, non sono abituato a bere vino.	=	No, I'm not used to drinking wine.

AVER BISOGNO DI	=	TO NEED
HA BISOGNO DI DENARO?	=	Do you need (some) money?
Sì, ne ho bisogno.	=	Yes, I need some.
No, non ne ho bisogno.	=	No, I don't need any.

translate, then answer in the negative with NE:

1) Do you want some coffee?
2) Does she need money?
3) Do you want to drink wine?
4) Do you sometimes eat potatoes?
5) Do you drink a lot of milk?
6) Do the students need another lesson?
7) Does he need a new car?
8) Do you sell cars?
9) Does your mother often buy cakes?
10) Do they take English lessons?
11) Have they a lot of sweaters?
12) Does he know any girls?
13) Do we need all these magazines?
14) Do they have some work to do today?
15) Am I afraid of their dogs?
16) Do you need a doctor?
17) Do you eat ham?
18) Do you want some tea?

translate, then answer in the negative with POCO, POCHI — POCA, POCHE.

1) Avete molti parenti?
2) Hanno molte sigarette?
3) Ha molti bei giocattoli quel bambino?
4) E' molto intelligente quell'uomo?
5) Studi italiano da molti mesi?
6) Leggete molti libri interessanti?
7) Ci sono molti impiegati nel Suo ufficio?
8) C'è molta gente nel ristorante?
9) Ci sono molte donne affascinanti?
10) Ci sono molti topi nella casa?
11) Volete molte carote?
12) Prendono molta verdura?

VOCABOLARIO

	traduzione	sinonimo-associato	contrario-associato
1. (la settimana) prossima	next (week)	la settimana seguente = the following week, tra una settimana = in a week	la settimana scorsa = last week
2. ottenere	to get	ricevere = to receive	
3. aver bisogno di	to need		mancare (di) = lack
4. /scherzare/Lei scherza!	/to kid/you're kidding!	prendere in giro = to tease, uno scherzo = a joke	
5. pare che	it seems	sembra che	
6. meraviglioso	wonderful, fantastic ≠ dreadful, horrible	formidabile, fantastico; affascinante = charming	orribile, orrendo, spaventoso, schifoso = shitty, senza valore = worthless, crummy
7. /(un) giornale /(una) carta	/newspaper /paper	/(una) rivista = magazine	
8. giocare	to play	giocare d'azzardo = to gamble, (un) gioco = game, (un) giocattolo = toy, (una) bambola = doll	
9. stupido	stupid, dumb ≠ intelligent	asino, scemo = an ass	intelligente, spiritoso
10. tutto	everything, all	qualche cosa = something, qualunque cosa = anything	niente = nothing, nessuno = none, nobody
11. cadere	to fall	lasciar cadere = to drop	raccogliere = to pick up
12. qualche	some	alcuni = few, some	nessuno = not any
13. – ogni quanto tempo? – da quando?	– how often? – how long?	da quanto tempo?	
14. /bello/carino	/beautiful/cute, pretty	stupendo	brutto = ugly
15. stasera	tonight ≠ last night	(la) sera = evening	ieri sera, domani sera = tomorrow night

LEZIONE 14

(NON) MAI, A VOLTE	=	NEVER, EVER
LEI FUMA, <u>A VOLTE?</u> <u>LE CAPITA DI</u> FUMARE?	=	Do you <u>ever</u> smoke?
No, <u>non</u> fumo <u>mai</u>.	=	No, <u>I never</u>/<u>don't ever</u> smoke.

translate, then answer in the negative:

1) Do you ever gamble?
2) Does he ever read the paper?
3) Does he ever tease his wife?
4) Do they ever go to the theatre?
5) Do you ever take trips?
6) Are we ever wrong?
7) Does she ever work part-time?
8) Are you ever lucky?

CHE = THAT		
CHE COSA DICE?	=	What is he saying?
Dice <u>che</u> hai ragione.	=	He says (that) you're right.

note: 'that' in English can be optional, but <u>che</u> in Italian is
obligatory.

translate:

1) I know (that) you need money.
2) They say you're lucky.
3) You don't have to tell me that I'm wrong.
4) I know the guy's a bastard.
5) Is it true (that) we need help?
6) I agree he must do it.

78

PUBLIC ENEMY NUMBER ONE — THE ITALIAN PRESENT!!!

LEGGO		
I'm reading now.	=	**Leggo ora.**
I often read.	=	**Leggo spesso.**
I've been reading for an hour.	=	**Leggo da un'ora (è un'ora che leggo).**

note: THE ITALIANS LIVE IN THE PRESENT! You must get used to
using it much more than we do in English.

Siamo sposati da cinque anni.	=	We've been married for five years.
Lavora qui da giugno.	=	He/she's been working here since June.
Sono qui da una settimana.	=	I've been here for a week.
Da quanto tempo è qui?	=	For how long have you been here?

translate, then put in the interrogative:

1) They've been here since January.
2) They've been in their new house since the summer.
3) The students have been on vacation for a month.
4) I haven't seen them for a long time.
5) My parents have been on the beach since this morning.
6) They always take trips during the summer.
7) I've been working here since the winter
8) She can't [doesn't] find a part-time job and must work full-time.
9) I've known him for ten years.
10) They've been living in Rome for three years. They usually live in Europe.
11) I know that he has been married for two years.
12) She's lucky now, and she's been lucky since last year.

PRESENT PARTICIPLE: **STARE + -ANDO/-ENDO** = TO BE + -ING

<u>sto</u> parl<u>ando</u>/prend<u>endo</u>/fin<u>endo</u>			=	I'm (in the midst) of speaking /taking/finishing
<u>stai</u>	"	"	"	=	you are, etc.
<u>sta</u>	"	"	"		
<u>stiamo</u>	"	"	"		
<u>state</u>	"	"	"		
<u>stanno</u>	"	"	"		

note: — to form the present participle, add '-ando' to the stem of the '-are' verbs, and '-endo' to the '-ere' and '-ire' verbs.

       — parlo = I'm speaking; for slight increase of emphasis use 'sto parlando', e.g. sto parlando da due ore = parlo da due ore = I've been speaking for two hours.

STA MANGIANDO?	=	Are you eating? (in the midst of eating?)
Sì, <u>sto</u> mang<u>iando</u>.	=	Yes, I'm eating.
No, non <u>sto</u> mang<u>iando</u>.	=	No, I'm not eating.

CAREFUL!!!

STA SCRIVENDO UNA LETTERA?	=	Are you writing a letter?
Sì, <u>sto scrivendo</u> una lettera.	=	Yes, I'm writing a letter.
Sì, <u>sto scrivendola</u>.	=	Yes, I'm writing it.

note: as with the infinitive, you attach the object, whether direct or indirect.

VERBI IRREGOLARI – PRESENT PARTICIPLE

fare (to do, to make) → facendo
bere (to drink) → bevendo
condurre (to lead) → conducendo
dire (to say) → dicendo
porre (to put) → ponendo
trarre (to draw) → traendo

translate using the emphatic form:

1) We've been eating for an hour.
2) They've been skiing since this morning.
3) We're waiting for the teacher now.
4) The kids have been playing for two hours.
5) He's gambling now. He always gambles on Saturdays.
6) She's talking now. She always talks a lot. She has been talking for two hours.
7) You've been reading the same book since yesterday.
8) The maid is doing the housework now. She always does it in the afternoon.
9) I'm writing a letter to my in-laws. I always write to them on Sundays.
10) She's eating now. She always eats at this hour.
11) You've been talking for an hour. You always talk too much.
12) I've been waiting for you for five hours. I always have to wait for you.
13) Stanno viaggiando ora i Suoi genitori?
14) Stiamo chiamandolo.
15) Sto aspettandoti.
16) Stanno ascoltandoci.
17) Sta piovendo, sta nevicando contemporaneamente.
18) Che cosa stanno facendo? Stanno camminando.
19) Sto chiudendo la finestra.
20) Sto dandoglieli.
21) Sta spiegandoci il problema.
22) Stai facendolo ora.

VOCABOLARIO

	traduzione	sinonimo-associato	contrario-associato
1. /buono/migliore /il migliore	/good/better /the best		/cattivo/peggiore /il peggiore = bad /worse/the worst
2. /viaggiare/(un) viaggio/(un) operatore turistico	/to travel/a trip /a travel agent	fare un viaggio = to take a trip, (un) soggiorno = a stay	
3. (un') andata semplice	one way ticket ≠ return (round trip)		un'andata-e-ritorno
4. prenotare	to reserve ≠ to cancel	completo = booked	disdire (la prenotazione)
5. /(una) città,/(un) villaggio	/city/village	(un) paese = a country	
6. in vacanza	on vacation		
7. /(una) spiaggia /(una) costume da bagno	/beach/bathing suit	in riva al mare = seaside, la sabbia = the sand, nuotare = to swim, la piscina = pool	
8. /(una) montagna, /in campagna	/mountain/in the country	sciare = to ski	(una) valle = valley
9. sono per	I'm for ≠ against	in favore di	contro
10. (il) denaro	money	i soldi, i quattrini, (la) grana = dough, (il) resto = change	in contanti = cash
11. /(un) assegno /(una) banca	/cheque (US check) bank		
12. (una) macchina fotografica	camera	film = film	
13. (un) posto simpatico	a nice place	(un) luogo = spot	
14. /(una) doccia /(un) bagno	/shower/bath	(una) vasca da bagno = a bathtub	
15. (un) colpo di sole	sunburn	(una) tintarella = tan	
16. /(una) commedia /(un) attore/(un) teatro	/a play/actor/theatre	(un) commediante = comedian	

LEZIONE 15

FUTURE VERBS IN '-ARE' AND '-ERE': PARLARE, PRENDERE

parlerò	I'll speak	**non parlerò**	I won't speak, etc.
parlerai	you'll speak	**non parlerai**	
parlerà	{ he she'll speak you'll speak	**non parlerà**	
parleremo	we'll speak	**non parleremo**	
parlerete	you'll speak	**non parlerete**	
parleranno	{ they'll speak you'll speak	**non parleranno**	

note: — the above endings are added to the stem of the -ARE and -ERE
verbs, e.g. portare = to bring → porterò (I'll bring), prendere = to
take → prenderò (I'll take).
— all verbs in -CARE and -GARE add an 'h' to the stem of the verb
before the endings, e.g. giocare = to play → giocherò (I'll play),
pagare = to pay → pagherò (I'll pay).
— the verbs in -IARE lose the 'i', e.g. mangiare = to eat → mangerò (I'll
eat), cominciare = to begin → comincerò (I'll begin).

GLI PARLERAI DOMANI/TRA DUE GIORNI/LA SETTIMANA
PROSSIMA?

Will you speak to him tomorrow?/in two days?/next week?

Sì, gli parlerò domani.   Yes, I'll speak to him tomorrow.
No, non gli parlerò domani.   No, I won't speak to him tomorrow.

FUTURE VERBS IN '-IRE': PARTIRE

partirò	= I'll leave	**non partirò**	= I won't leave, etc.
partirai	= you'll leave	**non partirai**	
partirà	he = she'll leave } you	**non partirà**	
partiremo	= we'll leave	**non partiremo**	
partirete	= you'll leave	**non partirete**	
partiranno	= they you'll leave }	**non partiranno**	

note: — the above endings are added to the stem of the -IRE verbs,
e.g. uscire = to go out → uscirò (I'll go out).
— those -IRE verbs which add 'isc' in the present are regular in the
future, e.g. finire = to finish → finirò (I'll finish), capire = to
understand → capirò (I'll understand).

MI DIRA' LA VERITA'?

Sì, Le dirò la verità.
No, non Le dirò la verità.

Will you tell me the truth?

Yes, I'll tell you the truth.
No, I won't tell you the truth.

SOME IRREGULAR VERBS

andare = to go andrò, andrai, andrà, andremo, andrete, andranno	**avere** = to have avrò, avrai, avrà, avremo, avrete, avranno	**bere** = to drink berrò, berrai, berrà, berremo, berrete, berranno
cadere = to fall cadrò, cadrai, etc.	**condurre** = to lead condurrò	**dare** = to give darò
dolere = to ache dorrò	**dovere** = must dovrò	**essere** = to be sarò
fare = to do, to make farò	**morire** = to die morirò, morrò	**parere** = to seem parrò
porre = to put porrò	**potere** = can potrò	**rimanere** = to remain rimarrò
sapere = to know saprò	**stare** = to stay starò	**tenere** = to keep terrò
trarre = to draw trarrò	**valere** = to be worth varrò	**vedere** = to see vedrò
venire = to come verrò	**vivere** = to live vivrò	**volere** = to want vorrò

SPECIAL USE OF THE FUTURE

CHE ORA E'?	What's the time?
<u>Sarà</u> mezzogiorno.	It's probably noon.

note: the future in Italian is employed to express what is probable, even
      when no idea of future is implied.

translate:

1) I'll answer your letter tomorrow.
2) We'll take a trip next week.
3) I'll be able to do it in a week.
4) He'll come tomorrow.
5) She'll write sometimes, I hope.
6) They'll buy a car instead of a bike.
7) We'll do the housework next Sunday.
8) I'll be on time.
9) You probably think I'm wrong.
10) I'll drink four glasses of wine tonight.
11) At last I'll live in Rome!
12) They'll have a lot of cash with them.
13) He'll leave a tip for the waiter.
14) Will you be able to come in two weeks?
15) I'll have to go tomorrow.
16) You'll catch a cold because of the weather.
17) I'll be ready at ten.
18) He'll need a tablet for his headache.

translate:

1) Sarò a casa questo pomeriggio.
2) Avrai bisogno di denaro?
3) Sono sicuro che sarà fortunata.
4) Lo porterò con me stasera.
5) Vi vedremo la settimana prossima?
6) Sai se ci aiuteranno?
7) Smetteremo di lavorare tra un'ora.
8) Avremo presto fame.
9) Dice che non comprerà un'altra macchina bianca.
10) Te lo dirà domani.
11) Non sanno se potranno farlo o no.
12) Quanti anni ha il tuo capufficio? — Avrà cinquant'anni.
13) Quanti chilometri ci saranno da Roma a Genova? — Ci saranno cinquecento chilometri.

VOCABOLARIO

	traduzione	sinonimo-associato	contrario-associato
1. stanco	tired, dead-beat	stanco morto, sfinito = exhausted	sentirsi bene = to feel great
2. malato	ill ≠ well	essere in piena forma, star benone	star bene, stare meglio = to feel better
3. prendersi un raffreddore	to catch a cold	l'influenza = flu, la febbre = fever	
4. starnuta(i)re	to sneeze	salute! = God bless you!	
5. tossire	to cough	(un) mal di gola = a sore throat	
6. (una) medicina	medicine	(una) pillola = a tablet, a pill, la pillola = the Pill	
7. /(un) dentista /(un) mal di denti	/dentist/toothache	i denti = teeth	
8. /(un) mal di testa /(un) mal di pancia	/headache /stomachache	(lo) stomaco, (il) ventre = tummy	
9. – fa male – Le fa male?	– it hurts – does it hurt?	(un) dolore = pain	
10. pronto?	/ready?/hello?(phone)	sono pronto = I'm ready	
11. succedere	to happen, occur	capitare, aver luogo	
12. riposarsi	to rest	non si arrabbi! calma! = take it easy!	
13. ridere	to laugh ≠ to cry	un sorriso = a smile	piangere, (una, delle) lagrime = tears
14. avere un buon aspetto	to look well		
15. ne dubito	I doubt it	ne ero sicuro = I thought as much	non ne dubito = I don't doubt it
16. lo stesso di	the same as ≠ different from	uguale a = similar to	diverso da
17. star male/poco bene	to be ill/sick		

LEZIONE 16

CONDITIONAL — first form

SE HO IL DENARO, COMPRO UNA MACCHINA.
   present   present

Se <u>ha</u> il denaro, <u>compra</u> una macchina?	= If you have the money, will you buy a car?
Sì, se <u>ho</u> il denaro, <u>compro</u> una macchina.	= Yes, if I have the money, I'll buy a car.
No, se <u>ho</u> il denaro, non <u>compro</u> una macchina.	= No, if I have the money, I won't buy a car.

note: in Italian when the condition is on the point of being realized you use the present tense in *both* parts of the sentences. 'Se ho il denaro, compro una macchina' means that the speaker only has to count his money before going to buy a car.

SE AVRO' IL DENARO/QUANDO AVRO' IL DENARO, COMPRERO'
   future   **UNA MACCHINA.**   future

Se <u>avrà</u> il denaro, <u>comprerà</u> una macchina?	= If you have the money, will you buy a car?
Sì, se <u>avrò</u> il denaro, <u>comprerò</u> une macchina.	= Yes, if I have the money (one day), I'll buy a car.
No, se <u>avrò</u> il denaro, non <u>comprerò</u> una macchina.	= No, If I have the money (one day), I won't buy a car.

<u>QUANDO</u> VERRA', GLI DARO' LA LETTERA.
    future   future

When he comes, I'll give him the letter.

---

note: the future is employed in Italian in subordinate clauses *referring to the future* which are introduced either by <u>se</u> (= if) or by a conjunction of time (<u>quando</u> = when).

translate, then answer affirmatively:

1) Se sei stanco, vai a letto?
2) Se hai mal di gola, prendi delle pillole?
3) Se ho fame, mi dai qualche cosa da mangiare?
4) Se il libro è noioso, lo leggi lo stesso?
5) Se avete abbastanza denaro, comprate una nuova casa?
6) Se non capite il professore, glielo dite?
7) Se fa bel tempo, andiamo al cinema lo stesso?
8) Se potete andarci domani, ci andate?
9) Se c'è un bel film, me lo dici?
10) Se la carne non è cotta, la mangi?

translate, then give the negative answer:

1) If she drinks too much, will her husband be happy?
2) If you need help, will you call me?
3) If you are ill, will you go to the doctor?
4) If I must take a trip next week, will you come with me?
5) If I ask you a question, will you answer me?
6) If I need money, will you lend me some?
7) If you like her cake, will you tell her?
8) If they don't understand, will the teacher help them?
9) If she doesn't call you tonight, will you call her?
10) If you can't do it, will you tell me?
11) If you can't come, will you call and tell me?
12) If you don't like the meal, what will you do?
13) If you need cash, will you go to the bank?
14) If we don't answer, will the teacher go crazy?
15) If the cop's a bastard, will we be able to do something?
16) If the restaurant's expensive, will we go in any case?
17) If your wife loves you, will you be happy?
18) If the boss comes late, shall we too?

1. **più presto è, meglio è**	the sooner the better	16. **solo** — **ho solo**	only — I only have
2. **il giorno dopo**	the next day	17. **ogni due settimane**	every other week
3. **la vigilia**	the day/night before	18. **non appena**	as soon as
4. **mentre**	while, during	19. **apposta**	on purpose
5. **ogni quanto tempo?**	how often?	20. **per quanto riguarda**	as far as
6. **in media**	on the average	21. **parecchi**	several
7. **soprattutto**	above all	22. — **inoltre** — **per di più**	— besides — what's more
8. **per ogni evenienza**	just in case	23. — **nell'insieme** — **in generale** — **la maggior parte di**	— on the whole — in general — most of
9. **presto**	soon	
10. **ancora una volta**	once more, again	
11. **secondo**	according to	24. **in quanto a (me)**	as for (me)
12. **da, a partire da**	as of . . . from on . . .	25. **nella misura in cui**	in so far as
13. — **dato che** — **poiché**	— given that — since	26. **tra due settimane**	in a fortnight
14. — **recente- mente** — **non molto tempo fa**	— recently — not long ago	27. **lo stesso**	all the same
		28. **da quando?**	how long?
15. **abbastanza**	enough	

VOCABOLARIO

	traduzione	sinonimo-associato	contrario-associato
1. telefonare	to call (up)	chiamare al telefono, una telefonata = a call	
2. riattaccare	to hang up ≠ to pick up		staccare (il ricevitore)
3. rimanga in linea	hold on		
4. chi parla?	Who's speaking?	Chi lo/la vuole?	Il signor . . . La desidera al telefono
5. Le passo . . .	I'll put you through to . . .		
6. /dare un esame /superare un esame	/to take a test /to pass a test		far scena muta = to flunk
7. sono occupato	I'm busy ≠ free		libero
8. come vuole	as you like		
9. (un) articolo	item	qualche cosa = something	
10. /(una) storia /(un) romanzo	/story/novel	(una) novella, (un) racconto = short story	
11. buffo	funny ≠ a drag	divertente	noioso, barboso
12. (un) amico	friend ≠ enemy	compagno = pal	nemico
13. – a causa di/ – perché	on account of		perché? = why?
14. pigro	lazy ≠ hardworking		sgobbone
15. me ne restano due	I have two left		non me ne restano più = I don't have any more
16. provare	to try	tentare di	
17. (un) appunta-mento(dare appuntamento)	an appointment (to make an . . .)		
18. ecco . . .	– here is, are		

LEZIONE 17

TO KNOW = **CONOSCERE** (to be familiar   **SAPERE** (to have
                      with)   knowledge of)

        conoscere qualcuno =   **sapere qualche cosa** =
        to know someone   to know something

        conoscere un posto =
        to know a place

note: I know <u>how to</u> drive = I <u>can</u> drive = <u>so</u> guidare, <u>I know how</u> to swim =
       I <u>can</u> swim = <u>so</u> nuotare, etc.

           / **Milano?**   / **ciò?**
Conosce – **quest 'uomo?**   **Sa** – **l'inglese?**
           \ **questo ristorante?**   \ **nuotare?**

              / Milan?   that?
Do you know – this man?   Do you know – English?
           \ this restaurant?   \ how to swim?

translate:

1) I know Jane.
2) Do you know London?
3) Do you know how to drive?
4) Do you know the answer?
5) Do you know his wife?
6) Do you know that store?
7) Do you know his family?
8) Do you know your lesson?
9) Do they know her relatives?
10) Do you know Italian?

CIO' CHE/QUELLO CHE = WHAT

E' ciò che vuole?	Is that what you want?
Sì, è ciò che voglio.	Yes, that's what I want.
No, non è ciò che voglio.	No, it isn't what I want.

note: Remember: What? (simple question) = (Che) cosa?

So ciò che vuole.	= I know what he wants.
So che . . .	= I know that . . .
Quello/ciò che so è che . . .	= What I know is that . . .
So che verrà.	= I know (that) he'll come.
E' ciò che voglio dire.	= That's what I mean.
So ciò che vuole dire.	= I know what he means.
Ciò che voglio dire è . . .	= What I mean is . . .

note: there's no difference between ciò che and quello che.

translate:

1) Non è ciò che pensi.
2) Non è ciò che voglio dire.
3) Non capisco ciò che volete.
4) So quello che ti dirà.
5) Sapete ciò che interessa a lui?

translate:

1) Do you know what you want to eat?
2) I'm not sure what she thinks.
3) We know what we must do.
4) That's what worries me.
5) That's what interests me.

VOCABOLARIO

	traduzione	sinonimo-associato	contrario-associato
1. è un gioco da bambini	it's a cinch ≠ hard	facile = easy	difficile, duro = it's rough = bisogna farlo
2. /(una) tasca/(un) portafoglio	/pocket/wallet		
3. /la scena/il regista	/the stage/the director	(il) cineasta = film-producer	
4. (un) complesso	a hang-up	(un) impedimento	
5. nervoso	nervous ≠ calm	innervosito = uptight	calmo
6. falso	false ≠ true, real	contraffatto = phony, fake, (una) bidonata, (una) patacca	vero
7. oggi stesso	this very day		
8. cavarsela	to swing something, to manage	se la cava bene = you get on well	
9. gettare	to throw		acchiappare = to catch
10. vincente	winner ≠ loser		perdente
11. e allora?	so what?	allora?, dunque? = so?	
12. guarda un po'!	well! well!		
13. /(un) passatempo /(un) tifoso	/hobby/fan	manìa	
14. serio	serious	grave	
15. /Natale/Pasqua	/Christmas/Easter	il veglione di San Silvestro = New Year's Eve party	
16. scegliere	to choose	selezionare	
17. ingiusto	unfair ≠ fair		giusto, retto = straight
18. essere preoccupato	to be worried, anxious	ansioso; I'm worried = sono preoccupato	non si preoccupi = don't worry

LEZIONE 18

COMPARATIVE, RELATIVE SUPERLATIVE

un uomo ricco   a rich man
un uomo più ricco   a richer man
l'uomo più ricco   the richest man

E' più giovane di me.   He/she's younger than me.
E' meno giovane di me.   He/she isn't as young as me.
E' giovane come/quanto me.   He/she's as young as me.
Non è giovane come me.   He/she isn't as young as me.
E' meno intelligente di me.   He/she's less intelligent than me.
E' così giovane che . . .   He/she's so young that . . .

THE ABSOLUTE SUPERLATIVE

un uomo altissimo/molto alto   a very tall man
una donna bellissima/molto bella   a very beautiful woman
una signora gentilissima/molto   a very kind lady
  gentile
un uomo ricchissimo/molto ricco   a very rich man

Sono giocattoli carissimi/molto   They're very expensive toys.
cari.
Sono ragazze intelligentissime/   They're very clever girls.
molto intelligenti.

note: — the absolute superlative is formed either by adding -issimo to the
adjective after its last vowel has been dropped, or by placing molto
(invariable) before the adjective.
— the adjectives ending in -co and -go, in adding the suffix -issimo,
undergo an orthographic change: lungo (long) → lunghissimo.

```
IRREGULAR COMPARISON
        COMPARATIVE    REL. SUPERLATIVE-ABS. SUPERLATIVE
  buono    migliore       il/la migliore   ottimo
  cattivo  peggiore       il/la peggiore   pessimo
```

translate:

1) She's the tallest in the family.
2) He isn't as rich as my brother.
3) He's the worst boss in the company.
4) I'm as broke as you are.
5) She's a very beautiful girl.

put in the relative superlative:

1) Questa macchina fotografica è . . . (buono) del negozio.
2) Questa regione è . . . (povero) d'Europa.
3) Questa drogheria è . . . (caro).
4) Questo supermercato è . . . (vicino) alla casa.
5) La tua collana è . . . (lungo) di tutte.
6) Questo affare è . . . (buono) dell'anno.
7) Questo macellaio è . . . (cattivo) della strada.
8) Questo film è . . . (noioso) di tutti.

put in the comparative:

1) Questa ragazza è . . . (serio) . . . me.
2) Questa spiaggia è . . . (bello) . . . quella.
3) Il primo piano è . . . (pulito) . . . pianterreno.
4) Il fornaio è . . . (vicino) . . . macellaio.
5) Il tuo anello è . . . (caro) . . . mio braccialetto.
6) Sua moglie è . . . (brutto) . . . tua.
7) Questa lezione è . . . (interessante) . . . altra.
8) Il suo nuovo romanzo è . . . (buono) . . . primo.
9) Sua figlia è . . . (carino) . . . moglie.
10) Questa somma è . . . (importante) . . . quella della settimana scorsa.

translate, then give the seven possible forms (corto: più corto di, meno corto di, corto come, il più corto, il meno corto, molto corto, cortissimo):

alto	caro
lungo	attento
cattivo	intelligente
caldo	cortese
forte	giusto
triste	schifoso
pesante	vecchio
profondo	buono
debole	stupido
pericoloso	affollato
difficile	duro

translate, then put in the comparative, e.g.:
She's as pretty as my sister:
— E' carina come mia sorella.
— E' più carina di mia sorella.

1) Our trip is as interesting as yours.
2) My shoes are as cheap as theirs.
3) Your jewellery is as beautiful as hers.
4) This book's as crummy as that one.
5) Your hobby's as boring as mine.
6) This lesson's as much of a cinch as the last one.
7) Your wallet's as full as mine.
8) My shower is as hot as Jane's.
9) This restaurant's as crowded as the other one.
10) My room's as sloppy as yours.
11) These mountains are as high as the sky.
12) My dress is as short as yours.
13) He's as lazy as his father.
14) They're as well-off as their parents.
15) The teachers are as poor as the students.

vero (true), feminine **vera** → **vera**<u>mente</u>

facile (easy), feminine **facile** → **faci**<u>lmente</u>

folle (mad), feminine **folle** → **folle**<u>mente</u>

note: — most are formed by adding — <u>mente</u> to the feminine singular of the
adjective.
— adjectives ending in -le or -re (single 'l' or 'r') drop the final 'e'
before adding -<u>mente</u>.
— buono → bene.
— cattivo → male.

give the adverb:

triste	rapido
duro	pronto
buono	felice
cattivo	secco
serio	raro
facile	grande
lungo	stupido
cortese	intelligente
frequente	caro
dolce	improvviso
profondo	probabile
stanco	difficile
folle	pesante
lento	forte

VOCABOLARIO

	traduzione	sinonimo-associato	contrario-associato
1. (un) regalo	gift	regalare = to give	
2. importante	important ≠ beside the point		fuori tema, irrilevante
3. che misura?	what size?	(il) numero (shoes)	
4. (un) reparto (da signora)	(ladies) department		
5. (il) primo piano	first floor	pianterreno = ground floor	
6. /(una) drogheria /(un) fornaio /(un) macellaio	/grocery/baker /butcher	(un) supermercato = supermarket	
7. in liquidazione	on sale	un affare = a bargain	
8. me l'aspettavo	I expected it	non mi sorprenderebbe = it would not surprise me	inatteso = unexpected
9. ricco	rich ≠ poor, broke	benestante, agiato	squattrinato, al verde, in bolletta
10. ne valeva la pena	it was worth it		non ne valeva la pena
11. (una) somma	amount	totale, quantità = quantity	
12. perdiana!	goodness!	Dio mio! porco cane! che rabbia!	grazie a Dio! = thank goodness!
13. quanti anni ha (hai, avete)?	how old are you?		
14. (la) giovinezza	youth ≠ old age	adolescenza = teenage	(la) vecchiaia
15. /(i) gioielli /(un) anello /(una) collana	/jewellery/ring /necklace	(un) braccialetto = bracelet	
16. qualcuno	someone ≠ no one	chiunque = anyone, tutti = everybody	nessuno
17. dappertutto	everywhere ≠ nowhere		in nessun posto
18. è la stessa cosa	it's the same thing		

LEZIONE 19

PAST (PASSATO PROSSIMO = PRESENT PERFECT)

Ieri
La settimana scorsa — **ho giocato**   I played tennis — yesterday.
Due giorni fa / **a tennis.**   — last week.
                                                                  two days ago.

---

ho giocato	**non ho giocato**
hai giocato	**non hai giocato**
ha giocato	**non ha giocato**
abbiamo giocato	**non abbiamo giocato**
avete giocato	**non avete giocato**
hanno giocato	**non hanno giocato**

note: the 'passato prossimo' is formed with the present of 'avere' and the
     past participle of the verb.

HA GIOCATO A TENNIS?   Did you play tennis?
                                Have you played tennis?

Sì, ho giocato a tennis.   Yes, I (have) played tennis.
No, non ho giocato a tennis.   No, I didn't play/haven't played
                                tennis.

PAST PARTICIPLE

parlare	→	parlato	(spoke, have spoken)
vendere	→	venduto	(sold, have sold)
finire	→	finito	(finished, have finished)

da ripetere:

Non ho parlato a nessuno.	= I didn't speak to anyone.
Non gli ho mai parlato.	= I never spoke to him.
Non ho ancora finito.	= I haven't finished yet.
Non mi ha dato niente.	= He/she didn't give me anything.
Mi ha dato solo due dollari.	= He/she only gave me two dollars.
Non l'abbiamo più visto(a).	= We didn't see him/her any more.

translate:

1) It's on the left.
2) I slept two hours.
3) I got divorced two years ago.
4) We began Italian lessons last month.
5) Did you eat a lot this morning?
6) He called me two hours ago.
7) I talked for two hours yesterday.
8) I only had kids four years ago.
9) They finished their lesson last night.
10) He left his office at ten.

```
AVERE – PASSATO PROSSIMO
ho avuto      =   I had
hai avuto

ha avuto

abbiamo avuto
avete avuto

hanno avuto
```

put in the negative:

1) Abbiamo visitato il museo.
2) Ho dimenticato il tuo nome.
3) Trovo che hai avuto torto.
4) Ho amato molto quel tipo.
5) Ha venduto la macchina a mia cugina.
6) Ti abbiamo aspettato per mangiare.
7) Abbiamo mangiato senza pane.
8) E' ciò che ho visto.
9) Hanno guardato la televisione ieri sera.
10) Oggi abbiamo mangiato spaghetti alla bolognese.

translate, then give the negative answer:

1) Did your teeth ache last week?
2) Did you sneeze a little while ago?
3) Did you have a sore throat two weeks ago?
4) Did she rest after her work yesterday?
5) Did you bring the books alone?
6) Did you have to pay?
7) Were you afraid of the dogs?
8) Did you have a nice day?

translate, then give the past participle of the following verbs:

to hope	to wait
to sleep	to find
to look	to receive
to be able to	to feel
to have to	to complete
to eat	to hold
to buy	to call
to want	to throw
to know (something)	to follow
to know (someone)	to recognize
to understand	to repeat
to prefer	to give
to forbid	to speak
to drive	to try

VERBI IRREGOLARI – PARTICIPIO PASSATO (con AVERE)
PRIMO GRUPPO

fare (to do, to make)   →   **fatto**

SECONDO GRUPPO

participio passato in **-so**:

accendere (to light)	→ **acceso**	**muovere** (to move)	→ **mosso**
appendere (to hang)	→ **appeso**	**perdere** (to lose)	→ **perso**
chiudere (to shut)	→ **chiuso**	**persuadere** (to persuade)	→ **persuaso**
concedere (to grant)	→ **concesso**	**prendere** (to take)	→ **preso**
decidere (to decide)	→ **deciso**	**radere** (to shave)	→ **raso**
discutere (to discuss)	→ **discusso**	**rendere** (to return)	→ **reso**
dividere (to share)	→ **diviso**	**ridere** (to laugh)	→ **riso**
mettere (to put)	→ **messo**	**sorridere** (to smile)	→ **sorriso**
mordere (to bite)	→ **morso**	**spendere** (to spend)	→ **speso**
		uccidere (to kill)	→ **ucciso**

participio passato in -to:

bere (to drink)	→ **bevuto**	**proteggere** (to protect)	→ **protetto**
cogliere (to gather)	→ **colto**	**scegliere** (to choose)	→ **scelto**
cuocere (to cook)	→ **cotto**	**scorgere** (to perceive)	→ **scorto**
dipingere (to paint)	→ **dipinto**	**scrivere** (to write)	→ **scritto**
fingere (to pretend)	→ **finto**	**spingere** (to push)	→ **spinto**
leggere (to read)	→ **letto**	**togliere** (to remove)	→ **tolto**
piangere (to cry)	→ **pianto**	**vedere** (to see)	→ **visto**
porre (to put on)	→ **posto**		**(veduto)**
chiedere (to ask)	→ **chiesto**	**rispondere** (to answer)	→ **risposto**

TERZO GRUPPO

aprire (to open)	→ **aperto**	**soffrire** (to suffer)	→ **sofferto**
coprire (to cover)	→ **coperto**	**dire** (to say)	→ **detto**
offrire (to offer)	→ **offerto**		

translate:

1) I've never taken the underground.
2) Has she already spent all the money?
3) What did you do last night?
4) Did they tell you that yesterday?
5) Have you finished the lesson?
6) Did you hear what she said?
7) Did you write down his address?
8) Did she have to do it a week ago?
9) Did the tourists have time to see a museum this morning?
10) Did they send you the books on time?

Put in the negative:

1) Gli alunni hanno risposto alle domande.
2) Mi hai fatto un bel regalo.
3) Il bambino ha pianto molto durante la notte.
4) Hanno bevuto troppo vino.
5) Ho letto il libro e ho visto la commedia.
6) Abbiamo offerto il pranzo a tutti.

CONTRARI 4 (VERBI)

1. **amare** to love	≠	**odiare** to hate
2. **stare in piedi** to stand up	≠	**sedersi** to sit down
3. **vestirsi** to get dressed	≠	**spogliarsi** to get undressed
4. **fare in fretta** to hurry up	≠	**fare con calma** to take one's time
5. **tornare** to come back	≠	**partire/uscire** to go away/out
6. **trovare** to find	≠	**perdere** to lose
7. **dimenticare** to forget	≠	**ricordarsi** (di) to remember
8. **comprare** to buy	≠	**vendere** to sell
9. **vincere** to win	≠	**perdere** to lose
10. **mettere** (il cappotto) to put on (coat)	≠	**togliere** to take off
11. **essere d'accordo con** to agree with	≠	**non essere d'accordo con** to disagree with
12. **atterrare** to land (plane)	≠	**decollare** to take off
13. **accendere** to put on, to turn on	≠	**spegnere** to turn off
14. **addormentarsi** to fall asleep	≠	**svegliarsi** to wake up
15. **fare attenzione a** to pay attention to	≠	**non fare attenzione a** to ignore
16. **domandare** to ask	≠	**rispondere** to answer
17. **spingere** to push	≠	**tirare** to pull
18. **ridere** to laugh	≠	**piangere** to cry
19. **dare** to give	≠	**prendere** to take
20. **uscire** to go out	≠	**restare a casa** to stay in
21. **essere presente** to be there	≠	**essere assente** not to be there

VOCABOLARIO

	traduzione	sinonimo-associato	contrario-associato
1. probabile	likely ≠ unlikely	molto probabile = most likely	poco probabile, impossibile
2. /(una) scuola /(un) liceo /(una) classe	/school/secondary (US) high) school /class, form (US grade)	(un') università = college, (un') aula = classroom, (un) voto = mark	
3. necessario	necessary	è obbligatorio = it's a must	facoltativo = optional
4. (un) diploma	diploma	laureato = graduated	
5. essere bocciato	to fail ≠ to succeed		riuscire, avere successo = to be successful
6. un successo	a hit ≠ failure		(un) insuccesso, (un) fallimento, (un) fiasco
7. sorprendente	amazing, surprising	stupefacente, sbalorditivo, incredibile	
8. preferito	favourite		
9. sposarsi	to get married	(una) luna di miele = honeymoon, matrimonio = marriage	divorziare = to get divorced
10. visitare	to sightsee	fare visita a qualcuno = to visit someone	
11. appartenere	to belong to		possedere = to own
12. il mio proprio	my own	il mio = mine	
13. (un, una) turista	tourist		
14. (un) museo	museum	(un') arte = art, (una) chiesa = church, (un) monumento = monument	
15. sempre dritto	straight ahead		
16. a destra	to the right ≠ to the left		a sinistra
17. silenzio!	keep quiet!	chiudi il becco! shut up!	
18. (un) indirizzo	address		

LEZIONE 20

PAST (PASSATO PROSSIMO) seguito — continued

Ieri
La settimana scorsa <u>sono andato</u> = I went — yesterday.
Due giorni fa — last week.
— two days ago.

note: some verbs are conjugated with ESSERE in the past and agree with the subject, e.g. Giovanna è andata.

ANDARE = TO GO

<u>sono</u> <u>andato</u>(a) = I went/have gone   <u>non</u> <u>sono</u> <u>andato</u>(a) = I didn't go
                                                                              /haven't gone
<u>sei</u> andato(a)   <u>non</u> <u>sei</u> andato(a)
è <u>andato</u>(a)   <u>non</u> è <u>andato</u>(a)
<u>siamo</u> andati(e)   <u>non</u> <u>siamo</u> andati(e)
<u>siete</u> andati(e)   <u>non</u> <u>siete</u> andati(e)
<u>sono</u> andati(e)   <u>non</u> <u>sono</u> andati(e)

E' ANDATA?   Did she go?/Has she gone?

Sì, <u>ci è andata.</u>   Yes, she went/has gone (there).
No, <u>non ci è andata.</u>   No, she didn't go/hasn't gone.

note: <u>ci</u> = there — placed before the verb.

Non ci sono andato con **nessuno.**	I didn't go with anyone.
Non è **ancora** andato.	He didn't go/hasn't gone yet.
Non sono **mai** andato a **Nuova York.**	I've never gone/been to New York.
Ci sono andato **solo** per il **weekend.**	I only went for the weekend.
Non ci siamo **più** andati da allora.	We haven't been there since.
Non è accaduto/successo **niente.**	Nothing happened.

VERBI CONIUGATI con ESSERE – PARTICIPIO PASSATO

andare (to go)	→ **andato**	**ringiovanire** (to get younger)	→ **ringiovanito**
venire (to come)	→ **venuto**	**migliorare** (to get better)	→ **migliorato**
giungere (to arrive)	→ **giunto**	**peggiorare** (to get worse)	→ **peggiorato**
partire (to leave)	→ **partito**	**calare** (to decrease)	→ **calato**
tornare (to come back)	→ **tornato**	**diminuire** (to diminish)	→ **diminuito**
(re)stare (to stay)	→ **(re)stato**	**apparire** (to appear)	→ **apparso**
entrare (to come in)	→ **entrato**	**parere** (to seem)	→ **parso**
uscire (to go out)	→ **uscito**	**sembrare** (to seem)	→ **sembrato**
salire (to go up)	→ **salito**	**accadere** (to happen)	→ **accaduto**
scendere (to go down)	→ **sceso**	**succedere** (to happen)	→ **successo**
cadere (to fall)	→ **caduto**	**bastare** (to be enough)	→ **bastato**
correre (to run)	→ **corso**	**bisognare** (to be necessary)	→ **bisognato**
nascere (to be born)	→ **nato**	**occorrere** (to be necessary)	→ **occorso**
crescere (to grow)	→ **cresciuto**	**riuscire** (to succeed)	→ **riuscito**
vivere (to live)	→ **vissuto**	**costare** (to cost)	→ **costato**
morire (to die)	→ **morto**	**piacere** (to like)	→ **piaciuto**
rimanere (to remain)	→ **rimasto**	**dispiacere** (to be sorry)	→ **dispiaciuto**
divenire (to become)	→ **divenuto**	**piovere** (to rain)	→ **piovuto**
diventare (to become)	→ **diventato**	**nevicare** (to snow)	→ **nevicato**
ingrassare (to grow fat)	→ **ingrassato**	**gelare** (to freeze)	→ **gelato**
dimagrire (to grow thin)	→ **dimagrito**		
invecchiare (to grow old)	→ **invecchiato**		

```
ESSERE — PASSATO PROSSIMO

sono stato(a) = I was/have been
sei stato(a)

è stato(a)

siamo stati(e)
siete stati(e)

sono stati(e)
```

translate:

1) Non siamo mai andati a Cicago.
2) Non sono stata a Nuova York da molto tempo.
3) E' uscito con lei ieri sera.
4) L'incidente è accaduto di notte.
5) E' nato a Rio di Gianeiro.
6) E' morta l'anno scorso.
7) Non sono mai caduto.
8) Siamo tornati a casa dopo il lavoro.
9) E' salita.
10) Mi domando se Lei è già stato negli Stati Uniti.

translate:

1) Have you ever been to the movies with him?
2) Have you ever seen a first-rate movie?
3) She fell and broke her arm.
4) She's Italian but in spite of that was born in New York.
5) Why did you come only once to see me?
6) The husband and the wife died together.
7) He hasn't returned to the house today.
8) I've often gone to the beach.
9) We have never been to China.
10) I only went once to the zoo.
11) She was born in Europe.
12) Where were you born? — I was born in Rome.

VOCABOLARIO

	traduzione	sinonimo-associato	contrario-associato
1. Lei è fortunato(a)	you're lucky	un colpo di fortuna = a lucky break	E' sfortunato(a) = you're out of luck
2. poco fa	a little while ago		tra poco = in a little while
3. gente	company	avere gente = to have company	
4. /(un, dei) bagagli/fare le valigie	/baggage/to pack		disfare le valigie = to unpack
5. (uno) scopo	aim	(un) bersaglio = target	
6. nei guai	in a jam, in a spot	in un bel pasticcio, (una, delle) grane = a snag	
7. essere fiero	to be proud ≠ to be ashamed		avere vergogna
8. entusiasta	enthusiastic		indifferente
9. (un) sogno	dream	(un) incubo = nightmare	
10. (uno) sbaglio	mistake	(una) colpa = error	
11. (una) ditta	company, firm	società	
12. (un) pacco	package	(un) pacchetto	
13. Mi ricordi di . . .	remind me to . . .		
14. di prima qualità	first rate ≠ second rate		di qualità scadente, perdita di tempo = waste of time
15. riconoscere	to recognize	scoprire, individuare = to spot	
16. criticare	to criticize ≠ to praise	discreditare = to down	lodare, elogiare
17. fare progressi	to make progress	migliorare = to improve	
18. dritto	straight ≠ crooked		storto
19. (la) folla	crowd, mob	(la) gente = people	

LEZIONE 21

STARE PER + INFINITIVE   = GOING TO . . .

Sto per mangiare.   = I'm going to eat.

Stiamo per partire.   = We're going to leave.

AVERE/ESSERE APPENA + PAST PARTICIPLE = TO HAVE JUST

Abbiamo appena finito.   = We've just finished.

E' appena partito.   = He has just left.

---

translate:

1) Ho appena finito di scrivere una lettera.
2) Abbiamo appena finito di bere il caffè.
3) E' appena salita.
4) Sta per uscire.
5) L'aeroplano sta per decollare.
6) Quella povera donna sta per morire.

translate:

1) I've just finished reading the book.
2) Jane has just left.
3) Make up your mind!
4) They've just bought a new apartment.
5) He just went out.
6) He's going to go out in a little while.
7) We've just finished packing.
8) She's cheating on her husband.

ANCORA = MORE

Ancora pane per favore!	= More bread please!
Ne vuole ancora?	= Do you want some more?

---

note: -- in a restaurant, you use 'ancora': More water please! =
   Ancora acqua per favore!
   -- ancora uno(a) = another one please.
   -- ancora un po' = another little bit.

SEMPRE/ANCORA = STILL

E ⟨ancora / sempre⟩ malato?	= Is he still sick?
Sì, è ⟨ancora / sempre⟩ malato.	= Yes, he's still sick.
No, non è più malato.	= No, he isn't sick any more.

---

note: SEMPRE also means 'always'.

SI = (TO) EACH OTHER

Ci si vede spesso.	= We often see each other.
Ci si ama molto.	= We love each other a lot.
Ci si vede venerdì?	= Will we see each other Friday?
Si parlano molto.	= They often talk to each other.

---

note: REMEMBER: 'si' also means 'one', 'you' etc. e.g. Si beve molto vino
   in Italia = One (you) drink(s) a lot of wine in Italy.

. . . PIACE?	= DO YOU LIKE?
Le piace il caffè?	= Do you like coffee?
Sì, mi piace il caffè.	= Yes, I like coffee.
No, non mi piace il caffè.	= No, I don't like coffee.

note: — Le piacciono questi quadri? = Do you like these pictures?
— gli piace il caffè = he likes coffee.
— le piace il caffé = she likes coffee.
— il caffè piace loro = they like coffee.

translate:

1) Vuole ancora del vino?
2) Non è più malata.
3) Ci si parla spesso.
4) Io non voglio più pane. Lei ne vuole ancora?
5) Ci si scrive molto tutto l'anno.
6) Avete sempre intenzione di divorziare?
7) Volete ancora qualche cosa?
8) Si amano molto.
9) Ancora dell' acqua, per favore!
10) Avete ancora problemi con il capufficio?
11) Hai intenzione di domandare ancora soldi a tuo padre?
12) Le piace il caffè? — No, non mi piace.
13) Le piacciono i gelati italiani? — Sì, mi piacciono molto.
14) Qui si parla italiano.

translate:

1) They still love each other.
2) Are they still living in New York?
3) Do you still want to take a trip with me?
4) They often talk to each other.
5) Is she still worried about her kids' health?
6) Do you want some more bread? — No, I don't want any more, thank you.
7) Are you still taking medicine for your sore throat?
8) Does it still hurt?
9) Do you like carrots? - - Yes, I like them.
10) One eats a lot of fish in Italy.

note: remember our present perfect can also be translated by the Italian present.

translate:

1) We've been working for two hours, but he only worked one hour.
2) They've been eating since noon. They've already eaten all the chicken.
3) We've been taking Italian lessons for two years. We took fifty lessons last year.
4) Have you ever been to New York? — Yes, I went last year.
5) She's been sleeping for ten hours. She slept ten hours last night too.
6) You've been watching TV for an hour. You watched it all day long yesterday.
7) They've been living in Rome for five years. Before that they lived in Paris for a year.
8) The kids have been playing for two hours. They played with their pals yesterday for two hours also.
9) He's been working for this company for twelve years. He worked for the other one only two years.
10) They've been quarrelling for half an hour. They quarrelled all day long yesterday.

1. **circa (un'ora)**	(an hour) or so	14. **dall'inizio**	from the first
2. **davvero**	indeed	15. **– definitiva-mente**	– for good
3. **– ancora** **– sempre**	still	**– permanente-mente**	– permanently
4. **uno su dieci**	one out of ten	16. **– tutto il giorno**	– all the day long
5. **per sbaglio**	by mistake	**– durante tutto il giorno**	
6. **a meno che**	unless		
7. **inoltre**	furthermore	17. **– fortunata-mente**	– fortunately
8. **lo stesso**	all the same	**– per fortuna**	– luckily
9. **– poco fa (passato)**	– a little while ago	18. **– dappertutto**	– all over
– tra poco (futuro)	– in a little while	**– in qualunque posto**	– anywhere
10. **per un certo tempo**	for a while	19. **– in qualche posto**	– somewhere
11. **– di gran lunga**	by far	**– in nessun posto**	– nowhere
– di molto		20. **– come al solito**	– as usual
12. **– di fatto**	– in fact	21. **in più**	in addition to
– effettiva-mente	– as a matter of fact	22. **in questo caso**	if so
13. **di qui a (l'inverno)**	by (winter)	23. **per così dire**	so to speak
		24. **come**	as
		25. **– tuttavia** **– lo stesso**	still, all the same

VOCABOLARIO

	traduzione	sinonimo-associato	contrario-associato
1. arrabbiato	angry ≠ satisfied	furioso, andare in collera = to lose one's temper	soddisfatto, contento = pleased
2. avere intenzione di	to plan to	sto per = I'm going to	
3. coraggioso	brave ≠ cowardly		vigliacco, codardo
4. prepararsi	to get ready	lavarsi = to get washed	sono pronto(a) = I'm ready
5. solito	usual ≠ unusual	tipico = typical	insolito, raro
6. /molto/piuttosto	/very/rather	del tutto = quite	appena = hardly
7. pulito	clean ≠ dirty		sporco
8. (un) compleanno	birthday	rallegramenti = congratulations	
9. raggiungere	to catch up ≠ to fall behind		restare indietro
10. – ancora qualche cosa?	– something else?	qualcun altro = someone else, altrove = somewhere else	nient'altro = nothing else
– chi altro?	– who else?		
– che cos'altro?	– what else?		
11. ho paura	I'm afraid	sono spaventato = I'm frightened	
12. (un) tiro	a trick	(una) trappola = a trap	
13. Lei imbroglia	you're cheating	note: to cheat on s.o. = ingannare qualcuno	
14. secondo	according to		
15. ho paura che	I'm afraid that		
16. Si decida	make up your mind		indeciso = undecided
17. (un) risultato	result	(una) conclusione, (una) soluzione	
18. (un, un') idiota	idiot, fool	un cretino, uno sciocco, un'asino = an ass	

LEZIONE 22

PAST IMPERFECT (IMPERFETTO) = WAS + ING

Guardavo la televisione $<$ **mentre leggeva.**
quando è venuto.

I was watching TV $<$ while he/she was reading.
when he came in.

---

note: — this tense is most often used for an action that was going on at a certain time.
— what is VITAL is to distinguish between the passato (I went/have gone) and the imperfetto, which is usually used with another verb in a sentence and which implies duration: I was eating while he was talking = mangiavo mentre parlava.
— it answers the question: what were you doing when . . . ?

IMPERFETTO

VERBI IN '-ARE'

parlavo	= I was speaking when . . .
parlavi	= you were speaking
parlava	$<$ he/she was speaking / you were speaking
parlavamo	= we were speaking
parlavate	= you were speaking
parlavano	$<$ they / you were speaking

---

note: the above endings are added to the stem of the verb.

IMPERFETTO

VERBI IN '-ERE'	VERBI IN '-IRE'
prendevo = I was taking	**finivo** = I was finishing
prendevi	**finivi**
prendeva	**finiva**
prendevamo	**finivamo**
prendevate	**finivate**
prendevano	**finivano**

note: the above endings are added to the stem of the verb.

IRREGULAR VERBS – VERBI IRREGOLARI

IMPERFETTO

bere = to drink	**condurre** = to lead	**dire** = to say
bevevo	conducevo	dicevo
bevevi	conducevi	dicevi
beveva	conduceva	diceva
bevevamo	conducevamo	dicevamo
bevevate	conducevate	dicevate
bevevano	conducevano	dicevano
essere = to be	**fare** = to do	**porre**
ero	facevo	ponevo
eri	facevi	ponevi
era	faceva	poneva
eravamo	facevamo	ponevamo
eravate	facevate	ponevate
erano	facevano	ponevano

insert the *passato prossimo* or the *imperfetto:*

1) Pietro . . . (venire) quando noi . . . (mangiare).
2) Tu . . . (leggere) un libro quando io . . . (venire).
3) Giovanni . . . (parlare) col direttore quando io . . . (entrare) nell'ufficio.
4) Alle otto Maria . . . (partire) mentre noi . . . (lavorare) ancora.
5) Le segretarie . . . (parlare) quando il direttore . . . (entrare) nella stanza.
6) Quando io . . . (uscire), . . . (piovere).
7) Quando tu mi . . . (telefonare), io . . . (fare) il bagno.
8) Tu . . . (avere) un'aria triste quando io ti . . . (incontrare) ieri.

DORMIVA QUANDO LE HO   = Were you sleeping when I called?
TELEFONATO?
Sì, dormivo quando mi ha telefonato.
No, non dormivo quando mi ha telefonato.

PARLAVANO MENTRE   = Were they talking while you were
SCRIVEVA?   writing?
Sì, parlavano mentre scrivevo.
No, non parlavano mentre scrivevo.

translate:

1) Were you crying when I came in?
2) What were you doing when I called?
3) They were drinking wine while we were watching TV.
4) She was reading while he was talking with his boss.
5) We were celebrating my birthday when it happened.
6) What were you saying when she entered the room?
7) I was working while you were playing with the kids.
8) I did that experiment when I was working for him.

translate:

1) Che facevate ieri mentre dormivo?
2) Mangiavo quando sei venuto.
3) Rispondevo alle domande mentre gli altri alunni ascoltavano.
4) I bambini guardavano la televisione mentre i genitori leggevano.
5) Bevevamo mentre tu lavoravi.
6) Quando mi hai telefonato, facevo la doccia.
7) Facevo il bagno quando sei entrato nella stanza da bagno.
8) Stava venendo a trovarci quando è successo l'incidente.

1. **così da**	so as to	15. **se solo**	if only
2. **– ora**	– at present	16. **poichè è così**	in the
– al momento	– for the time being		circumstances
		17. **sicuramente**	definitely
3. **– a proposito**	– by the way	18. **definitivamente**	for good
– incidental-mente	– incidentally	19. **completamente**	altogether
4. **in un modo o in un altro**	somehow	20. **il colmo**	the limit
		21. **ogni conto fatto**	all in all
5. **– a tutti i costi**	– by all means	22. **che altro?**	what else?
– con ogni mezzo	– by any means	23. **non importa**	no matter
6. **in qualche modo**	in a way	24. **più tardi**	later on
7. **dopo tutto**	after all	25. **dal momento che**	as long as
8. **sempre più**	more and more	26. **qualunque**	whatever
9. **la sera dopo**	the following night	27. **fino a qui**	up to now
10. **– tra una settimana**	– a week from today	28. **fino a domani**	till tomorrow
– oggi a otto		29. **fino a quando?**	how long?
11. **poco tempo prima**	shortly before	30. **fino (place)**	as far as
12. **indipendente-mente da**	apart from	**– fino alla stazione**	– as far as the station
13. **qualunque sia**	regardless	**– fino là**	– as far as that
14. **in breve**	to make a long story short		

VOCABOLARIO

	traduzione	sinonimo-associato	contrario-associato
1. preferirei andarci	I'd prefer going	mi piacerebbe di più = I'd rather	
2. (un) ospite	guest	invitato	(un) ospite = host
3. /deludere /(una) delusione	/to disappoint /disappointment	mi ha deluso = he let me down	
4. guadagnare soldi	to earn	guadagnar da vivere = to earn one's living	(la) disoccupazione = unemployment
5. si diverta	enjoy yourself	ci siamo divertiti molto = we had a good time	
6. esagerare	to exaggerate	passare i limiti = to go too far	
7. un esperimento	an experiment		
8. capita che	it happens that		
9. trovo che	I feel that	penso che = I think that	
10. proteggere	to protect		
11. controlli che	make sure (that)		
12. cattivo	naughty ≠ good	un ragazzaccio = a brat	buono
13. ricevere	/to receive /to entertain	(un) ricevimento = party, festeggiare = to celebrate	
14. permettere	to permit ≠ to forbid		proibire
15. piuttosto che	rather than		
16. benvenuto!	welcome!	faccia come a casa Sua = to make yourself at home	
17. urlare	to yell	gridare = to shout	sussurrare = whisper
18. battersi	to fight	lottare = to struggle	
19. (un) pederasta	a queer ≠ lesbienne	omosessuale = homosexual	(una) lesbica
20. (una) squillo	call girl, prostitute	(un) casino, (un) bordello = brothel	(un,una) ruffiano(a), (un) magnaccia = pimp, Madam

LEZIONE 23

CONDITIONAL — second form

SE <u>AVESSI</u> IL DENARO, <u>COMPREREI</u> UNA MACCHINA.'
past subjunctive + conditional

If I <u>had</u> the money, I <u>would</u> buy a car.

SE LEI AVESSE IL DENARO, COMPREREBBE UNA MACCHINA?

If you had the money, would you buy a car?

Sì, se <u>avessi</u> il denaro, <u>comprerei</u> una macchina.
No, se <u>avessi</u> il denaro, <u>non comprerei</u> una macchina.

note: this is not a problem as it follows the same structure as in English,
except that you form the first part of the sentence with the <u>past</u>
<u>subjunctive</u> (imperfetto congiuntivo): <u>se avessi</u> (both 'se ho avuto'
and 'se avevo' are wrong).

CONDITIONAL

VERBI IN '-ARE' **'-ERE'**		**VERBS IN '-IRE'**	
comp<u>rerei</u>		fin<u>irei</u>	
comp<u>reresti</u>		fin<u>iresti</u>	
comp<u>rerebbe</u>	would buy	fin<u>irebbe</u>	would finish
comp<u>reremmo</u>		fin<u>iremmo</u>	
comp<u>rereste</u>		fin<u>ireste</u>	
comp<u>rerebbero</u>		fin<u>irebbero</u>	

note: add the above endings to the stem of the verb.

note: all verbs with an irregular future have the same irregularity in the conditional, only the endings change: e.g. andare (to go): future → andrò, conditional → andrei, andresti, andrebbe, andremmo, andreste, andrebbero; bere (to drink): future → berrò, conditional → berrei, berresti, berrebbe, berremmo, berreste, berrebbero; venire (to come): future → verrò, conditional → verrei, verresti, etc.

PAST SUBJUNCTIVE

VERBS IN '-ARE'	VERBS IN '-ERE'	VERBS IN '-IRE'
(se) parlassi	(se) vedessi	(se) capissi
parlassi	vedessi	capissi
parlasse	vedesse	capisse
parlassimo	vedessimo	capissimo
parlaste	vedeste	capiste
parlassero	vedessero	capissero

note: add the above endings to the stem of the verb.

IRREGULAR VERBS – VERBI IRREGOLARI

PAST SUBJUNCTIVE

bere (to drink)	→ bevessi	essere (to be)	→ fossi
condurre (to lead)	→ conducessi	fare (to do)	→ facessi
dare (to give)	→ dessi	porre (to put)	→ ponessi
dire (to say)	→ dicessi	stare (to stay)	→ stessi

compare:

Se sono malato, vado dal dottore.	If I'm sick, I'll go to the doctor.
Se fossi malato, andrei dal dottore.	If I were sick, I would go to the doctor.
Se hanno tempo, vengono.	If they have time, they'll come.
Se avessero tempo, verrebbero.	If they had time, they'd come.
Se devo farlo, mi arrabbio.	If I have to do it, I'll be angry.
Se dovessi farlo, mi arrabbierei.	If I had to do it, I'd be angry.

123

translate, then put in the first IF form:

e.g. Se tu fossi malato, andresti dal dottore?
- If you were sick would you go to the doctor?
- Se sei malato, vai dal dottore?

1) Se tu avessi i soldi, compreresti un nuovo appartamento?
2) Se Lei potesse, mi aiuterebbe?
3) Se i turisti avessero tempo, andrebbero a vedere i musei?
4) Se la commedia fosse un fiasco, andremmo a vederla lo stesso?
5) Se Lei non capisse, me lo direbbe?
6) Se la ditta avesse successo, il padrone sarebbe contento.
7) Se tu divorziassi, saresti infelice?
8) Se piovesse, prenderemmo un ombrello.
9) Se dovessimo farlo, lo faremmo.
10) Se facesse brutto tempo, non faremmo la passeggiata.
11) Se avessimo fame, finiremmo la carne di ieri sera.
12) Se lei non potesse venire, tu verresti solo?

translate, then answer in the negative:

1) If that book belonged to you, would you lend it to me?
2) If you were late, would you call me up?
3) If you were a tourist would you go to the New York Museum of Modern Art?
4) If you were tired would you go to sleep in my bedroom?
5) If they were rich, would they travel?
6) If we had to choose a dentist, would we choose that one?
7) If you failed the test, would you go on working?
8) If I had to choose a husband, would I take yours?
9) If we didn't have so much money, could we go to Paris?
10) If you could buy those cigarettes, would you give me some?
11) If she found a pretty apartment, would she buy it?
12) If that dress were on sale, would I take it?
13) If it rains, will we go anyway?
14) If it were sunny outside, would we stay at home?
15) If you work part-time, can you earn enough money?
16) If her husband criticises her all the time, will she leave him?

VOCABOLARIO

	traduzione	sinonimo-associato	contrario-associato
1. colpire	to hit	picchiare, battere = to beat, dare una sculacciata = to spank	
2. mentire	to lie ≠ to tell the truth	(una) bugia = a lie	dire la verità
3. sembrare	to look	sembra stanco = you look tired	
4. come se	as though		
5. mi sembra vada bene	it sounds good		
6. che disordine!	what a mess!		
7. /ho nostalgia della famiglia /la famiglia sente la mia mancanza	/I miss my family /my family misses me		
8. andiamo!	let's go!	su, andiamo! = come on!	
9. incinta	pregnant		(un) aborto = abortion
10. timido	shy ≠ outgoing		sfrontato
11. (il) nord	North	sud, est, ovest	
12. /(la) Francia /(gli) Stati-Uniti /(l') Italia/(la) Cina	/France/the United States/Italy/China	francese, americano, italiano, cinese	
13. – Germania – Spagna – Inghilterra – Africa	– Germany – Spain – England – Africa	tedesco, spagnolo, inglese, africano	
14. precedente	previous		l'ultimo = the latter
15. quante storie!	what a fuss!	fare storie = to make a fuss	
16. indovinare	to guess	a caso = by guess-work	
17. /senz'altro/sono stufo(a)!	/you bet!/I'm fed up!		

LEZIONE 24

HELP!!!

CONDITIONAL — third form

Compare with first form page 88

Se <u>ho</u> denaro, <u>compro</u> una macchina.
If I have money, I'll buy a car.

second form page 122

Se <u>avessi</u> denaro, <u>comprerei</u> una macchina.
If I had money, I'd buy a car.

third form

SE <u>AVESSI AVUTO</u> DENARO, <u>AVREI COMPRATO</u> UNA MACCHINA.
IF I <u>HAD HAD</u> MONEY, I <u>WOULD HAVE BOUGHT</u> A CAR.

note: this is extremely complex — **the killer!!!**

PAST PERFECT SUBJUNCTIVE = PAST SUBJUNCTIVE OF AVERE + PAST PARTICIPLE		PAST CONDITIONAL = CONDITIONAL OF AVERE + PAST PARTICIPLE	
Se avessi		avrei	
avessi		avresti	
avesse	avuto	avrebbe	comprato
avessimo		avremmo	
aveste		avreste	
avessero		avrebbero	

note: the verbs conjugated with ESSERE in the past are also conjugated with ESSERE in these tenses as in all other COMPOUND TENSES (see page 108 for the list).

SE AVESSE AVUTO DENARO AVREBBE COMPRATO UNA
MACCHINA?
If you had had money, would you have bought a car?

Sì, se _avessi_ avuto denaro, _avrei comprato_ una macchina.
No, se _avessi avuto_ denaro, _non avrei comprato_ una macchina.

SE FOSSE STATO MALATO SAREBBE ANDATO A LETTO?
If you had been sick, would you have gone to bed?

Sì, se _fossi stato_ malato, _sarei andato_ a letto.
No, se _fossi stato_ malato, _non sarei andato_ a letto.

SE E' NECESSARIO FARLO, LO FARO'.
If I have to do it, I'll do it.

SE FOSSE NECESSARIO FARLO, LO FAREI.
If I had to do it, I'd do it.

SE FOSSE STATO NECESSARIO FARLO, LO AVREI FATTO.
If I had had to do it, I would have done it.

SE POSSO, VENGO.
If I can I'll come.

SE POTESSI, VERREI.
If I could, I'd come.

SE AVESSI POTUTO, SAREI VENUTO.
If I could have, I would have come.

SE SONO MALATO, VADO DAL MEDICO.
If I'm sick, I'll go to the doctor.

SE FOSSI MALATO, ANDREI DAL MEDICO.
If I were sick, I'd go to the doctor.

SE FOSSI STATO MALATO, SAREI ANDATO DAL MEDICO.
If I had been sick, I would have gone to the doctor.

SE SONO RICCO, COMPRO UNA MACCHINA.
If I'm rich, I'll buy a car.

SE FOSSI RICCO, COMPREREI UNA MACCHINA.
If I were rich, I'd buy a car.

SE FOSSI STATO RICCO, AVREI COMPRATO UNA MACCHINA.
If I had been rich, I would have bought a car.

give the second and third forms of IF:

e.g. Se Giovanna viene, mi aiuta.
   — Se Giovanna venisse, mi aiuterebbe.
   — Se Giovanna fosse venuta, mi avrebbe aiutato.

1) Se non devo lavorare, gioco col gatto.
2) Se piove, non andiamo.
3) Se Lei non mi impresta denaro, non posso comprare una macchina.
4) Se ho tempo, cerco un lavoro migliore.
5) Se vuole, andiamo al cinema.
6) Se posso scegliere, prendo questo.
7) Se il museo è aperto, ci andiamo.
8) Se il telefono suona, non rispondo.
9) Se ho i soldi, compro una casa in campagna.
10) Se Mario arriva oggi, sono contento.

translate into the three Italian conditional forms:

e.g. If I'm sick, I'll go to the doctor.
   — Se sono malato, vado dal medico.
   — Se fossi malato, andrei dal medico.
   — Se fossi stato malato, sarei andato dal medico.

1) If I work part-time, I won't have enough money.
2) If I have to do the dishes, will you help me?
3) If everything goes wrong, I'll go to bed.
4) If she can't write, she'll call.
5) If you continue to yell, I'll hang up.
6) If you disappoint me again, I'll leave you.
7) If he earns a lot of money, I'll marry him.
8) If you have a headache, you can rest.
9) If you're good, I won't spank you.
10) If you plan to go, you must tell me.
11) If you lie again, I'll be fed up.
12) If you want to get your plane, you must pack now.

VOCABOLARIO

	traduzione	sinonimo-associato	contrario-associato
1. orario ridotto	part-time ≠ full-time	a mezza giornata	orario completo, a tempo pieno
2. (un) sindacato	union	far sciopero = to go on strike	
3. famoso	famous		sconosciuto = unknown
4. lamentarsi	to complain ≠ to be satisfied	protestare, brontolare = to kick (grumble)	essere soddisfatto, esser/contento (di)
5. (una) ragione	reason	(una) spiegazione = explanation, (un) particolare = detail	(un) fatto = fact
6. (un') idea	idea	(un) pensiero = thought	
7. si rende conto?	do you realize?		non mi sono reso conto = I didn't realize
8. (un) incidente	accident	(un) disastro, (una) catastrofe	
9. /disturbare /dare fastidio	/to annoy, bother /to disturb	seccare, scocciare = to bug	
10. /che seccatura! /che scocciatura!	what a nuisance!		
11. romper le scatole (a)	to be a pain in the neck	(un) rompiscatole = a pain in the ass	
12. aver la sfacciataggine (di)	to have guts	(la) faccia tosta = nerve	
13. litigare	to argue ≠ to get on	bisticciare = to quarrel	andare d'accordo
14. (una) disputa	an argument	(una) lite, (un) litigio = a quarrel	
15. principale	main	dominante = leading	
16. persuadere	to persuade	convincere = to convince	
17. chiaro	clear ≠ vague	evidente = obvious	vago, impreciso
18. non so (guidare)	I don't know how (to drive)		

LEZIONE 25

SEQUENCE OF TENSES = CONCORDANZA DEI TEMPI

Dice che verrà.
present + future

He says he'll come.

Ha detto
Diceva che sarebbe venuto.
past + past conditional.

He said he'd come/he said he
would have come.

---

note: — note the use of the past conditional (and not the present conditional)
for the sequence of tenses. The Italians say: he said he 'would have'
come, to mean 'he said he would come'.
— note the use of either the past or the imperfect (ha detto . . . ,
diceva . . .)

HA DETTO CHE AVREBBE
TELEFONATO?

Did he say he would call?
/he would have called?

Sì, ha detto che avrebbe
telefonato.

Yes, he said he would call/
he would have called.

No, ha detto che non avrebbe
telefonato.

No, he said he wouldn't call
/he wouldn't have called.

---

put in the past:

1) Dice che farà subito le valigie.
2) Ti dico che partirò domenica.
3) Scrive che verrà la settimana prossima.
4) Sappiamo già che saremo bocciati all'esame.
5) So che un giorno o l'altro tornerà a casa.
6) Sappiamo che con questo libro parleremo presto e bene l'italiano.
7) Ti dico che andrò in Italia per le vacanze.
8) Scrivono che passeranno da Roma in settembre.
9) Mi rendo conto che non parlerò italiano in pochi giorni.
10) Ha la faccia tosta di dire che pagherà più tardi.
11) Stanno litigando per sapere chi non farà i lavori di casa.
12) Non si rende conto che se non uscirà alle otto perderà il treno.
13) Vanno sempre d'accordo quando si tratta di decidere quale film guarderanno alla televisione.
14) Quel rompiscatole dice che aspetterà anche due ore per parlare con Lei.

put in the present:

1) Sapevo che sarebbe venuto.
2) Abbiamo detto che saremmo andati al cinema.
3) Lo scrittore pensava che il suo libro sarebbe stato il migliore dell'anno.
4) Mi ha detto che gli sarebbe piaciuto lavorare a orario ridotto.
5) Si rendeva conto che il fatto di scrivere questo libro gli avrebbe preso troppo tempo.
6) Sapevo che non saresti stato capace di farlo.
7) Mi sono reso subito conto che quello scocciatore non sarebbe partito subito.
8) Abbiamo letto nel giornale che il tempo sarebbe stato pessimo.
9) Dicevano che avrebbero fatto sciopero.
10) Il medico diceva che sarebbe morto.
11) Il bandito non pensava che sarebbe stato arrestato sul luogo della rapina.
12) Quella carogna diceva che avrebbe accettato con piacere una bustarella.

translate:

1) I knew that you would help us.
2) I knew you wouldn't be satisfied.
3) She said that she'd know how to drive by Christmas time.
4) I knew you'd quarrel with my mother.
5) I thought I could do it.
6) All of us thought the prices would go down.
7) The candidate thought they'd vote for him.
8) I knew you'd be lucky.
9) He said he'd arrive on time.
10) I didn't think he'd kick about the decision.
11) We thought that you'd be able to write.
12) Didn't you realize that I could help you?

answer in Italian in the negative:
e.g. Non sapevi che sarei venuto a trovarti?
     No, non sapevo che saresti venuto a trovarmi.

1) Non pensavi che avrei telefonato prima delle otto?
2) Non sapevate che oggi avremmo fatto sciopero?
3) Non avete pensato che il bandito avrebbe tirato?
4) Non immaginava che quel tipo avrebbe voluto una bustarella?
5) Non pensavi che oggi sarebbe piovuto?
6) Non mi ha detto che avrebbe finito quel lavoro per martedì?
7) Non sapeva che L'avrei amata pazzamente?
8) Non pensava che si sarebbe trovata nei guai?
9) Non immaginava che Suo marito L'avrebbe ingannata?
10) Non sapevano che il padre li avrebbe puniti?
11) Non ha pensato che avrei potuto aiutarLa?
12) Non ha detto la Sua segretaria ieri che avrebbe subito scritto e spedito la lettera?

VOCABOLARIO

	traduzione	sinonimo-associato	contrario-associato
1. (un) fuoco	fire	(un) pompiere = fireman	
2. /(un) gangster /(un) truffatore	/gangster/crook	(un) malvivente, (un) bandito = robber, (un) ladro = thief	
3. rubare	to steal, to swipe		
4. (una) prigione	jail, prison	in guardina = in the clink	
5. arrestare	to arrest ≠ to release	pizzicare = to nab	rilasciare
6. un furto con scasso	a burglary	(una) rapina = hold-up	
7. /uccidere/(un) assassino/(un) delitto	/to kill/a murderer /a murder	un sicario = a killer	
8. /tirare/abbattere	/to shoot/to gun down	(una) rivoltella = gun, (una) pallottola = bullet	
9. onesto	honest ≠ crooked	retto = straight	disonesto, losco
10. (una) carognata	dirty trick	(un) colpo mancino, (un) brutto tiro = low deal	
11. (una) bustarella	bribe	unger le ruote = to buy s.o.	
12. (un,una) giornalista	journalist	(un,una) cronista = reporter	
13. /(un) politico /(un) politicante	/politician/dabbler in politics	la politica = politics	
14. (un) candidato	candidate	votare = to vote	
15. (una,delle) circostanze	circumstances		
16. la droga	drugs	l'haschisc = pot	
17. evadere	to escape	scappare = to get away	
18. infinocchiare	to hustle	farsi beffe di = to take s.o. in	
19. la malavita	the underworld		
20. la sua tattica è . . .	his policy is . . .		

VOCABOLARIO

	traduzione	sinonimo-associato	contrario-associato
21. raggiungere	to reach	arrivare a = to get to	
22. fin troppo bene	only too well		
23. non poter trattenersi da	can't help+ing	non ho potuto trattenermi dal ridere = I couldn't help laughing	
24. essere lì lì per	almost + verb	sono stato lì lì per cadere = I almost fell	
25. su, via!	come now!	non la bevo = I don't buy it	
26. (una) forza	strength ≠ weakness	il forte = strong point	debolezza, il punto debole = weak point
27. La disturbo se ...?	would you mind if ...?		non mi disturba affatto = I don't mind
28. ci ho messo un'ora	it took me an hour		
29. e inoltre	in addition to that	così come = as well as	
30. sveglio	awake ≠ asleep		addormentato
31. /(una) vita /vivo	/life/alive		a morte = death, morto = dead
32. morire	to die		nascere = to be born
33. notare	to notice		
34. (una, delle) sciocchezze	nonsense	sciocco, stupido = silly	
35. terribilmente	like crazy!	maledettamente!	
36. (Che) cosa mai...	what on earth ...	Che diavolo ... Dio mio! = My God!	
37. /suggerire/(un) suggerimento	/to suggest /suggestion	proporre, consigliare = to advise un consiglio = a piece of advice	
38. è colpa mia	it's my fault		
39. in caso che	in case		

LEZIONE 26

PAST PERFECT (TRAPASSATO PROSSIMO)

QUANDO SONO ENTRATO $\swarrow$ **AVEVANO GIA' MANGIATO.**
                                    ERANO GIA' USCITI.

When I came in

they <u>had</u> already <u>eaten</u>.
they <u>had</u> already <u>gone</u> out.

---

note: — this is the same structure as in English (an action 'paster' than another action).
— the verbs conjugated with ESSERE in the past are also conjugated with ESSERE in this tense (see page 108 for the list).

translate:

1) He said he had seen a tiger in the zoo.
2) I was sure that I had seen him before.
3) By the time he came we had already eaten.
4) She said she had got divorced because he had cheated on her.
5) When she refused this job, she had already accepted another one.
6) She didn't believe him any more, because he hadn't always told her the truth.
7) He was afraid because someone had followed him.
8) She told me she had found a great diet.
9) He had already gone out when I called.
10) She wanted to know what had happened between them.

136

complete the following sentences using the TRAPASSATO PROSSIMO:

1) Ha detto che ti ... (aspettare) tutto il giorno.
2) Ha detto che ... (venire) invano.
3) Ha detto che ... (prendere) l'aereo.
4) Ha scoperto tardi che sua moglie l' ... (ingannare).
5) Mi sono reso conto che il signor Bianchi ... (fare) uno sbaglio quando ho verificato il libro dei conti.
6) Quando sono arrivata, essi già ... (affittare) la casa.
7) (Tu) ... (finire) i compiti quando sono entrato?
8) Avete detto che già ... (vedere) il film?
9) Perchè avete detto che ... (perdere) la grana?
10) Non avete pensato che quel tipo ... (fare) il poliziotto quando era giovane.
11) Ti ho detto che ... (perdere) la borsetta e che ne (comprare) un'altra?
12) Maria ti ha detto che ... (venire) in bicicletta?
13) L'artista ... (morire) quando i suoi dipinti sono diventati celebri.
14) Perchè non mi hai detto che tuo marito ti ... (mentire)?
15) Perchè sua moglie gli ha detto che ... (partire)?
16) Quando ti ho telefonato noi ... (finire) di mangiare.
17) Il ladro correva perchè ... (vedere) i poliziotti.
18) Il commerciante era soddisfatto perchè ... (guadagnare) molto denaro.
19) Gli studenti erano contenti perchè le vacanze ... (cominciare).
20) Non ho mangiato il pompelmo perchè già ... (mangiare) una mela e due pesche.
21) Ha cominciato una dieta perchè ... (ingrassare) troppo.
22) Quando la polizia lo ha arrestato, il bandito ... (tirare) già due volte.
23) Quando il proprietario è arrivato, il ladro ... (rubare) i gioielli e il denaro.
24) Quando ho visto quel film ci ho messo un'ora a scoprire chi ... (pagare) il sicario per uccidere il testimone.

TO GET: how to translate

RICEVERE, AVERE

L'ho avuto/ricevuto ieri.
I got it yesterday.

Quando lo avrò?
When will I get it?

DIVENTARE

Diventa vecchio.
He's getting old.

Diventa interessante.
It's getting interesting.

ARRIVARE

Siamo arrivati tardi.
We got there late.

Non arriviamo in nessun luogo.
We're getting nowhere.

SGRIDARE

Ti farai sgridare!
You are going to get it!

Mi sono veramente fatto sgridare quando sono rincasato tardi.
I really got it when I came back late.

CAPIRE

Capito?
Get it?

Non La capisco.
I don't get you.

PROCURARE

Può procurarmi quel libro?
Can you get me that book?

Se lo è procurato al mercato.
He got it in the market.

AVERE LA COMUNICAZIONE
(phone), **PARLARE CON**

Hai potuto parlare con lui?
Did you get him?

Non ho potuto parlare con lei.
I didn't get her.

GUADAGNARE

Guadagno sei mila lire all'ora.
I get six thousand lires an hour.

Spero di guadagnare di più il mese prossimo.
I hope, I'll get more money next month.

translate:

1) Soon it'll get dark earlier.
2) Could you repeat it please? I didn't get it.
3) If you don't shut up, you're going to get it.
4) Did you get here yesterday or this morning?
5) When you go to Italy, can you get me some Italian wine?
6) Where did he get this beautiful jacket?
7) Could you explain it to me? I don't get it.
8) I think you should try to get your diploma this year.

138

VOCABOLARIO

	traduzione	sinonimo-associato	contrario-associato
1. terminare	to complete ≠ to start	finire = to finish	cominciare, iniziare, avviare
2. (una) condizione	condition	(una) posizione, (uno) stato = state	
3. andar male	to go wrong	peggiorare = to get worse	migliorare = to get better
4. (un) esempio	example	(uno) stato = state	
5. (una) luce	light		(un') oscurità = dark
6. /(un) frutto /(una) pesca /(una) mela	/fruit/peach /apple	un pompelmo = a grapefruit, (un') arancia = orange	
7. così così	so-so ≠ great	non formidabile = no great shakes	formidabile
8. (una) barba	beard	rasarsi = to shave	
9. /(un) quadro /(un) artista	/a picture/an artist	dipingere = to paint, un dipinto = a painting	
10. uno scrittore	a writer	(un) romanzo = novel	
11. /(una) figura /(una) dieta	/figure/diet	la linea, (un) viso = face	
12. (un) corpo	body	(un) collo = neck, (una) spalla = shoulder	
13. troppo magro	underweight ≠ overweight	snello = slim	troppo grasso
14. dimagrire	to lose weight		ingrassare = to gain weight
15. /(un) istituto di bellezza (una) messa in piega	/beauty parlour /wash and set	(un) parrucchiere = hairdresser, (un) barbiere = barber	
16. /(uno) zoo/(un) animale/(un) animale domestico	/zoo/animal/pet	(una) tigre = a tiger, (un) leone = a lion, (un) elefante = an elephant, (un) uccello = a bird, (una) scimmia = a monkey, (un) orso = a bear, (un') anitra = a duck	

LEZIONE 27

---

translate:

1) I'm tired but still I want to go out to dinner.
2) He's cheating on her but still she loves him.
3) It's raining but still I want to do some shopping.
4) Non voglio fare i lavori di casa ma li faccio lo stesso.
5) Sono stanco di traslocare, tuttavia ho accettato questo nuovo posto.
6) E' malata ma lavora molto lo stesso.

PARLANDO – PRESENT PARTICIPLE

par<u>lando</u>   <u>while</u> speaking
ved<u>endola</u>   <u>on</u> seeing her

---

note: — remember: you form the present participle by adding -ANDO to
the stem of the '-ARE' verbs and by adding -ENDO to the stem of
the '-ERE' and '-IRE' verbs (see page 80).
— remember: as with the infinitive you attach the object, whether
direct or indirect.

```
-ING → INFINITIVE

senza pagare                    without paying
dopo avere mangiato             after eating/having eaten
prima di andare                 before going
invece di mangiare              instead of eating
per essere venuto               for coming/having come
```

translate:

1) He went out without paying.
2) Instead of smoking you should go out for a walk.
3) He left without having eaten.
4) Before going to the movies, I'll have a sandwich.
5) After having telephoned, he went to bed.
6) She went out without talking to him.
7) She passed her exam without working.
8) The gangsters fled without stealing anything.
9) Instead of arguing we should decide what to do.
10) After reading this book, I'll write a letter to my father.
11) Without saying anything, she hit him.
12) Instead of eating now, do you want to go and see her at the hospital?
13) Thank you for coming.
14) I had already lost a lot of weight before meeting him.
15) Instead of working he was reading a paper.
16) I'm looking forward to finishing this wretched book.

```
┌─────────────────────────────────────────────────────────────┐
│ DI CUI                        = WHOSE, OF WHICH, ABOUT        │
│ La donna di cui Le ho mostrato    The woman whose picture I showed │
│ la foto . . .                     you . . .                   │
│ L'uomo di cui Le ho parlato . . . The man I spoke to you about . . . │
│ La casa di cui vedo il tetto . . . The house whose roof I can see . . . │
└─────────────────────────────────────────────────────────────┘
```

note: — parlare di: l'uomo di cui parlo = the man I'm speaking about.
        avere bisogno di: l'uomo di cui ho bisogno = the man I need.

```
┌─────────────────────────────────────────────────────────────┐
│ A CUI                         = (TO) WHOM                     │
│ La donna a cui parlo . . .        The woman whom I talk to . . . │
│ L'uomo a cui penso . . .          The man I'm thinking of . . . │
│ Il cane a cui ho dato da          The dog to which I gave something │
│ mangiare . . .                    to eat . . .                │
│ I bambini a cui ho dato           The children (to) whom I gave │
│ del pane . . .                    some bread . . .            │
└─────────────────────────────────────────────────────────────┘
```

note: — parlare a = to speak to
         pensare a = to think of
         dare a = to give to
         essere abituato a = to be used to
     — IN CUI = in which, SU CUI = on which, DA CUI = from which,
        PER CUI = for which.

translate:

1) The man I was telling you about is my best friend.
2) The woman whose guy's French is very sexy.
3) The man whom I'm thinking about hasn't come yet.
4) Can you give me the money I need?
5) I would like the kind of coffee I'm used to.
6) He's the kind of man I need.
7) That's what I'm talking to you about.

8) The man whose brother I know will come and see you tomorrow.
9) The year in which I was born was a good year for wine.
10) The house in which I'm living belongs to my father.
11) The bridge on which we are is one way only.
12) The room in which they are is very cold.
13) The chair on which you're sitting is very old.
14) The bed on which you are is mine.

GIA' – NON ANCORA	= ALREADY – NOT YET
E' già venuto?	Has he/Did he come already?
Sì, è già venuto.	Yes, he has come already.
No, non è ancora venuto.	No, he hasn't come yet.
No, non ancora.	No, not yet.

---

translate:

1) He has already eaten.
2) Has he already finished his work?
3) Have they already called? – No, not yet.
4) I've already done it.
5) He hasn't answered yet.
6) Is he already sleeping? – No, not yet.

put in the negative:

1) Ha già telefonato.
2) Ha già trovato una nuova fidanzata.
3) Hai già comprato un'Alfa Romeo?
4) Abbiamo già dato un esame.
5) Siete già andati a vedere l'Aida?
6) Ho già visto questo film.

VOCABOLARIO

	traduzione	sinonimo-associato	contrario-associato
1. farebbe meglio a	you'd better + verb		
2. /(un) ufficio postale/(un) francobollo	/post office /stamp	posta aerea = by air mail	
3. /(una) busta /(una) cartolina	/envelope /postcard	(una) lettera = letter (la) firma = signature	
4. firmare	to sign		
5. La metto in guardia (contro)	I warn you	avvertire, minacciare = to threaten	
6. testardo	stubborn	ostinato = obstinate	
7. accettare	to accept ≠ to refuse	ammettere = to admit	rifiutare, negare = to deny
8. a parer mio	in my opinion	per me = as for me	
9. deciso	settled	stabilito = set	non deciso = up in the air
10. (un) posto	job, work	(un) impiego, (una) funzione = function	
11. andare in pensione	to retire	dare le dimissioni = to resign	
12. traslocare	to move	stabilirsi = to move in	
13. (un) camion	lorry, truck	(il) furgone = van	
14. (una) parte	part ≠ the whole	(la) metà = half	il tutto
15. a senso unico	one way		
16. /(una) terra/(la) terra/(il) mondo	/land/earth /world	(una) proprietà = property	
17. Com'è carina!	How pretty she is!		
18. /(una) montagna /(un) lago	/mountain/lake	(un) fiume = river	
19. sembra	it looks like	sembra che = it seems that	
20. descrivere	to describe	dipingere = to depict	
21. questo dannato libro	this wretched book	questo maledetto libro	
22. Non vedo l'ora di ...	I'm looking forward to ...		

LEZIONE 28

BISOGNARE, DOVERE, ESSERE OBBLIGATO A =
TO HAVE TO, MUST

present		past
I must/have to work	→	I had to work

— **bisogna**		**bisognava**
— **devo** **lavorare**	→	**dovevo/ho dovuto** **lavorare**
— **sono obbligato a**		**ero/sono stato obbligato a**

| I'm supposed to work | → | I was supposed to work |

— **devo** **lavorare**	→	**devevo/ho dovuto** **lavorare**
— **sono tenuto a**		**ero/sono stato tenuto a**

note: — BISOGNA = you, one, we, etc. must.
      — DOVERE is much used and you must get used to using it.
      Special uses: — Deve essere malato = he must be sick. = sarà malato.
      Deve essere stato malato = He must have been sick = sarà stato
      malato; (see page 85 for the use of the future).

translate:

1) You must go today.
2) She was supposed to tell you the truth.
3) He must have left.
4) You must be tired.
5) Do we have to work so late?
6) You weren't supposed to ask him.
7) I didn't have to tell you the truth.
8) They must not have understood.

translate:

1) Il giornalista doveva scrivere un articolo sul nuovo candidato.
2) Perchè non è venuto? Deve essere a Roma.
3) Non l'ho visto da molto tempo, dev'essere di nuovo in prigione.
4) Non ero tenuto ad andare ieri.
5) Le strade sono bagnate. Deve essere piovuto.

```
SHOULD – SHOULD HAVE

Ora
Domani  dovrebbe lavorare.

Now,
Tomorrow  you should work.

Ieri, avrebbe dovuto lavorare.

Yesterday you should have worked.
```

```
You should see her.              Dovrebbe vederla.
You should have seen her.        Avrebbe dovuto vederla.

We should tell her.              Dovremmo dirglielo.
We should have told her.         Avremmo dovuto dirglielo.
```

translate:

1) You should have bought more vegetables.
2) He should call her.
3) You should never have said that.
4) Why should I write to him?
5) I don't think you should write now, but you should have written last week.
6) Why shouldn't the kids have eaten at five?
7) He shouldn't have lied.
8) You're right. We should have told you.

translate:

1) Avrebbe dovuto ascoltarti.
2) Avresti dovuto aspettare l'autobus.
3) Non dovresti aver paura del buio.
4) Avrei dovuto comprare quel quadro.
5) Non avrebbero dovuto dargli una bustarella.
6) Cosa mai avremmo dovuto fare?
7) Non penso che dovresti andare.
8) Siete tenuti a saperlo.

THE IMPERATIVE — FOR FRIENDS AND LOVERS!

VERBI IN '-ARE'	**VERBI IN '-ERE'**	**VERBI IN '-IRE'**
mangia! = eat!	**chiudi!** = close!	**apri!** = open!
mangiate! = eat! (plural)	**chiudete!** = close! (plural)	**aprite!** = open! (plural)
non mangiare! = don't eat!	**non chiudere!** = don't close!	**non aprire!** = don't open!
non mangiate! = don't eat! (plural)	**non chiudete!** = don't close! (plural)	**non aprite!** = don't open! (plural)

note: — the few irregular verbs which add -ISC in the present, follow
the example of FINIRE in the imperative: finisci! finite! = finish!
— non finire! non finite! = don't finish! (see page 55 for the list).
— as with the infinitive and the present participle you attach the
object, whether direct or indirect, e.g. chiudila! chiudetela! = close
it! (la porta).

Mangia quella minestra, Pietro!	= Eat that soup, Peter!
Non chiudere la porta, Maria!	Don't close the door, Mary!
Aprite le finestre, ragazze!	Open the windows, girls!

IRREGULAR VERBS – VERBI IRREGOLARI
IMPERATIVES

essere (to be)	→ **sii, siate**	**bere** (to drink)	→ **bevi, bevete**
avere (to have)	→ **abbi, abbiate**	**sapere** (to know)	→ **sappi, sappiate**
andare (to go)	→ **va', andate**	**volere** (to want)	→ **vogli, vogliate**
dare (to give)	→ **dà, date**	**dire** (to say)	→ **dì, dite**
porre (to put)	→ **poni, ponete**	**venire** (to come)	→ **vieni, venite**

translate:

1) Chiudi la finestra, Giovanni!
2) Non aprire la porta, Maria!
3) Manda una cartolina a tua madre, Davide, mandala oggi!
4) Bambini, finite presto i compiti!
5) Antonio e Marco, non toccate i miei libri!
6) Pietro, prendi una penna e scrivi subito a tuo padre!

Insert the imperative (singular) affirmative and negative:
e.g. (accendere) la televisione → accendi la televisione! = put the TV on!
   – non accendere la televisione = don't put the TV on!

1) (Fumare) una sigaretta Nazionale.
2) (Guardare) dalla finestra la gente che passa.
3) (Lavorare) tutta la notte.
4) (Bere) un altro caffè.
5) (Scendere) al pianterreno.
6) (Comprare) una bottiglia di vino buono.

Insert the imperative (plural) affirmative and negative:
e.g. (venire) ad incontrarci alla stazione – venite ad incontrarci alla
   stazione! = come to meet us at the station! – non venite ad incontrarci
   alla stazione! = don't come to meet us at the station!

1) (Finire) questo lavoro per stasera.
2) (Andare) alla piscina.
3) (Fare) attenzione a quello che dice Marco.
4) (Dire) quello che pensate.
5) (Bere) una Coca Cola dopo aver nuotato.
6) (Pulire) la cucina dopo aver mangiato.

THE IMPERATIVE — FORMAL/BUSINESS USAGE

VERBI IN '-ARE'	VERBI IN '-ERE'	VERBI IN '-IRE'
mang<u>i</u>! = eat!	chiud<u>a</u>! = close!	apr<u>a</u>! = open!
mang<u>ino</u>! = eat! (plural)	chiud<u>ano</u>! = close! (plural)	apr<u>ano</u>! = open! (plural)
<u>non</u> mang<u>i</u>! = don't eat!	<u>non</u> chiud<u>a</u>! = don't close!	<u>non</u> apr<u>a</u>! = don't open!
<u>non</u> mang<u>ino</u>! = don't eat! (plural)	<u>non</u> chiud<u>ano</u>! = don't close! (plural)	<u>non</u> apr<u>ano</u>! = don't open! (plural)

note: — this is for formal use only (to waiters, in hotel, in business, etc . . .)
  — this tense is in fact the 'present subjunctive'.
  — personal pronouns precede this tense, e.g. chiuda la porta, per
    favore, signor Bianchi, <u>la</u> chiuda! = close the door, please Mr Bianchi,
    close it!
  — the verbs with an irregular present to form this tense change the final
    vowel of the present into -<u>a</u>, e.g. porre (to put): present indicative =
    pong<u>o</u>, present subjunctive = pong<u>a</u>.

Mi porti un caffè, cameriere!   = <u>Bring</u> me a coffee waiter!
<u>Scriva</u> il Suo nome, Signora!   = <u>Write</u> your name, Madam!
Non aprano le finestre, Signore   = <u>Don't open</u> the windows, ladies
e Signori!   and gentlemen!

```
IRREGULAR VERBS — VERBI IRREGOLARI
           THE 'FORMAL' IMPERATIVE
essere (to be)   → sia! siano!     stare (to stay)   → stia! stiano!
avere (to have)  → abbia! abbiano! sapere (to know)  → sappia! sappiano!
dare (to give)   → dia! diano!
```

translate:

1) Venga qui per favore, signora Smith!
2) Apra la porta, signorina Brown!
3) Non chiuda la finestra, signor Peters!
4) Ascolti attentamente ciò che dico, signor White!
5) Non ha ancora pagato il conto dell'albergo, signore? Lo paghi ora, per favore!
6) Vada ora a fare le spese, se vuole. I negozi sono ancora aperti.
7) Beva un altro bicchiere di vino!
8) Entrino in questa sala, signore e signori, e ammirino questo quadro del Tintoretto!
9) Mi dia quelle scarpe nere che sono in vetrina!
10) Eccole, signore, venga a provarle!
11) Signor Brown, dica al Suo inquilino di non fare tanto rumore di notte, per favore!
12) Cambi da gas a gasolio, costa meno!

translate:

1) Excuse me, Madam!
2) Listen to me, Sir!
3) Bring me a scotch, waiter!
4) Call me tonight, darling!
5) Take this book to your mother, young man!
6) You should drink some water, Sir!
7) You should sublet a part of your house, Mrs Smith!
8) Excuse me, Sir, can you tell me where's the post-office? —
   Take the first road on the right and then the second on the left. —
   Thank you very much.

VOCABOLARIO

	traduzione	sinonimo-associato	contrario-associato
1. affittare	to rent, to let	dare in affitto = to let, prendere in affitto = to rent subaffittare = to sublet	
2. (un) proprietario	owner ≠ tenant		(un) inquilino
3. /(un) metodo /(un) modo	/method/way	(un) sistema = system, (uno) stile = style	
4. ordinario	ordinary ≠ exceptional	qualunque = commonplace	eccezionale, straordinario
5. alla moda	fashionable ≠ old fashioned	moderno = modern, di vecchio stampo = of the old style	fuori moda, antiquato
6. (una) parola	word	(una) frase = sentence	
7. (il) gas	gas	petrolio = oil	
8. scarso	scarce ≠ abundant		abbondante
9. (un) rumore	noise ≠ silence	(un) chiasso, (uno) schiamazzo	(il) silenzio
10. – in autobus – in macchina	– by bus – by car	in aereo = by plane	
11. invano	in vain, useless	inutile, non serve a nulla = it's no avail	
12. non posso sopportarlo	I can't bear him	non posso vederlo	sono pazzo per = I'm wild about
13. causare	to cause	scatenare = to bring on	
14. E' il colmo!	That beats all! That's the limit!		
15. (un) credulone	sucker	(un) merlo, (un) tonto, (un) sempliciotto	
16. assurdo	absurd ≠ logical	ridicolo = ridiculous	logico, pratico = practical
17. degli affari	business	fare affari = to do business	
18. caro(a)	darling	tesoro	

LEZIONE 29

COSI' = SO

E' così malato che non può lavorare.　　　He's so sick that he can't work.

TANTO = SO MUCH

Ha tanto denaro!　　　He has so much money!

Parla tanto!　　　He speaks so much!

---

translate:

1) Il capufficio era così arrabbiato che è uscito urlando.
2) Parli tanto!
3) Mangia tanto che ingrassa molto.
4) E' così stanca che resterà a letto.
5) Abbiamo tanto riso!
6) Hanno avuto tanto lavoro ieri che hanno lasciato l'ufficio alle dieci di sera.

translate:

1) She's so stubborn she won't listen to you.
2) She's so frank that it hurts.
3) They're so rich!
4) He drank so much coffee he couldn't sleep.
5) We're so unhappy we should get divorced.
6) It's so cold outside that I'll stay at home.

STAVO + PRESENT PARTICIPLE	= WAS + -ING, WAS IN THE MIDST OF
Stavo scrivendoti quando mi hai telefonato.	I <u>was</u> just <u>writing</u> to you when you called.

translate:

1) I'm in the midst of eating and I was in the midst of eating when you called.
2) They were in the midst of having an Italian lesson when he arrived.
3) We were in the midst of reading when your brother turned the TV on.
4) We were just coming to see you when we met your mother-in-law.

NE = SOME	
N<u>e</u> ho.	= I have <u>some of it/them</u>, etc.
N<u>e</u> vuole?	Do you want <u>some of it/them</u>, etc.
Gli<u>ene</u> parlerò.	I'll speak to him/her <u>about it</u>.

note: — frequent use of NE with verbs followed by 'di':
    — aver bisogno di → n<u>e</u> ho bisogno = I need it/some.
    — parlare di → se n<u>e</u> parlerà = we'll speak about it.
    — pensare di → che n<u>e</u> pensa? = what do you think about it?

give the affirmative and negative answers using n<u>e</u>:

1) Ha denaro?
2) Parlavate bene di lui quando è entrato?
3) Avete molta fame?
4) Ha bisogno di parecchie segretarie il capufficio?
5) Parlano molto dei loro problemi i bambini?
6) Vendete molti libri come questo?
7) Regali qualche volta dei fiori alla tua ragazza?
8) Hanno due macchine i Cattaruzza?

CI = THERE

CI VA STASERA?	= Are you going <u>there</u> tonight?
Sì, ci vado stasera.	Yes, I'm going <u>there</u> tonight.
No, non ci vado stasera.	No, I'm not going <u>there</u> tonight.

---

translate:

1) I lived there for a year.
2) Are we going there at once?
3) He went there with me.

C'ERA = THERE WAS

C'ERA UN UOMO NELLA STANZA?	= <u>Was there</u> a man in the room?
Sì, c'era.	Yes, <u>there was.</u>
Sì, c'era un uomo nella stanza.	Yes, <u>there was</u> a man in the room.

C'ERANO = THERE WERE

C'ERANO MOLTI FIORI NEL GIARDINO?	= <u>Were there</u> many flowers in the garden?
Sì, ce n'erano molti.	Yes, <u>there were.</u>
Sì, c'erano molti fiori.	Yes, <u>there were</u> many flowers.

CI SARA'/CI SARANNO. = THERE WILL BE

CI SARANNO MOLTI REGALI?	<u>Will there be</u> many presents?
Sì, ce ne saranno molti.	Yes, <u>there will be</u> many.
Sì, ci saranno molti regali.	Yes, <u>there will be</u> many presents.

---

translate:

1) Was there a lot of snow in winter?
2) Will there be a lot of work to do?
3) There were many children playing in the park.
4) Were there any problems with the last lesson?
5) There were only four people in the restaurant.
6) There were many passengers delighted with the trip.
7) There will be a crowd in the house.
8) There are always many tourists in Rome.

NON = NOT TO

Ti ho detto di <u>non</u> farlo.   I told you <u>not to</u> do it.

---

translate:

1) I told you not to work too much.
2) He warned me not to go.
3) You promised me not to leave me.
4) She wrote not to wait for her.
5) I asked him not to call.

LA.RAGIONE PER CUI/PER   = THE REASON WHY
LA QUALE

E' la ragione <u>per cui</u> non verrò.   = That's the reason <u>why</u> I won't
                                                come.

---

translate:

1) That's the reason why he wants to go abroad.
2) That's the reason why it fits me.
3) I'm disappointed and that's the reason why I'm leaving.
4) I don't know and that's the reason why I'm beating around the bush.
5) I'm not sure and that's the reason why I can't answer.
6) We're poor and that's the reason why we need money.
7) He's an ass and that's the reason why I'm getting divorced.

VOCABOLARIO

	traduzione	sinonimo-associato	contrario-associato
1. enorme	huge ≠ tiny	immenso	minuscolo
2. /(uno) straniero /(uno) sconosciuto	/foreigner /stranger	all'estero = abroad	
3. /sincero /sinceramente	/frank/frankly	onestamente = honestly	menare il can per l'aia = to beat around the bush
4. (un') abitudine	habit	abituarsi = to get used to	
5. guidare	to drive	cavalcare = to ride (a horse)	
6. immaginare	to imagine	fare come se = to pretend	
7. aumentare	to increase ≠ to decrease, go down	salire = to go up	diminuire
8. mi va bene	/it fits/it's suitable		largo = loose, stretto = tight
9. abituarsi a . . .	to get used to . . .	prendere l'abitudine di	
10. un'occasione	a chance	una possibilità	
11. gentile	friendly	amichevole ≠ ostile	sgarbato, freddo = cold
12. (un) passeggero	passenger ≠ driver		(un) conducente
13. (una) sosta	a break	una pausa = a pause	
14. il fatto è che . . .	the point is ≠ that's not the point		non è questo il nocciolo della questione
15. contento (di)	delighted	soddisfatto	deluso = disappointed
16. calmo	calm ≠ excited		agitato
17. in ogni caso	anyway, in any case	in ogni modo	
18. (una) folla	crowd		

LEZIONE 30

REFLEXIVE VERBS (VERBI RIFLESSIVI)

LAVARSI = TO GET WASHED (WASH ONESELF)

mi lavo = I'm getting washed
      /I wash myself

non mi lavo = I'm not getting washed
       /I'm not washing myself

ti lavi
si lava
ci laviamo
vi lavate
si lavano

non ti lavi
non si lava
non ci laviamo
non vi lavate
non si lavano

note: — reflexive verbs are extremely frequent in Italian.
      — mistakes are not very important, but you should try to get used to
         the structure 'I wash myself'.

SI LAVA TUTTI I GIORNI?   = Do you wash/get washed every day?

Sì, mi lavo tutti i giorni.   Yes, I wash/get washed every day.
No, non mi lavo tutti i giorni.   No, I don't wash/get washed every
         day.

MI LAVO.   = I wash myself.
MI LAVO LE MANI.   I wash my hands.

TI LAVI.   You wash yourself.
TI LAVI LE MANI.   You wash your hands.

note: no possessive pronouns for the parts of your body.

SOME REFLEXIVE VERBS

addormentarsi = to go to sleep
svegliarsi = to wake up
alzarsi = to get up
sedersi = to sit down
spogliarsi = to get undressed
vestirsi = to get dressed
cambiarsi = to change one's clothes
radersi = to shave
lavarsi = to get washed
spicciarsi = to hurry up
pettinarsi = to comb one's hair
sentirsi = to feel
vergognarsi (di) = to be ashamed (of)
preoccuparsi = to worry about
sbagliarsi = to make mistakes
lamentarsi = to complain
avverarsi = to come true
fidanzarsi = to get engaged

sposarsi = to get married
rallegrarsi = to be glad about
divertirsi = to have a good time
meravigliarsi = to be astonished
arrabbiarsi = to get angry
calmarsi = to calm down
burlarsi (di) = to make fun of
abituarsi (a) = to get used to
rendersi conto di = to realize
interessarsi (a) = to be interested (in)
ricordarsi (di) = to remember
dimenticarsi (di) = to forget
domandarsi = to wander
perdersi = to lose one's way
decidersi = to make up's one's mind
infischiarsi = not to give a darn
servirsi = to help oneself
chiamarsi = to be named

note: — many of these verbs can be used reflexively or not:
— Veste il bambino = she dresses the kid. BUT (**MA**):
— Si veste = she's getting dressed.

SI = EACH OTHER

Ci <u>si</u> parla spesso.   = We often speak to each other.
Ci <u>si</u> ama = <u>ci</u> amiamo.   We love each other.
Ci <u>si</u> vede spesso = <u>ci</u> vediamo   We often see each other.
spesso.

translate, then answer in the negative:

1) Si sbaglia spesso?
2) Ti ricordi delle tue ultime vacanze?
3) Si chiama Smith?
4) Vi infischiate di ciò che dico?
5) Vi siete sposati in chiesa?
6) Si alzano presto tutti i giorni?
7) Si addormenta tardi di solito il bambino?
8) Non ti senti bene?
9) Tony e Maria si sono fidanzati ieri?
10) Vi siete decisi o no?
11) Si sono arrabbiati molto i suoi genitori?
12) Ti spogli davanti a tuo marito?

translate:

1) I'm washing and getting dressed for the party.
2) We're wondering why you told him not to come.
3) They're getting married tomorrow.
4) Tonight I want to have a good time.
5) I make mistakes all the time.
6) Do you realize what you're saying?
7) I don't remember him.
8) He's always complaining. — What's he complaining about?
9) I can't make up my mind.
10) I don't give a darn about anything.
11) Hurry up! (3 translations)
12) I shaved while she was changing.
13) If he made up his mind we wouldn't have to worry any longer.
14) If we got married now we'd get divorced soon.
15) You'll get used to this toothpaste.
16) All dreams don't come true.
17) Our neighbours aren't ashamed of stealing flowers from our garden.
18) Excuse yourself! (3 translations)
19) I lost my way when I was coming back from the station.
20) I wonder whether my translation's correct.

VOCABOLARIO

	traduzione	sinonimo-associato	contrario-associato
1. evidentemente	evidently ≠ doubtfully	senza alcun dubbio = without a doubt	non . . . sicuramente
2. /(un) sapone /(un) asciugamani /(uno) spazzolino da denti	/soap/towel /toothbrush	(il) dentifricio = toothpaste	
3. /praticamente tutto/tanto	/practically all /so very much	quasi tutto = nearly all, tutto ciò che = all that	affatto = not at all, così poco = so little
4. /(una) coperta /(un) cuscino	/blanket/pillow	(un) lenzuolo = sheet	
5. /in qualunque momento/ dovunque /qualunque cosa	/whenever/wherever /whatever	ogni volta che = every time, in qualunque posto = anywhere	
6. (una) conversazione	conversation	chiacchierare = to chat	
7. avverarsi	to come true		
8. (delle) raccomandazioni	contacts	relazioni = connections, legami = ties	
9. permanente	permanent ≠		temporaneo
10. /(un) albero/(un) fiore/(un) giardino/(un) cortile	/tree/flower /garden/yard	(un) parco = park, (una) foresta = forest, (un') erba = grass	
11. /(un) cielo/(una, delle/ stelle	/sky/stars	la luna = the moon	
12. (un) grattacielo	skyscraper	(una) vista = sight	
13. più lontano	further		più vicino = nearer
14. (un) pettegolezzo	gossip	chiacchiere	
15. fresco	fresh		stantìo = stale
16. (di) fuori	outside ≠ indoors		dentro
17. svenire	to faint		
18. /tale quale/d'allora	/as is/ever since		
20. prendere in giro	to make fun of	burlarsi di	

LEZIONE 31

IO STESSO = MYSELF

io stesso(a)	myself
tu stesso(a)	yourself
egli stesso	himself
essa stessa	herself
se stesso(i)	oneself
Lei stesso(a)	yourself
noi stessi(e)	ourselves
voi stessi(e)	yourselves
essi stessi	themselves
esse stesse	

L'HO COMPRATO IO STESSO.
I bought it myself.

LO FARA' EGLI STESSO.
He will do it himself.

note: — I did it myself = l'ho fatto io stesso = l'ho fatto da solo = I did it alone, she got dressed herself = si è vestita da sola, etc.

fill in the reflexive:

1) Avresti dovuto invitarlo . . .
2) Abbiamo preparato il pasto . . .
3) Avete organizzato . . . la riunione?
4) Lo ha licenziato . . .
5) Hanno costruito . . . la loro casa.
6) Penso di poter finire il lavoro . . .
7) Ce ne occuperemo . . .
8) Se avessi potuto farlo . . . lo avrei fatto.
9) Glielo dica . . . !

REFLEXIVE VERBS — VERBI REFLESSIVI

PAST = THE PRESENT OF ESSERE + PAST PARTICIPLE

Mi sono lavato(a) ieri	Non mi sono lavato(a) ieri
ti sei lavato(a) ieri	non ti sei lavato(a) ieri
si è lavato(a) ieri	non si è lavato(a) ieri
ci siamo lavati(e) ieri	non ci siamo lavati(e) ieri
vi siete lavati(e) ieri	non vi siete lavati(e) ieri
si sono lavati(e) ieri	non si sono lavati(e) ieri

note: — the reflexive verbs are conjugated with ESSERE in all compound
tenses, e.g. mi ero già lavato quando è mancata l'acqua = I had
already washed when the water was cut.

TI SEI SVEGLIATO TARDI?   Did you wake up late?

Sì, mi sono svegliato tardi.   Yes, I woke up late.
No, non mi sono svegliato tardi.   No, I didn't wake up late.

Put into the past:

1) Mi domando se verrà.
2) Non si rende conto di ciò che dice.
3) Mio nonno si abitua a non fumare più.
4) Ti burli troppo spesso di me.
5) Ti ricordi della nostra prima notte assieme?
6) Donatella si lava e si veste in un quarto d'ora.
7) Si spiccia per uscire con te.
8) Non ci lamentiamo di niente.
9) Mi diverto sempre quando esco con voi.
10) La vecchia signora si siede sempre dietro il conducente.
11) Gli operai si rendono conto che saranno licenziati.
12) Il commesso si ricorda di quel cliente.

translate:

1) We always woke up late on vacation and now we wake early for work.
2) I didn't make mistakes yesterday and I'm not making mistakes now.
3) We had a good time last night. We always have a good time.
4) I hurried up but you didn't realize that I wanted to see you sooner.
5) He never makes up his mind early enough. Have you made up your mind yet?
6) You made fun of me yesterday. I'm fed up with you.
7) She got married again. I wonder if she remembers all her husbands.
8) Practically all were interested in the conversation.
9) You should be ashamed to take her gossip seriously.
10) I can't get used to the new car.
11) I cut myself when I tried to shave quickly.
12) If I had hurried, I wouldn't have been late.

VOCABOLARIO

	traduzione	sinonimo-associato	contrario-associato
1. fabbricare	to manufacture	fare = to make	
2. (una) riunione	meeting		
3. (una) fabbrica	factory	operai = workers	
4. il mercato	the market		
5. organizzare	to organize	avviare = to set up	
6. al minuto	retail ≠ wholesale		all'ingrosso
7. (il) personale	staff		
8. assumere	to hire ≠ to fire		licenziare
9. /(un) ingegnere /(un) ponte	/engineer /bridge		
10. /intesi/è un grosso affare /affari importanti	/it's a deal/it's a big deal/big business	avviare un affare = to put a deal together	
11. costruire	to build		
12. (una) macchina	machine	(un) calcolatore = calculator, or computer; (un) computer also = computer	
13. (un') inserzione	an ad	fare pubblicità = to advertise	
14. (una) pubblicità commerciale	a commercial		
15. (un) cliente	customer ≠ salesman, client		commesso
16. /(un) reddito /(una,delle) tasse	/income/taxes		
17. (uno) stipendio	salary	(una) paga = pay	
18. /(un) rischio /arrischiato	/risk/risky	rischioso, correre il rischio = to take a chance	affare fatto, è nel sacco = it's a sure thing
19. esige che . . .	he requires that . . .		
20. se l'è cavata	he swung it	è riuscito a . . . = he managed to . . .	

LEZIONE 32

VERB REVIEW

PRESENTE — THE problem!

Lavoro tutti i giorni.	I work everyday.
Ora lavoro.	I'm working now.
Lavoro da un'ora.	I've been working for an hour.
Domani lavoro.	I'm going to work tomorrow.

---

note: the Italian PRESENT is so extensively used that its meaning can be tricky to grasp.

FUTURO

Lavorerò ⟨ **tra due giorni.** / **la settimana prossima.**   I'll work ⟨ in two days. / next week.

Sarà malato.   He's probably ill.

PASSATO PROSSIMO

Ho lavorato ⟨ **ieri.** / **la settimana scorsa.** / **due giorni fa.**   I worked / I (have) worked ⟨ yesterday. / last week. / two days ago.

165

IMPERFETTO — the other problem!

Lavoravo ⟨ **quando sei venuto.** = I <u>was</u> working ⟨<u>when</u> you came.
         ⟨ **mentre tu parlavi.**   ⟨<u>while</u> you were talking.

note: — distinguish between:
      — I worked yesterday = ho lavorato ieri.
      — I was working when you called = lavoravo quando tu hai telefonato.

TRAPASSATO PROSSIMO

Mi ha detto che ti <u>aveva visto</u>.   He told me he <u>had seen</u> you.

Ho pensato che <u>eri</u> già <u>partito</u>.   I thought that you <u>had</u> already <u>left</u>.

SE = IF

Se <u>ho</u> i soldi, <u>compro</u> una macchina.
If I have the money, I'll buy a car.

Se <u>avessi</u> i soldi, <u>comprerei</u> una macchina.
If I had the money, I'd buy a car.

Se <u>avessi avuto</u> i soldi, <u>avrei comprato</u> una macchina.
If I had had the money, I would have bought a car.

insert the correct tense (the pronouns in square brackets are for guidance in choosing the correct verb form only):

1) [Noi] . . . (addormentarsi) tardi ieri.
2) [Tu] . . . (fare) i lavori di casa oggi? — No, li . . . (fare) domani.
3) [Lei] . . . (guardare) la televisione da due ore.
4) [Voi] . . . (andare) al cinema due settimane fa?
5) [Egli] . . . (leggere) mentre io . . . (dormire).
6) [Essi] . . . (litigare) da un'ora.
7) [Tu] . . . (essere) già in Inghilterra?
8) Da quando [voi] . . . (essere) qui?
9) [Egli] . . . (guidare) la Fiat quando . . . (succedere) l'incidente.
10) [Essi] . . . (essere sposati) da un anno.
11) [Essa] . . . (dormire) nonostante la pioggia.
12) Quando la polizia . . . (arrestare) il ladro, egli . . . (rubare) già molto denaro.
13) [Io] . . . (pensare) che tu . . . (finire) di mangiare.
14) Noi . . . (studiare) l'italiano da un anno.
15) Voi . . . (vedere) già questo film?
16) Io . . . (andare) dal dentista ieri.
17) Che cosa [tu] . . . (fare) quando io . . . (entrare)?
18) [Essa] . . . (essere) infelice dal giorno del suo matrimonio.
19) [Noi] . . . (cominciare) un'altra lezione domani.
20) [Io] non . . . (potere) farlo ieri e non . . . (potere) farlo domani.
21) Da stamattina io . . . (tentare) di telefonarti.
22) [Essa] . . . (cucinare) quando tu . . . (tornare) a casa?
23) [Egli] . . . (riparare) la macchina che non . . . (funzionare) più?
24) [Noi] . . . (lavarsi) stamattina. [Noi] . . . (lavarsi) ogni giorno.
25) [Egli] . . . (ricordarsi) di ciò che [egli] . . . (dire) quando tu lo . . . (incontrare) la settimana scorsa?
26) Tu mi . . . (dire) la stessa cosa da stamattina.
27) Io . . . (insegnare) all'Università di Roma prima di venire negli Stati Uniti.
28) [Essi] . . . (essere divorziati) da sei mesi. Da quando . . . (essere divorziati) voi?

translate, then give the second and the third form of IF:

1) If I can, I'll go with him.
2) If they love each other, why don't they get married?
3) If you make fun of me, I'll leave you.
4) If we don't have to do the work ourselves, we'll go for a walk.
5) If he doesn't work, he won't pass his exam.
6) If they're rich next year, they'll buy a new house.
7) If we can help, we'll call you.
8) If you want to sell your car, I'll buy it.
9) If he's an ass his wife won't love him any more.
10) If your sister takes the pill, she won't get pregnant.
11) If we take our coats to the dry cleaners, it will be expensive.
12) If the workers go on strike, the unions will be happy.
13) If there's another war, we'll all be killed.
14) If you continue the bullshit, I'll leave you.
15) If we don't take a walk, I'm going to scream.
16) If you want to take a trip, I'll come with you.
17) If her lover can't screw any more, she'll be disappointed.
18) If the commercial is bad, that will be nothing new.
19) If politicians don't take bribes, that will be amazing.
20) If we have to pay our taxes early, we'll be in a jam.
21) If soldiers refuse to go to war, the world will at last be happy.
22) If we don't take the highway, the trip will take longer.
23) If his policy is so stupid, we won't vote for him.
24) If I have to lose weight, I'll try to.
25) If I don't have to do the housework, I'll play with the children.
26) If you can't manage, I'll help you.
27) If they put up the prices, they'll lose a lot of money.
28) If the cops can catch the gangster, they'll put him in jail.

translate:

1) She's been cooking the meal since this morning.
2) He was saying such a lot of bullshit that she walked out.
3) He was whispering while I was talking aloud.
4) My arm has been hurting me all day.
5) I'm going to get washed and dressed to go out.
6) She lived in New York for ten years when she was young and now she's been living in Rome for two years.
7) Do you realize how stupid they are!
8) I couldn't remember his name.
9) The commercial was so bad yesterday that I turned off the TV.
10) They've been selling retail since Christmas.
11) We've been manufacturing computers for a long time.
12) I need to know if you can come.
13) I have to tell you something important.
14) You should have repaired the car yesterday. You never listen when I tell you you should repair it.
15) I didn't have to do it for today. I have to do it for tomorrow.
16) They were putting the deal together when the cops came in.
17) You mustn't wash this sweater.
18) I'm not used to eating Italian food.
19) You should have called and told me you were in a jam.
20) He didn't know what to do, so I told him that he should see the boss.
21) If you were one of his friends you should be used to his drinking so much.
22) What a sucker you are! You shouldn't have believed him.
23) I couldn't bear him, and I don't understand why she's wild about him.
24) Did you hear their stupid conversation?
25) He was going to retire when his wife got sick.
26) I don't have to help you as you didn't help me when I needed it.

translate:

1) They've been engaged since Christmas. Do you think they're going to get married soon?
2) I was laughing while you were making fun of me.
3) You should give her a gift for her birthday and you should have given her one last year.
4) I've been trying for two hours to get that damn guy on the phone.
5) I didn't expect it, but it doesn't surprise me.
6) I don't see anyone and I don't hear anything.
7) I only have a little dough. Can you lend me some?
8) Our company has been supplying the factory with computers for years and years.
9) He didn't understand anything. He never understands anything.
10) I was getting divorced when I met him.
11) He's been cheating on his wife since their marriage.
12) You have to catch up if you don't want to fall behind too much.
13) The crooks were celebrating their burglary when the cops came in.
14) You shouldn't have taken those drugs.
15) I can't help you. I'm too tired.
16) He's been hitting his wife since their baby was born.
17) For how long have you been pregnant?
18) My leg has been hurting me since the accident.
19) Would you mind if I smoked while you're eating?
20) I had to leave a big tip. You should have left one too.
21) I couldn't stay honest in politics. Could you?
22) The underworld is so strong that we're all afraid.
23) For how long have you been married?
24) Did you know he was making love with his secretary while you were on your trip?
25) You should have got used to his jokes a long time ago.
26) You don't have to take your own soap with you.
27) We're paying high taxes and we're going broke at the same time.
28) You should have told me earlier that you weren't going to come.

VOCABOLARIO

	traduzione	sinonimo-associato	contrario-associato
1. /(una) promessa /(un) segreto	/a promise /a secret	promettere = to promise	
2. /(un') informazione/(un) indizio	/a tip/a clue	fare allusione (a), lasciar capire = to hint	
3. riparare	to repair ≠ to break		rompere
4. (una) ricompensa	reward	(un) premio = prize	
5. /(una) strada /(un') autostrada	/road/highway, motorway		
6. Che intende dire?	What do you mean?		
7. fare all'amore	to make love	un amante = a lover, avere rapporti = to have sex, chiavare, scopare = to screw	
8. a voce bassa	in a whisper ≠ aloud		a voce alta
9. fornire	to supply		
10. rovinare	to damage	fare male (a) = to harm	
11. rovinarsi	to go broke	fallire, fare fallimento, fare bancarotta = to become bankrupt	
12. (la) pace	peace ≠ war	(un) esercito = army, (la) guerra (un) soldato = soldier	
13. cucinare	to cook	bollire = to boil, far cuocer arrosto = to roast	
14. (un) ambiente	atmosphere	un ambiente simpatico = a nice atmosphere	
15. /cucire/(un) ago	/to sew/needle	(un) filo = thread, (un) ferro = iron, stirare = to iron, lavare = to wash	
16. fare practica(di)	to practise	esercitarsi = to exercise	
17. (un) nastro	a tape	(un) registratore = a tape recorder	
18. (una) biblioteca	library		
19. (una, delle) fesserie	bullshit	sei fesso, sei cretino = you're an ass	
20. /(una) tintoria /(una) pulitura a secco	/laundry/dry cleaning	il bucato = the laundry	

VERBS AND PREPOSITIONS 1 The case of the missing preposition.
WATCH OUT! This can be tricky. In some cases, there is a preposition in English, but NOT IN ITALIAN.

1. I'm listening to you.	L'ascolto.
2. He's waiting for me.	Mi aspetta.
3. I'm looking for one like this.	Ne cerco uno così.
4. Look at this!	Guardi questo!
5. How much did you pay for it?	Quanto l'ha pagato?
6. Call me back later.	Mi richiami più tardi.
7. I asked him for one.	Gliene ho domandato uno.
8. Call me up tonight.	Mi telefoni stasera.
9. Hurry up!	Faccia presto/si spicci!
10. According to him . . .	Secondo lui . . .
11. Can I try it on?	Posso provarlo?
12. Turn on/turn off the T.V.	Accenda/spenga la televisione.
13. In spite of the weather . . .	malgrado il tempo . . .
14. He came back late.	E' tornato tardi.
15. Put on/take off your coat.	Metta/tolga il cappotto.
16. Is six okay for you?	Le va bene alle sei?
17. I give up.	Desisto./Abbandono./Mi arrendo.
18. What about a coffee?	E se prendessimo un caffè?
19. He's getting/waking up.	Si alza/si sveglia.
20. I'm sitting down ≠ standing up.	Mi siedo ≠ mi alzo.
21. Go on! Keep on!	Vada avanti!/Continui!
22. He's in ≠ He's out.	C'è/E' in casa ≠ Non c'è/E' fuori.
23. I'm mixed up.	Faccio confusione.
24. Bring it to me!	Me lo porti!
25. Show it to me!	Me lo mostri!
26. Give it to me!	Me lo dia!
27. I'll give it back.	Lo restituirò.
28. I'm going out now.	Esco adesso.
29. There were a lot of people.	C'era molta gente.
30. Do you know how to drive?	Sa guidare?

VERBS AND PREPOSITIONS 2

a) fill in the blanks in the second column as far as you can;
b) fold the page back to check your answer;
c) read the translation of the sentence for further clarification.

1. to come in	E' entrato . . . stanza.
2. a. to speak to/to talk to	— Vorrei parlare . . . signore Bianchi.
b. to speak about	— Si parlava . . . Lei.
3. to depend on	Questo dipende . . . Lei.
4. to agree with	Sono d'accordo . . . Lei.
5. to take care of	Mi occuperò . . . ciò (o: me ne occuperò).
6. to be fond of	Non vado pazzo . . . gli spaghetti.
7. to live in	Abita . . . Nuova York.
8. to be married to	E' sposata . . . un americano.
9. to go to	E' andato . . . Napoli.
	. . . ufficio.
	. . . Pamela.
	. . . il parrucchiere.
10. to belong to	. . . chi è questo cane? (ma: it belongs to me = è mio).
11. to be afraid of	Ho paura . . . lui.
12. to be mad at	Sono arrabbiato . . . lui.
13. to be sick of	Sono stufo . . . vederlo sempre triste.
14. to be worried about	Sono preoccupato . . . la sua salute.
15. to be ashamed of ≠	— Ha vergogna . . . la moglie.
to be proud of	— Va orgoglioso . . . la moglie.
16. to feel like	Ho voglia . . . caffè.
17. to look like/to take after	Assomiglia . . . suo padre.
	— Ha preso . . . suo padre.
18. a. to get used to	— Non mi abituerò mai . . . suo modo di parlare.
b. to be used to	— Si è abituato . . . suoi modi di fare?
19. to be interested in	Mi interesso . . . la pittura moderna.
20. to leave with	Può lasciare i bambini . . . me.

VERBS AND PREPOSITIONS 2

1. entrare nel, nella . . .	He came into the room.
2. a. parlare con	— I would like to speak to/with Mr Bianchi.
b. parlare di	— We were speaking about you.
3. dipendere da	It depends on you.
4. essere d'accordo con	I agree with you.
5. occuparsi di	I'll take care of it.
6. andar pazzo per	I'm not fond of spaghetti.
7. abitare a	She lives in New York.
8. essere sposato con	She's married to an American.
9. /andare a/in/da/dal, dalla . . .	He went — to Naples.
	— to the office.
	— to Pamela's.
	— to the hairdresser's.
10. essere di	Who does this dog belong to?
11. aver paura di	I'm afraid of him.
12. essere arrabbiato con	I'm mad at him.
13. essere stufo di	I'm sick of seeing him sad all the time.
14. essere preoccupato per	I'm worried about his health.
15. avere vergogna di ≠ andare orgoglioso di	— He's ashamed of ≠ proud of his wife.
16. avere voglia di	I feel like coffee.
17. assomigliare a /prendere da	— He looks like his father. — He takes after his father.
18. a. abituarsi a	— I'll never get used to his way of speaking.
b. essere abituato a	— Are you used to his manners?
19. interessarsi a (interessarsi di = to deal in)	I'm interested in modern painting.
20. lasciare a	You can leave the kids with me.

VERBS AND PREPOSITIONS 3

1. a. to think about/over
   b. to think of, about s.o.
   c. to think about (opinion)
   d. to think about (in general)
2. to explain to
3. to get in ≠ to get out
4. to get on ≠ to get off
5. to stop
6. to laugh at
7. to have a share in the business
8. to need
9. on behalf of
10. near ≠ far from
11. to write to

12. to be about
13. to be in the midst of
14. to apologize
15. to look like
16. to realize
17. as for (me)
18. to succeed in
19. to be worth it
20. to have just
21. to be good at
22. to regret
23. to doubt
24. to plan to

— Pensi . . . ciò che ha detto! (o: ci pensi!)
— Penso . . . te.
— Che cosa pensa . . . ciò che ha detto?

— . . . che pensa?

Ora . . . spiego.
Entri . . . la macchina/Esca . . . la macchina.
Salga . . . l'autobus/Scenda . . . l'autobus.
Ha smesso . . . fumare.
Non rida . . . me.
E' socio . . . l'azienda?
Ha una partecipazione . . . l'azienda?
Ho bisogno . . . molto amore (o: ne ho bisogno).
Telefono . . . parte . . . Tommaso.
Abita vicino . . . me ≠ lontano . . . me.
Ho scritto una lettera . . . mio padre (o: gli ho scritto).
. . . che cosa si tratta?
Mia sorella . . . mangiando.
Mi scuso . . . averLa disturbata.
Ho avuto l'aria . . . un idiota.
Non mi sono reso conto . . . problema.
In quanto . . . me, non andrò.
Sono riuscito . . . farlo.
Vale la pena . . . andare?
E' . . . andato via.
E' bravo . . . matematica.
Mi è spiaciuto . . . non averlo visto.
Dubita . . . me?
Mi propongo . . . andarci questa settimana.

1. a. pensare a	— Think over what he said.
b. pensare a	— I'm thinking about you.
c. pensare di	— What do you think about what he said?
d. pensare a	— What are you thinking about?
2. spiegare a	I'm going to explain it to you.
3. entrare in ≠ uscire da	Get in ≠ out of the car.
4. salire su ≠ scendere da	Get on ≠ off the bus.
5. smettere di	He stopped smoking.
6. ridere di/burlarsi di /prendersi gioco di	Don't laugh at me.
7. essere socio di /avere una partecipazione in	Have you a share in the business?
8. avere bisogno di	I need a lot of love.
9. da parte di	I'm calling you on behalf of Tom.
10. vicino a ≠ lontano da	He lives near me ≠ far from me.
11. scrivere a	I wrote to my father.
12. trattarsi di	What's about?
13. stare + present participle	My sister's in the midst of eating.
14. scusarsi di	I apologize for having disturbed you.
15. avere l'aria di	I looked like a fool.
16. rendersi conto di	I didn't realize the problem.
17. in quanto a	As for me, I won't go.
18. riuscire a	I succeeded in doing it.
19. valere la pena di	Is it worth going?
20. essere/avere appena	He just left.
21. essere bravo in	He's good at maths.
22. (di)spiacere di	I regret not having seen him.
23. dubitare di	Do you doubt me?
24. proporsi di	I plan to get there this week.

VERBS AND PREPOSITIONS 4

1. to manage to	Sono riuscito . . . farlo.
2. to come back from	Sta per tornare . . . Londra.
3. to ask to	Mi ha domandato . . . farlo.
(note: to ask for something = domandare qualche cosa — without preposition)	
4. you'd better	Farebbe meglio . . . andare via ora.
5. you're right	Ha — ragione . . . andare via subito.
≠ you're wrong	— torto . . .
6. I'd be happy to	Sarei felice . . . rivederLa.
7. to refuse to	Ha rifiutato . . . farlo.
8. to be glad to	Sono contento . . . andare.
9. to remember	Si ricorda . . . lui o si è dimenticato . . . lui?
≠ to forget	
10. a. to come to	— Quando viene . . . noi?
b. to come from	— Vengo . . . Palermo.
11. to answer	Perchè risponde . . . lui e non . . . me?
12. a. to learn to	— Impariamo . . . parlare italiano.
b. to teach	— Ti insegnerò io . . . essere educato!
13. /to start/begin	— Cominciamo . . . mangiare proprio ora.
≠ to finish	— Ha finito . . . mangiare?
14. to complain about	Non si lamenti . . . me!
15. to tell about	Mi parlava . . . ciò.
16. to intend to	Abbiamo intenzione . . . andare all'estero quest'estate.
17. concerning, relating to	Il capufficio desidera vederLa a proposito . . . quell'affare.
18. to go to	— Vado . . . mia zia.
(note: — for places: to go to = andare a	— Vado . . . Venezia.
— to go and + verb = andare a)	— Vado . . . comprare qualche cosa da mangiare.

VERBS AND PREPOSITIONS 4

1. riuscire a	I managed to do it.
2. tornare da	He's going to come back from London.
3. domandare di	He asked me to do it.
4. farebbe meglio a	You'd better go now.
5. ha ragione di ≠ ha torto a	You're right to ≠ wrong to go at once.
6. sarei felice di	I'd be happy to see you again.
7. rifiutare di	He refused to do it.
8. essere contento di	I'm glad to go.
9. ricordarsi di ≠ dimenticarsi di	Do you remember him or did you forget him?
10. venire da	— When will you come to see us? — I'm coming from Palermo.
11. rispondere a	Why do you answer him and not me?
12. a. imparare a	— We're learning to speak Italian.
b. insegnare a	— I'll teach you to be polite.
13. (in)cominciare a ≠ finire di	We're just starting eating now. Have you finished eating?
14. lamentarsi di	Don't complain about me!
15. parlare di	He was telling me about that.
16. avere intenzione di	We intend to go abroad this summer.
17. a proposito di, riguardo a	The boss wants to see you concerning that affair.
18. a. andare da	— I'm going to my aunt's.
b. andare a (for places)	— I'm going to Venice.
c. andare a (verbs of movement followed by an infinitive)	— I'm going to buy something to eat.

IDIOMS 1

1. to go for a walk	**Andiamo a . . .**
2. all the same	**Grazie . . .**
3. /I don't care/It's all the same to me.	**Per me . . .**
4. /I'd like you to meet /. . . pleased to meet you.	**— Paolo, vorrei/mi piacerebbe . . . Giacomo.** **— . . . !**
5. It doesn't matter.	**Non . . .**
6. /That's the limit! /That beats all!	**E' il . . . !**
7. /to be on the line /to hold on	**Il signore Bianchi . . . al telefono!** **. . . in linea!**
8. to make a mistake	**Ho fatto . . .** **Mi sono . . .**
9. /How are you?/Fine, thank you and you?	**— Come . . . ?** **— Bene, grazie, e . . . ?**
10. Straight or on the rocks?	**Liscio o con ghiaccio?**
11. Do you have a light?	**Ha da . . . ?**
12. to have a drink	**Vuol venire a . . . qualcosa stasera?**
13. Too bad! ≠ All the better!	**. . . !/Tanto . . . !**
14. on the other hand	**Non è intelligente ma . . . è molto bella.**
15. to have a dream	**Ho . . . un brutto sogno ieri sera.**
16. /to be sick of/fed up	**Sono . . . !**
17. It isn't worth it.	**Non ne vale . . .**
18. /How goes it?/It's no good!	**Come . . . ?/. . . !**
19. I feel that	**Mi . . . che sbagli.**
20. I'm starving ≠ I'm full.	**Muoio di . . . ≠ Sono . . .**
21. some more . . .	**. . . pane, per favore.**
22. to change one's mind	**Ho cambiato . . .**

IDIOMS 1

1. /andare a passeggio /fare una passeggiata	Let's go for a walk!
2. lo stesso	Thank you all the same.
3. per me fa lo stesso	— I don't care. — It's all the same to me.
4. /mi piacerebbe presen- tarLe . . . /Piacere!	— Paolo, I'd like you to meet Giacomo. — Pleased to meet you!
5. Non importa.	It doesn't matter.
6. E' il colmo!	— That's the limit! — That beats all!
7. /essere al telefono /Rimanga in linea!	— Mr Bianchi's on the line! — Hold on!
8. /fare uno sbaglio /sbagliarsi	I made a mistake.
9. /Come sta? /Bene, grazie, e Lei?	— How are you? — Fine, thank you, and you?
10. Liscio o con ghiaccio?	Straight or on the rocks?
11. Ha da accendere?	Do you have a light?
12. bere qualcosa	Do you want to come and have a drink tonight?
13. Pazienza! ≠ Tanto meglio!	Too bad! ≠ All the better!
14. in compenso	She isn't bright, but on the other hand she's very beautiful.
15. fare un sogno	I had a bad dream last night.
16. essere stufo di . . .	I'm sick of it.
17. Non ne vale la pena.	It isn't worth it.
18. /Come va?/Male!	— How goes it?/— No good!
19. mi pare che . . .	I feel that you're wrong.
20. muoio di fame ≠ sono pieno	I'm starving ≠ I'm full.
21. ancora . . .	Some more bread, please!
22. cambiare idea	I changed my mind.

IDIOMS 2

1. to make a fortune	Ha fatto . . . in America.
2. to do someone a favour	Potrebbe farmi . . . ?
3. to stand in line	Bisogna fare . . . per andare al cinema.
4. /to earn a living	— Guadagna bene da . . . ?
/to make (good) money	— Guadagna molti . . . ?
5. to make an appointment	— Vorrei . . . appuntamento lunedì.
	— Mi ha . . . appuntamento alle cinque.
6. to get on someone's nerves	/Mi . . . /Mi . . . noia.
7. to be late ≠ early	Arriva spesso . . . ≠ . . .
8. What's it like out?	Che . . . fa?
9. to do for a living	Che . . . fa?/Che . . . fa?
10. to make an effort	Bisogna fare uno . . .
11. to go shopping	Andiamo a fare . . .
12. to feel under the weather ≠ to feel great	Non sono in . . . ≠ Sono in piena . . .
13. to do the dishes	Tocca a voi fare . . .
14. We'll take turns.	Faremo a . . . !
15. You gotta be kidding!	Tu . . . !/Stai . . . !
16. What a pain in the neck!	Che . . . !
17. to mean	Che cosa . . . ?
18. to tell the truth	A . . . , non mi piace.
19. that goes without saying	Non occorre . . . / . . .
20. that's all the more reason	Ragion . . . per lasciarla!
21. help yourself (to some more)	Si . . . !/Ne . . . !
22. It's not my cup of tea.	Non mi . . . niente.

IDIOMS 2

1. fare fortuna	He made a fortune in America.
2. fare un favore a qualcuno	Could you do me a favour?
3. fare la coda	You must stand in line to go to the movies.
4. /guadagnare bene da vivere/guadagnare molti soldi	— Does he earn a good living? — Does he make (good) money?
5. — prendere/fissare un appuntamento — dare appuntamento	— I'd like to make an appointment for Monday. — He made an appointment with me for five.
6. /infastidire/dare noia.	He gets on my nerves.
7. arrivare in ritardo ≠ arrivare in anticipo	He's often late ≠ early
8. Che tempo fa?	What's it like out?
9. fare un lavoro/fare un mestiere	What does he do for a living?
10. fare un sforzo	You must make an effort.
11. fare spese	Let's go shopping.
12. Non essere in forma ≠ essere in piena forma.	I feel under the weather ≠ I feel great.
13. fare i piatti	It's your turn to do the dishes.
14. fare a turno	We'll take turns!
15. Tu scherzi!/Stai scherzando!	You gotta be kidding!
16. Che seccatura!	What a pain in the neck!
17. intender dire	What do you mean?
18. a dire il vero	To tell the truth, I don't like it.
19. Non occorre dirlo/Beninteso!	That goes without saying.
20. ragion di più	That's all the more reason to drop her.
21. /Si serva!/Ne prenda ancora!	Help yourself!/Help yourself to some more!
22. Non mi dice niente.	It's not my cup of tea.

IDIOMS 3

1. to make a fuss	Smetti di fare . . . !
2. to be successful	La commedia ha avuto . . .
3. to take a nap	Sono stanco e vado a fare . . .
4. on the face of it	A giudicare . . . direi che ha ragione.
5. to hurt	Le fa . . . ?
6. I don't give a damn.	Me ne . . ./Me ne . . .
7. time's up!	E' . . . !
8. to fall behind ≠ to catch up	Sono restato . . . ≠ Devo ricuperare il tempo perso.
9. what's up?	Che cosa . . . ?
10. to be in a good ≠ bad mood	E' di buon . . . ≠ di cattivo . . .
11. /I don't want to put you out/You're not putting me out.	– Non voglio . . . – Lei non mi . . .
12. I can't get over it.	Non riesco a . . .
13. I didn't realize.	Non mi sono reso . . .
14. to worry	Si . . . per suo figlio.
15. We were cut off (phone)	La comunicazione è stata . . .
16. /Have a good time! /We had a good time.	– Si . . . ! – Ci siamo . . . molto.
17. to be lucky	Sono molto . . .
18. /Do you mind if . . . ? /I don't mind.	– La . . . se fumo? – Non mi . . . affatto.
19. to look tired ≠ to look good, well	– Ha . . . stanca. – Ha un buon . . ./una bella . . .
20. to be in a hurry	Ho . . .
21. /Did you enjoy it? /I enjoyed it.	– Ti è . . . ? – Sì, mi è . . .
22. kiss me/give me a kiss!	. . . !/Dammi un . . . !
23. Fuck you!	Va a farti . . . !
24. Leave me alone!	Lasciami in . . . !

IDIOMS 3

1. fare storie	Stop making such a fuss!
2. avere successo	The play was successful.
3. fare un sonnellino	I'm tired and I'm going to take a nap.
4. a giudicare dall'apparenza/a prima vista	On the face of it, I'd say you're right.
5. fare male	Does it hurt?
6. Me ne infischio/Me ne frego.	I don't give a damn.
7. E' ora!	Time's up!
8. restare indietro ≠ ricuperare il tempo perso	I've fallen behind. I must catch up.
9. Che cosa succede?	What's up?
10. essere di buon umore ≠ essere di cattivo umore	He's in a good ≠ bad mood.
11. /Non voglio distrubarLa /Lei non mi disturba affatto.	− I don't want to put you out. − You're not putting me out.
12. Non riesco a capacitarmi.	I can't get over it.
13. rendersi conto	I didn't realize.
14. preoccuparsi	She worries about her son.
15. La comunicazione è stata interrotta.	We were cut off.
16. /Si diverta! /Ci siamo divertiti molto.	− Have a good time! − We had a good time!
17. essere fortunato	I'm very lucky.
18. /La disturbo se . . . ? /Non mi disturba affatto.	− Do you mind if I smoke? − I don't mind.
19. avere l'aria stanca ≠ avere un buon aspetto, una bella cera	− You look tired. − You look good/well.
20. avere fretta	I'm in a hurry.
21. /Ti è piaciuto? /Sì, mi è piaciuto.	− Did you enjoy it? − Yes, I enjoyed it.
22. Baciami!/Dammi un bacio!	Kiss me/Give me a Kiss!
23. Va a farti fottere!	Fuck you!
24. Lasciami in pace!	Leave me alone!

CONGRATULATIONS!!

You are no longer a beginner. You can now go on to *Il Gimmick — L'Italiano Corrente* (the first uncensored, realistic vocabulary learning book).

Key/Soluzione

Lezione 1, pagina 1
1) E' un tavolo grande? 2) Non è una porta nera. 3) A più tardi! 4) E' un cane piccolo? 5) Accidenti! 6) Non è un grosso libro nero, ma un grosso libro blu. 7) Che cos'è? — E' un orologio. 8) E' un telefono rosso? 9) Non è una sedia piccola. 10) E' una sveglia bianca?

Lezione 1, pagina 2
1) Sì, è un gatto piccolo. — No, non è un gatto piccolo. 2) Sì, è un cane bianco. — No, non è un cane bianco. 3) Sì, è un telefono blu. — No, non è un telefono blu. 4) Sì, è un muro bianco. — No, non è un muro bianco. 5) Sì, è un libro grosso. — No, non è un libro grosso. 6) Sì, è una penna. — No, non è una penna. 7) Sì, è un orologio blu marino. — No, non è un orologio blu marino. 8) Sì, è una matita nera. — No, non è una matita nera. 9) Sì, è una sedia. — No, non è una sedia. 10) Sì, è una libreria grande. — No, non è una libreria grande. 11) Sì, è un topo bianco. — No, non è un topo bianco. 12) Sì, è una porta. — No, non è una porta. 13) Sì, è una porta verde. — No, non è una porta verde. 14) Sì, è una sveglia rosa. — No, non è una sveglia rosa.

Lezione 2, pagina 4
1) Come sta? — Bene, grazie, e Lei? 2) Sono sigarette? 3) Sono cappotti neri? 4) Mi dispiace. Chiedo scusa. 5) Sono libri grossi? 6) E' ora! 7) Che cosa sono? — Sono matite. 8) Esatto! 9) Sono bambini poveri. 10) Può ripetere, per favore?

Lezione 2, pagina 6
— tipi deboli — ragazze piccole — bimbi forti — donne ricche — calzini neri — cappotti lunghi — tipi grossi — uomini vecchi — ragazzi giovani — lapis lunghi — accendini corti — vecchie sveglie — buoni vecchi libri — notti lunghe — buoni alberghi — vie larghe — carte spesse — stanze piccole — libri rossi — chiavi grandi — scatole blu — bimbi miti — fiammiferi sottili — cappotti leggeri — tipi poveri — ultime lezioni — primi bambini — tavoli pesanti — vecchi cani — dischi italiani.

Lezione 2, pagine 6
1) Sì, sono donne interessanti. — No, non sono donne interessanti. — E' una donna interessante? 2) Sì, sono uomini forti. — No, non sono uomini forti. — E' un uomo forte? 3) Sì, sono bambini poveri. — No, non sono bambini poveri. — E' un bambino povero? 4) Sì, sono tipi miti. — No, non sono tipi

miti. — E' un tipo mite? 5) Sì, sono sigarette buone. — No, non sono
sigarette buone. — E' una sigaretta buona? 6) Sì, sono scarpe nere. — No,
non sono scarpe nere. — E' una scarpa nera? 7) Sì, sono pantofole rosse. —
No, non sono pantofole rosse. — E' una pantofola rossa? 8) Sì, sono calzini
bianchi. — No, non sono calzini bianchi. — E' un calzino bianco? 9) Sì,
sono stanze grandi. — No, non sono stanze grandi. — E' una stanza grande?
10) Sì, sono ragazze giovani. — No, non sono ragazze giovani. — E' una
ragazza giovane? 11) Sì, sono fiammiferi lunghi. — No, non sono fiammiferi
lunghi. — E'un fiammifero lungo? — etc.

Lezione 2, pagina 8
1) No, la donna non è alta. — No, le donne non sono alte. 2) No, l'uomo
non è debole. — No, gli uomini non sono deboli. 3) No, il libro non è
grosso. — No, i libri non sono grossi. 4) No, la stanza non è piccola. — No,
le stanze non sono piccole. 5) No, la lezione non è interessante. — No, le
lezioni non sono interessanti. 6) No, il tavolo non è pesante. — No, i tavoli
non sono pesanti. 7) No, l'impermeabile non è blu. — No, gli impermeabili
non sono blu. 8) No, la scarpa non è piccola. — No, le scarpe non sono
piccole. 9) No, il bambino non è magro. — No, i bambini non sono magri.
10) No, la donna non è giovane. — No, le donne non sono giovani. 11) No,
il cappello non è nero. — No, i cappelli non sono neri. 12) No, il tipo non
è basso. — No, i tipi non sono bassi. 13) No, la scarpa non è sopra il tavolo.
— No, le scarpe non sono sopra il tavolo. — etc.

Lezione 2, pagina 9
1) Are they blue watches? — No, non sono orologi blu. — No, non è un
orologio blu. 2) Are they fat men? — No, non sono uomini grassi. — No,
non è un uomo grasso. 3) Are they tall women? — No, non sono donne
alte. — No, non è una donna alta. 4) Are they yellow boxes? — No, non
sono scatole gialle. — No, non è una scatola gialla. 5) Are they big shoes?
— No, non sono scarpe grandi. — No, non è una scarpa grande. 6) Are they
short streets? — No, non sono vie corte. — No, non è una via corta. 7) Are
they beautiful kids? — No, non sono bambini belli. — No, non è un bel
bambino. 8) Are they long raincoats? — No, non sono impermeabili lunghi.
— No, non è un impermeabile lungo. 9) Are they green hats? — No, non
sono cappelli verdi. — No, non è un cappello verde. 10) Are they big rooms?
— No, non sono stanze grandi. — No, non è una stanza grande. 11) Are they
black cats? — No, non sono gatti neri. — No, non è un gatto nero. 12) Are
they yellow socks? etc. 13) Are they strong guys? 14) Are they thick
books? 15) Are they big bookshops? 16) Are they short lessons? 17) Are
they rich guys? 18) Are they big dogs? 19) Are they brown shoes?
20) Are they bad cigarettes? 21) Are they heavy coats? 22) Are they red
letter boxes? 23) Are they big keys? 24) Are they black boots? 25) Are
they white mice? 26) Are they low walls?

Lezione 2, pagina 10

1) E' una donna giovane? – Sono donne giovani? 2) E' una stanza piccola? – Sono stanze piccole? 3) E' una scatola grande? – Sono scatole grandi? 4) E' un portacenere giallo? – Sono portaceneri gialli? 5) E' una donna interessante? – Sono donne interessanti? 6) E' un bambino mite? – Sono bambini miti? 7) E' un fiammifero lungo? – Sono fiammiferi lunghi? – 8) E' un accendino bello? – Sono accendini belli? 9) E' una via stretta? – Sono vie strette? 10) E' un cappotto leggero? – Sono cappotti leggeri? 11) E' una donna vecchia? – Sono donne vecchie? 12) E' un tipo cattivo? – Sono tipi cattivi? 13) E' un cane nero? – Sono cani neri? 14) E' una sveglia verde? – Sono sveglie verdi? 15) E' un uomo ricco? – Sono uomini ricchi? 16) E' un muro alto? – Sono muri alti? 17) E' un libro vecchio? – Sono libri vecchi? 18) E' la prima lezione? – Sono le prime lezioni? 19) E' un giorno lungo? – Sono giorni lunghi? 20) E' una notte nera? – Sono notti nere? 21) E' un gatto bianco? – Sono gatti bianchi? 22) E' un libro sottile? – Sono libri sottili? 23) E' un tavolo pesante? – Sono tavoli pesanti? 24) E' un marmocchio buono? – Sono marmocchi buoni? 25) E' un impermeabile verde? – Sono impermeabili verdi? 26) E' un ragazzo debole? – Sono ragazzi deboli?

Lezione 2, pagina 11

1) Vuole ripetere, per favore? 2) Il bambino è sotto il tavolo. 3) Non è così. 4) Il portacenere non è sopra la sedia. 5) Le vie non sono larghe. 6) Mi dispiace. 7) La donna è grossa e grassa. 8) I tipi sono poveri ma interessanti. 9) E' ora! 10) Accidenti! 11) La buca è rossa. 12) Buon giorno. Come sta? 13) I libri non sono spessi. 14) La prima lezione è interessante. 15) La ragazza è magra, anch'io. 16) L'uomo non è grasso, neanch'io. 17) L'accendino è vecchio, ma buono. 18) I bimbi sono forti. 19) E' esatto. E' così. 20) Il cappello è piccolo. 21) La prima stanza è piccola. 22) Le scarpe sono grandi. 23) Il muro è rosso e blu. 24) Il cappotto è nero ma il cappello è blu marino. 25) Un libro è sopra il tavolo. 26) E' interessante una ragazza ricca? 27) Un telefono rosso è sopra la sedia 28) I calzini gialli sono sotto il tavolo.

Lezione 3, pagina 16

1) E' la Sua (tua, vostra) sciarpa? – No, è la sua. 2) Sono i suoi stivali? – No, sono i suoi. 3) Che cosa succede? 4) Di chi è la borsetta? 5) Non sono i miei maglioni, sono i suoi. 6) Grazie. – Prego. 7) I Suoi (tuoi, vostri) pantaloni sono troppo corti? 8) Capito? 9) Non sono le Sue (tue, vostre) cravatte, sono le mie. 10) Non importa. 11) Che c'è di nuovo? – Niente di speciale.

Lezione 3, pagina 16

1) i Suoi. 2) la mia. 3) le loro. 4) la sua. 5) il mio. 6) i tuoi. 7) i suoi. 8) la nostra. 9) il suo. 10) la nostra. 11) i loro. 12) i nostri. 13) la sua.

14) il suo. 15) il tuo. 16) la Sua. 17) i vostri. 18) la loro. 19) le nostre.
20) il vostro.

Lezione 3, pagina 17

— una cravatta nuova — delle donne gentili — il mio amico preferito — delle
gonne vecchie — i suoi vestiti nuovi — una camicia bianca — una lezione
noiosa — una donna infelice — delle scarpe nuove — dei guanti sporchi — una
borsetta cara — un compito difficile — dei lattanti asciutti — la prima lezione
— dei gatti neri — una ragazza matta — un uomo falso — una donna grossa —
un marmocchio sciocco — un bimbo felice — una camera schifosa — una
cravatta bianca.

Lezione 3, pagina 18

1) I nostri bambini sono infelici. 2) I tuoi calzini sono neri. 3) I suoi
dischi sono sensazionali. 4) I miei cappelli sono sopra i tavoli. 5) Queste
vie non sono larghe. 6) Le loro camere sono grandi. 7) Questi tavoli sono
pesanti. 8) Le sue camicie sono sporche. 9) Anche le mie cravatte sono
verdi e gialle. 10) Questi alberghi sono cari. 11) Sono i miei colori preferiti.
12) Sono ragazze sciocche.

Lezione 3, pagina 18

1) I suoi guanti non sono piccoli. 2) Il suo libro non è sopra il tavolo.
3) Il mio compito non è facile. 4) I Suoi (tuoi, vostri) stivali nuovi non sono
sporchi. 5) Il suo tipo non è pazzo. 6) I loro vestiti non sono vecchi.
7) I nostri maglioni non sono nuovi. 8) Questa lezione non è noiosa. 9) Il
suo vestito nuovo non è nero. 10) Le nostre camicie nuove non sono belle.
11) La sua gonna blu non è cara. 12) I miei calzoni non sono asciutti.
13) La nostra lavagna non è larga. 14) I loro bambini non sono gentili.
15) Il suo gilé non è sporco. 16) Le nostre pantofole non sono rosse.

Lezione 4, pagina 21

1) Gli occhi di Pietro sono verdi. 2) Come si scrive? 3) La bocca della
ragazza è larga. 4) I denti della donna sono bianchi. 5) Aspetti un
momento! 6) Il viso di Giovanna è bello. 7) Le gambe della ragazza sono
sottili. 8) Le mani dell'uomo sono dietro [di] me. 9) La macchina del
tipo è verde. 10) L'ombrello dello zio di Giovanna è nero.

Lezione 4, pagina 21

— dello studente — delle donne — della settimana — degli studenti — dei
bambini — della donna — dell'uomo — dell'anno — del ragazzo — della
ragazza — del bambino — delle ragazze — dei marmocchi — di Giovanna
— della mano — del piede — dei secoli — della stanza — delle vie — del cane
— degli uomini — del ragazzo — della giacca — dei bambini — del tipo —
del pomeriggio.

Lezione 4, pagina 22

— quale uomo? — quale libro? — quale naso? — quale secolo? — quali donne? — quale ragazzo? — quali occhi? — quale gatto? — quali finestre? — quali tipi? — quali anni? — quali mesi? — quale ombrello? — quale cane? — quale martedì? — quali mani? — quali studenti? — quali sedie? — quale orologio? — quali macchine? — quali stivali? — quale borsetta? — quali gonne? — quali cappotti? — quali vestiti? — quali orecchi? — quali gambe? — quali unghie? — quale settimana? — quali sigarette? — quale accendino? — quali giacche? — quali piedi? — quale lezione?

Lezione 4, pagina 24

1) Questa borsetta è sopra il tavolo. 2) Quella gonna è sotto la mia.
3) Questo vestito è piccolo per quel tipo. 4) Quel vestito è provocante.
5) Quest'orologio è il mio e quello è il vostro. 6) Questa camicia è la mia e quella è la vostra. 7) Quel libro è lontano da Giovanna, ma questo è vicino.
8) Quella macchina è nuova e cara. 9) Quella gatta è dietro la porta, ma questa è sotto il tavolo. 10) Quella donna è laggiù. 11) Questo tipo è ricco e quello è povero. 12) Questa prima lezione è noiosa e l'ultima lezione corta.
13) Quel viso è bello. 14) Questo stivale è nuovo e l'altro è vecchio.

Lezione 4, pagina 24

1) Quei tipi sono deboli. 2) Quei guanti sono nuovi, ma questi sono vecchi.
3) Quest'uomo è ricco, l'altro è povero ma buono. 4) Questa sedia non è in quella stanza. 5) Questa borsa è dietro il tavolo. 6) Questo libro è Suo (tuo), quello è mio. 7) Queste macchine sono dietro l'albergo, ma quelle sono laggiù. 8) Questa donna è pazza ma interessante. 9) E' noioso quel tipo? — Questo non [lo] è. 10) Sono ricche quelle donne? — Queste non [lo] sono. 11) Quella macchina è grossa, ma questa non [lo] è. 12) Quali lezioni sono interessanti? — Quelle. 13) Quale bimbo è il Suo (tuo)? Questo.

Lezione 5, p
Lezione 5, pagina 28
1) Quei tipi sono deboli. 2) Quei guanti sono nuovi, ma questi

Lezione 5, pagina 28

1) Ci sono trenta ore in un giorno? 2) Sono le tre e mezzo. 3) Sono pericolose queste strade? Quali [lo] sono? 4) Sono le dodici meno un quarto.
5) Ci sono tassì o autobus di sera? — No, non ce ne sono. 6) Per me fa lo stesso. 7) Quale soffitto è alto? — Questo. 8) Quale bottiglia è piena? — Quella. 9) La sua bicicletta è veloce. 10) Quella strada è pericolosa.
11) Ci sono bottiglie vuote sulla tavola? 12) Ci sono biciclette in questa strada? 13) Ci sono tre denti falsi. Quali sono? 14) Sono le quattro e un quarto. 15) Nemmeno per sogno! 16) Che ora è? — Sono le dieci.
17) Due tipi sono incapaci. — Quali? 18) La caramella è dolce o acida?

19) Come si chiama? Come ti chiami? — Mi chiamo Pietro. 20) Questa stanza è sporca ma quella è pulita. 21) Le lezioni di oggi sono facili o difficili? 22) E' bella o brutta la sua ragazza? — Quale ragazza? 23) Ci sono aerei sicuri d'inverno? 24) Che genere di bambini sono? 25) Ci sono dodici mesi in un anno? 26) Ci sono tre belle macchine in questa strada. Quali? 27) C'è una bottiglia piena sotto il tavolo. 28) C'è una lezione barbosa in questo libro. Quale?

Lezione 6, pagina 32

1) Io non sono sporco. E Lei? 2) Quell'uomo è medico. 3) Che cosa significa? 4) L'uomo d'affari è ricco e grasso. 5) Lei trova? 6) Lui non è francese, ma Lei sì. 7) Non siamo felici. 8) L'uno o l'altro.

Lezione 6, pagina 32

1) Non è uno sporco poliziotto. 2) Giovanni non è un padrone abbastanza gentile. 3) Non siete studenti molto interessanti. 4) Gli uomini d'affari non sono troppo ricchi. 5) Il problema non è troppo difficile. 6) Questo lavoro non è molto lungo. 7) Il mio lavoro non è noioso. 8) L'avvocato non è americano. 9) Non è molto violenta. 10) I professori di quest'anno non sono barbosi. 11) I giorni in dicembre non sono corti. 12) Grazie al cielo! 13) I battelli non sono veloci. 14) La bottiglia non è vuota. 15) La stanza non è sporca. 16) Non siamo interessanti. 17) Il film non è amaro. 18) Non è brutta. 19) Non è dietro la porta. 20) Non sono la segretaria del direttore.

Lezione 6, pagina 33

1) Il capufficio è simpatico, anch'io. — Il capufficio non è simpatico, neanch'io. 2) Lo studente è barboso, anche Lei (tu, voi). — Lo studente non è barboso, neanche Lei. 3) L'uomo d'affari è ricco, anche Lei. — L'uomo d'affari non è ricco, neanche Lei. 4) La segretaria è intelligente, anche il suo tipo. — La segretaria non è intelligente, neanche il suo tipo. 5) Io sono gentile, anche Lei. — Io non sono gentile, neanche Lei. 6) L'ufficio è lontano, anche la metropolitana. — L'ufficio non è lontano, neanche la metropolitana. 7) Il mio capufficio è grosso, anche la sua segretaria. — Il mio capufficio non è grosso, neanche la sua segretaria. 8) L'ospedale è vicino, anche la scuola. — L'ospedale non è vicino, neanche la scuola. 9) Sono donne d'affari, anche noi. — Non sono donne d'affari, neanche noi. 10) Siete studenti, anche noi. — Non siete studenti, neanche noi. 11) Siete schifosi, anche loro. — Non siete schifosi, neanche loro. 12) I Suoi (tuoi, vostri) problemi sono facili, anche i miei. — I Suoi problemi non sono facili, neanche i miei. 13) La sua bottiglia è vuota, anche la mia. — La sua bottiglia non è vuota, neanche la mia. 14) Il Suo (il tuo, il vostro) gatto è carino, anche il nostro. — Il Suo gatto non è carino, neanche il nostro. 15) Questa stanza è sporca, anche quella. — Questa stanza non è sporca,

neanche quella. 16) La sua bicicletta è veloce, anche la mia. — La sua bicicletta non è veloce, neanche la mia. 17) L'inverno è freddo, anche l'autunno. — L'inverno non è freddo, neanche l'autunno. 18) Il professore è barboso, anche Lei (tu, voi). — Il professore non è barboso, neanche Lei. 19) Il mio tipo è brutto, anche il tuo. — Il mio tipo non è brutto, neanche il tuo. 20) Io sono forte, anche loro. — Io non sono forte, neanche loro.

Lezione 6, pagina 34
1) Fa bel tempo oggi. 2) E' troppo tardi per andare. 3) E' noioso. 4) Fa freddo. 5) E' troppo presto. 6) E' simpatico. 7) E' molto caro. 8) E' interessante. 9) Fa caldo. 10) E' a buon mercato.

Lezione 7, pagina 37
1) Above all, we don't have the time today. — Soprattutto, non abbiamo tempo oggi? 2) He hasn't been here for two months. — Non è più qui da due mesi? 3) You never have a lot of money. — Non avete mai molto denaro? 4) There's nobody in the room. — Non c'è nessuno nella stanza? 5) She has nothing interesting. — Non ha niente d'interessante? 6) They aren't here yet. — Non sono ancora qui? 7) We don't have two cars yet. — Non abbiamo ancora due macchine? 8) We never have problems. — Non abbiamo mai problemi? 9) I don't have anything any more. — Non ho più niente? 10) He (she) is (you are) never in the office. — Non è mai in ufficio?

Lezione 7, pagina 38
1) E' ancora a Roma ≠ Non è più a Roma. 2) Abbiamo ancora molto tempo. ≠ Non abbiamo più molto tempo. 3) Il capufficio ha ancora una segretaria. ≠ Il capufficio non ha più una segretaria. 4) Non ha ancora niente. ≠ Non ha più niente. 5) Sono ancora giovani. ≠ Non sono più giovani.

Lezione 7, pagina 38
1) Non ha più lavoro questo mese. — Ha ancora lavoro questo mese? 2) Non c'è nessuno nella stanza. — C'è qualcuno nella stanza? 3) Ha solo due gonne. — Ha solo due gonne? 4) Non è mai qui la domenica. — E' qui qualche volta la domenica? 5) Non abbiamo niente d'interessante. — Abbiamo qualche cosa d'interessante? 6) Non è ancora giugno. — E' già giugno? 7) E' ancora in Italia. — E' ancora in Italia? 8) Non abbiamo più tempo. — Abbiamo ancora tempo? 9) Abbiamo ancora molto lavoro. Abbiamo ancora molto lavoro? 10) Lei ha solo una macchina. — Lei, ha solo una macchina? 11) E' già capufficio. — E' già capufficio? 12) Il suo film è più o meno schifoso. — E' più o meno schifoso il suo film? 13) Di solito non sono qui presto. — Sono qui presto, di solito? 14) Abbiamo la macchina da un anno. — Avete la macchina da un anno? 15) Hanno solo due bambini. — Hanno solo due bambini? 16) Non ha mai un lavoro. — Ha un lavoro qualche volta?

17) Abbiamo solo un professore. – Avete solo un professore? 18) I
bambini non sono mai a casa nel pomeriggio. – Sono qualche volta a casa i
bambini nel pomeriggio? 19) Ho solo due sigarette. – Ha solo due sigarette?
20) Non c'è nessuno. – C'è qualcuno?

Lezione 7, pagina 39

1) Il professore non ha sempre ragione. 2) L'uomo d'affari ha già successo.
3) Non ho fame ma sete. 4) In ogni modo ho paura. 5) Lei non ha ragione.
6) Non abbiamo mai denaro. 7) Ha quindici anni. 8) Ho spesso freddo in
inverno e caldo in estate. 9) Di rado ha sonno. 10) La segretaria del
capufficio non ha mai torto (non sbaglia mai). 11) Non ho mai fretta.
12) Hanno vergogna della loro casa.

Lezione 8, pagina 44

1) Non parliamo spesso italiano. 2) Va di solito al cinema la domenica?
3) Lavorano spesso assieme al capufficio? 4) A chi tocca? 5) Mangiamo.
6) Non ascolta più Giovanni. 7) Lei parla (tu parli) da un'ora. 8) Finalmente
comincio questo lavoro.

Lezione 8, pagina 44

1) Non mi piace molto la tua gonna. 2) Non lavoriamo spesso molto il
lunedì. 3) Non compri un vestito nuovo. 4) Non lavori presto la mattina.
5) Non ascoltate più o meno il professore. 6) Gli studenti non fanno
domande stupide. 7) Quel bambino non gioca senza parlare. – ecc (etc).

Lezione 8, pagina 45

1) Lavoriamo sempre presto la mattina. 2) Il mascalzone non parla a
nessuno. 3) Non ascolta mai Giovanni. 4) Lei mangia (tu mangi) troppo.
5) Lei mangia (tu mangi) da un'ora. 6) Parla solo inglese. 7) Desideriamo
andare con Maria. 8) Lei fuma (tu fumi) da un'ora. 9) Lavorano con il
capufficio. 10) Studia ancora italiano. 11) Studia italiano da tre anni.
12) Adoro il mio ragazzo (il mio tipo). 13) Non andiamo mai al cinema di
sera. 14) Vanno al cinema solo una volta al mese. 15) Vado spesso a
passeggio di sera. 16) Mando oggi il denaro. 17) Non fuma affatto.
18) Mangia ancora. 19) Sperano di andare con Giovanni. 20) Pensiamo a
Lei (a te). 21) Amo Maria. 22) Compra solo maglioni verdi.

Lezione 8, pagina 46

1) Che cosa fuma? (fumi?). 2) Chi lavora? 3) Che cosa compra? 4) Che
cosa spera (speri) di fare? 5) Chi parla a Sua (tua) sorella? 6) Chi ama?
(ami?). 7) Che cosa aspetta? (aspetti?).

Lezione 8, pagina 46

1) agli 2) a 3) ai 4) alla 5) alle.

Lezione 9, pagina 48

1) Scrive (scrivi) una lettera? 2) Legge un libro. 3) Che cosa vede (vedi) al cinema? 4) Prende (prendi) pane e burro? 5) Ride (ridi) o no?
6) Risponde al telefono.

Lezione 9, pagina 50

1) Vale solo poco. 2) Vedo solo un uomo che mangia. 3) Non facciamo mai [un] lavoro interessante. 4) Non vivono più a Nuova York. 5) Non compra niente. 6) Mangiamo da un'ora. 7) Oggi prendiamo una bistecca.
8) Legge il libro da una settimana. 9) Non beve più. 10) Prendiamo lezioni d'italiano quest'anno. 11) Vende solo macchine. 12) Vende macchine da cinque anni. 13) Una tazza di caffè, per favore! 14) Gli uomini che lavorano troppo sono infelici. 15) La macchina che compra (compri) è troppo cara.

Lezione 9, pagina 51

1) You can't see anything. 2) They don't sell sandwiches here any more.
3) They don't eat potatoes in Italy. 4) I don't want to answer this question any more. 5) The waiter doesn't want to work any more. 6) I only want a coffee. 7) I never get anything. 8) I can't see anybody.

Lezione 9, pagina 52

1) You must rest a little! 2) We have to leave now. 3) You must eat something! 4) You must write to the director. 5) They must take the 7.15 train. 6) It's necessary to drink water every day. 7) It's necessary to call Mr Bianchi in an hour. 8) Dobbiamo vedere quel film. 9) Devono mangiare al ristorante malgrado il prezzo. 10) Devo fare una domanda.
11) Deve (devi, dovete) andare ora? 12) Non deve (non devi, non dovete) parlare a Maria. 13) Si mangia bene in questo ristorante? 14) Posso avere la lista del giorno, per favore? 15) Invece di un pasto, mangio un panino.
16) Non prendono mai la metropolitana il sabato.

Lezione 10, pagina 56

1) Sente (senti, sentite) qualcuno? 2) Perchè non dice (dici, dite) niente?
3) Dormo di quando in quando nel pomeriggio. 4) I bambini non dormono ancora. 5) Non capisce mai la prima volta. 6) Non viene mai. 7) Sceglie dalla lista del giorno. 8) Io preferisco [il] vino, e Lei? (e tu? e voi?) 9) Non capiscono niente. 10) Prima di uscire dobbiamo pagare il conto.
11) Veniamo dalla stazione. 12) Dobbiamo partire? 13) Si costruiscono case nuove vicino a Roma. 14) Lavoro molto per finire presto.

Lezione 11, pagina 60

1) Li vedo. 2) Lo vuole. 3) L'ascoltiamo (ti ascoltiamo, vi ascoltiamo).
4) Lo (la) mangiamo. 5) Le lezioni sono troppo difficili e non le capiamo.
6) Io prendo la metropolitana. E Lei? (e tu? e voi?). 7) Batte Sua moglie

(batti tua moglie) di quando in quando? — No, non la batto mai. 8) Il professore è barboso e spesso non lo ascoltiamo.

Lezione 11, pagina 61
1) Non la capisco. 2) Lo mettono nel loro appartamento. 3) Non possiamo comprarla. 4) Lo mangio tutti i giorni. 5) La fanno entrare nel mio ufficio. 6) Lo prende a prestito di quando in quando. 7) La compra la settimana prossima. 8) Lo prendiamo alle otto di sera. 9) L'aprono ogni dieci minuti. 10) Lo fanno bene. 11) Non la riconosco. 12) Li mettete sulla tavola. 13) La sa. 14) Lo beviamo buono. 15) Lo posso vedere per un'ora. 16) Li impariamo. 17) La cominciamo con un controllo. 18) Non li vediamo spesso. 19) Maria ci aspetta spesso dopo la lezione. 20) Vi vedo spesso al cinema.

Lezione 11, pagina 62
1) Non mi piace questo dolce duro e non lo voglio. 2) Posso vederli con il direttore. 3) Non La (ti, vi) sentiamo. 4) Non lo mando. 5) Deve fare li suo letto. 6) Deve (devi, dovete) andare di sopra per trovarlo. 7) Questo diamante è caro ma mi piace veramente. 8) E' come il mio. 9) Questa lezione è difficile e non la capisco. 10) Può (puoi, potete) vederli spesso. 11) Non mi piace questa donna. 12) Li riconosce (riconosci, riconoscete)? 13) Lo vuole (vuoi, volete) per lunedì? 14) Le stanze di sopra sono piccole. 15) So molte cose interessanti. 16) Facciamo [literally mangiamo] solo due pasti al giorno. 17) La lezione comincia. La trova (trovi, trovate) difficile? 18) La parola è difficile. Non so scriverla. 19) Il lavoro è piuttosto lungo. Non voglio farlo. 20) Faccio un gioco meraviglioso. Lo conosce (conosci, conoscete)? 21) E' una splendida ragazza. La conosce (conosci, conoscete)? 22) Ho bisogno di sugarette e devo comprarle. 23) Il libro è difficile ma devo finirlo. 24) Ci chiamano. 25) Vede (vedi, vedete) quelle donne? — Sì, le vedo. 26) Ami i tuoi genitori. Giovannino? — Sì, li amo. 27) Lo vuole veramente? Può prenderlo. 28) Se vuole (vuoi, volete) prendere a prestito il mio impermeabile giallo, può (puoi, potete) prenderlo.

Lezione 12, pagina 67
1) Parlo spesso a lei ma non a lui. 2) Questi libri non appartengono al capufficio, appartengono a me. 3) Mia suocera non ci scrive spesso. 4) Amo i miei genitori e penso spesso a loro. 5) Mi dà il suo ultimo libro. 6) Ci raccontano sempre i loro problemi. 7) Non gli parlo mai. 8) Le (ti, vi) mandiamo i libri oggi.

Lezione 12, pagina 69
1) I write to him from time to time. 2) I tell you to do it! 3) You give her the time to work. 4) They're explaining the problem to us. 5) We're thinking of you a lot. 6) I find it easy. 7) Your sister gives him everything.

8) My uncle tells you silly things.   9) Her father teaches her Italian.   10) I'm going to show it to him (her).

Lezione 12, pagina 70
1) Posso vederlo solo una volta alla settimana.   2) Dovete dir loro tutto.
3) Tuo padre vuole offrirti un lavoro.   4) Devo lasciarla sola questa sera.
5) Che cosa La porto, signore?   6) Potete scrivermi subito?   7) Tu la conosci forse.   8) La suocera di lei è ancora una bella donna.   9) I genitori di lui abitano a Roma.   10) Il marito della mia segretaria non le dà mai denaro.   11) I nonni della mia fidanzata non la vedono da due anni.   12) I suoi nonni abitano in Italia e non li vede da due anni.   13) Può imprestarmi del denaro? — Mi dispiace, non posso imprestarglielo.   14) Mia moglie vuole una donna ad ore per fare i lavori di casa, ma non la trova.

Lezione 12, pagina 70
1) Conosco sua madre. Lei la conosce (tu la conosci, voi la conoscete)?
2) Fortunatamente la domestica fa i lavori di casa.   3) La macchina mi appartiene.   4) Racconta loro tutti i suoi problemi.   5) Le dà un bel maglione. Tu che cosa le dai? (Lei che cosa le dà, voi che cosa le date?).
6) Lavoro da molto tempo. Lei lavora (tu lavori, voi lavorate) ancora?
7) Pensa spesso a sua moglie.   8) Le parla (parli) spesso? — No, le parlo appena.   9) A chi appartiene quella casa?   10) Lo vedo ogni giorno.
11) Li vede (vedi) spesso? — No, li vedo di rado.   12) Posso prendere a prestito la Sua (tua, vostra) matita? — Sì, può (puoi, potete) prenderla a prestito.

Lezione 13, pagina 73
1) Is the shoe on the table?   2) Is the ashtray on the chair?   3) Is your pen on the bed?   4) Is the pencil on the book?   5) Is the cheese on the plate?
6) Are your in-laws in the garden?   7) Do you want a cigarette? — No, thanks, I have (some).   8) The secretary is in the director's office.   9) There is a red car in the street.   10) Is there some butter on the bread?   11) C'è un tappeto nella stanza?   12) Ci sono biciclette nella metropolitana?   13) C'è una lezione barbosa nel libro. Quale?   14) Ci sono professori barbosi nella stanza?   15) Lei può (tu puoi, voi potete) vederli nella via.   16) Ci sono topi nella cucina?   17) C'è vino nelle bottiglie?   18) C'è acqua nei bicchieri?
19) C'è del caffè nelle tazze?   20) Non ho giornali. Lei ne ha (tu ne hai, voi ne avete)?

Lezione 13, pagina 76
1) Vuole del caffè? — No, non ne voglio.   2) Ha bisogno di denaro? — No, non ne ha bisogno.   3) Vuole (vuoi, volete) bere del vino? — No, non voglio (vogliamo) berne.   4) Mangia (mangi, mangiate) qualche volta patate? — No, non ne mangio (non ne mangiamo) mai.   5) Beve (bevi, bevete) molto latte?

— No, ne bevo (beviamo) poco. 6) Hanno bisogno di un'altra lezione gli studenti? — No, non ne hanno bisogno. 7) Ha bisogno di una nuova macchina? — No, non ne ha bisogno. 8) Vende (vendi, vendete) macchine? — No, non ne vendo (non ne vendiamo). 9) Compra spesso dolci Sua (tua, vostra) madre? — No, ne compra di rado. 10) Prendono lezioni di inglese? — No, non ne prendono. 11) Hanno molti maglioni? — No, ne hanno pochi. 12) Conosce qualche ragazza? — No, non ne conosce. 13) Abbiamo bisogno di tutte queste riviste? — No, non ne abbiamo bisogno. 14) Hanno del lavoro da fare oggi? — No, non ne hanno. 15) Ho paura dei loro cani? — No, non ne ho. 16) Ha (hai, avete) bisogno di un dottore? — No, non ne ho (abbiamo) bisogno. 17) Mangia (mangi, mangiate) prosciutto? — No, non ne mangio (mangiamo). 18) Vuole (vuoi, volete) del tè? — No, non ne voglio (non ne vogliamo).

Lezione 13, pagina 76
1) Do you have a lot of relatives? — No, ho pochi parenti. 2) Do they have many cigarettes? — No, hanno poche sigarette. 3) Has that child (little boy) many beautiful toys? — No, quel bambino ha pochi bei giocattoli. 4) Is that man very intelligent? — No, quell'uomo è poco intelligente. 5) Have you been learning Italian for many months? — No, studio italiano da pochi mesi. 6) Do you read many interesting books? — No, leggiamo pochi libri interessanti. 7) Are there many employees in your office? — No, ci sono pochi impiegati nel mio ufficio. 8) Are there many people in the restaurant? — No, c'è poca gente nel ristorante. 9) Are there many charming women? — No, ci sono poche donne affascinanti. 10) Are there many mice in the house? — No, ci sono pochi topi nella casa. 11) Do you want a lot of carrots? — No, voglio (vogliamo) poche carote. 12) Do they take a lot of vegetables? — No, prendono poca verdura.

Lezione 14, pagina 78
1) Lei gioca d'azzardo, a volte? — No, non gioco mai d'azzardo. 2) Gli capita di leggere il giornale? — No, non legge mai il giornale. 3) Prende in giro sua moglie, a volte? — No, non prende mai in giro sua moglie. 4) Vanno a teatro, a volte? — No, non vanno mai a teatro. 5) Lei viaggia, a volte? — No, non viaggio mai. 6) Abbiamo torto, a volte? — No, non abbiamo mai torto. 7) Le capita di lavorare a orario ridotto? — No, non le capita mai di lavorare a orario ridotto. 8) Le (ti, vi) capita di essere fortunato? — No, non mi (ci) capita mai di essere fortunato (i).

Lezione 14, pagina 78
1) So che ha (hai, avete) bisogno di denaro. 2) Dicono che Lei è fortunato. 3) Non deve dirmi che ho torto. 4) So che quel tipo è un mascalzone. 5) E' vero che abbiamo bisogno di aiuto? 6) Convengo che deve farlo.

Lezione 14, pagina 79

1) Sono qui da gennaio. — Da quando sono qui? 2) Sono nella loro casa nuova dall'estate scorsa. — Da quando sono nella loro casa nuova? etc.
3) Gli studenti sono in vacanza da un mese. 4) Non li vedo da molto tempo.
5) I miei genitori sono sulla spiaggia da stamattina. (= questa mattina).
6) Fanno sempre viaggi durante l'estate. 7) Lavoro qui dall'inverno scorso.
8) Non trova un lavoro a orario ridotto e deve lavorare a orario completo.
9) Lo conosco da dieci anni. 10) Vivono a Roma da tre anni. Vivono di solito in Europa. 11) So che è sposato da due anni. 12) E' fortunata ora, ed è fortunata dall'anno scorso.

Lezione 14, pagina 81

1) Stiamo mangiando da un'ora. 2) Stanno sciando da stamattina.
3) Stiamo aspettando ora il professore. 4) I bimbi stanno giocando da due ore. 5) Sta giocando d'azzardo ora. Gioca sempre d'azzardo il sabato.
6) Sta parlando ora. Parla sempre molto. Sta parlando da due ore. 7) Sta (stai, state) leggendo lo stesso libro da ieri. 8) La domestica sta facendo i lavori di casa ora. Li fa sempre di pomeriggio. 9) Sto scrivendo una lettera ai miei suoceri. Scrivo sempre loro la domenica. 10) Sta mangiando ora. Mangia sempre a quest'ora. 11) Stai parlando da un'ora. Tu parli sempre troppo. 12) Sto aspettandoti da cinque ore. Devo sempre aspettartio.
13) Are your parents taking a trip now? 14) We're calling him. 15) I'm waiting for you. 16) They're listening to us. 17) It's raining, it's snowing at the same time. 18) What are they doing? They're walking. 19) I'm closing the window. 20) I'm giving them to him/her. 21) He/she's explaining the problem to us. 22) You're doing it now.

Lezione 15, pagina 86

1) Risponderò domani alla Sua (tua, vostra) lettera. 2) Faremo un viaggio la settimana prossima. 3) Potrò farlo tra una settimana. 4) Verrà domani.
5) Scriverà qualche volta, spero. 6) Compreranno una macchina invece di una bicicletta. 7) Faremo i lavori di casa domenica prossima. 8) Sarò in orario. 9) Forse Lei pensa (tu pensi, voi pensate) che ho torto. 10) Berrò quattro bicchieri di vino stasera. 11) Finalmente vivrò a Roma!
12) Avranno molti contanti con loro. 13) Lascerà una mancia per il cameriere. 14) Potrà (potrai, potrete) venire tra due settimane? 15) Dovrò andare domani. 16) Prenderà (prenderai, prenderete) un raffreddore a causa del tempo. 17) Sarò pronto alle dieci. 18) Avrà bisogno di una pillola per il mal di testa.

Lezione 15, pagina 86

1) I'll be at home this afternoon. 2) Will you need money? 3) I'm sure she'll be lucky. 4) I'll bring him (it) with me tonight. 5) Will we see you next week? 6) Do you know whether they'll help us? 7) We'll stop

working in an hour. 8) We'll soon be hungry. 9) He says he won't buy
another white car. 10) He will tell it to you tomorrow. 11) They don't
know whether or not they'll be able to do it. 12) How old is your boss?
— About fifty. 13) How far do you think it is from Rome to Genoa? —
About five hundred kilometres.

Lezione 16, pagina 89

1) If you're tired, will you go to bed? — Sì, se sono stanco, vado a letto.
2) If you've got a sore throat, will you take some tablets? — Sì, se ho mal di
gola, prendo delle pillole. 3) If I'm hungry, will you give me something to
eat? — Sì, se hai (ha) fame, ti (Le) do qualche cosa da mangiare. 4) If the
book's boring, will you read it all the same? — Sì, (anche) se il libro è noioso,
lo leggo lo stesso. 5) If you've enough money, will you buy a new house?
— Sì, se abbiamo abbastanza denaro, compriamo una nuova casa. 6) If you
don't understand the teacher, will you tell him? — Sì, se non capiamo il
professore, glielo diciamo. 7) If it's nice out, shall we still go the movies? —
Sì, (anche) se fa bel tempo, andiamo al cinema lo stesso. 8) If it's possible
for you to go there tomorrow, will you go? — Sì, se possiamo andarci
domani, ci andiamo. 9) If there's a good film, will you tell me? — Sì, se c'è
un bel film, glielo (te lo) dico. 10) If the meat's undercooked, will you eat
it? — Sì, (anche) se la carne non è cotta, la mangio.

Lezione 16, pagina 89

1) Se beve troppo, suo marito è contento? — No, se beve troppo, suo marito
non è contento. 2) Se ha (hai, avete) bisogno di aiuto, mi chiama (chiami,
chiamate)? — No, se ho (abbiamo) bisogno di aiuto, non La (ti, vi) chiamo
(chiamiamo). 3) Se stai male (se starai male), vai (va, andate) dal dottore?
(andrai, andrà, andrete dal dottore?) — No, se sto (starò) male, non vado (non
andiamo) dal dottore (non andrò, non andremo) dal dottore. 4) Se dovrò
fare un viaggio la settimana prossima, verrai (verrà) con me? — No, se dovrai
(dovrà) fare un viaggio la settimana prossima, non verrò con te (Lei). 5) Se
Le (ti, vi) faccio una domanda, mi risponde (rispondi, rispondete)? — No, se
mi fa (mi fai, mi fate) una domanda, non Le (ti, vi) rispondo (rispondiamo).
6) Se ho bisogno di denaro, me ne presti (presta, prestate)? — No, se ha (hai,
avete) bisogno di denaro, non gliene (te ne, ve ne) presto (prestiamo). 7) Se
ti (Le, vi) piace il suo dolce, glielo dici (dice, dite)? — No, se mi (ci) piace il
suo dolce, non glielo dico (diciamo). 8) Se non capiscono, il professore li
aiuta? — No, se non capiscono, il professore non li aiuta. 9) Se non Le (ti,
vi) telefona stasera, le telefona Lei (le telefoni tu, le telefonate voi)? — No,
se non mi (ci) telefona stasera, io non le telefono (noi non le telefoniamo)
10) Se non può (puoi, potete) farlo, me lo dice (dici, dite)? — No, se non posso
(possiamo) farlo, non glielo (te lo, ve lo) dico (diciamo). 11) Se non può
(. . .) venire, mi telefona per dirmelo? — No, se non posso venire, non Le
telefono per dirglielo. 12) Se non Le piace il pranzo, che cosa fa? — Se non

mi piace il pranzo, non faccio niente.   13) Se ha bisogno di contanti, va in banca? — No, se ho bisogno di contanti, non vado in banca.   14) Se non rispondiamo, si arrabbia il professore? — No, se non rispondiamo, il professore non si arrabbia.   15) Se il poliziotto è un mascalzone, possiamo fare qualche cosa? — No, se il poliziotto è un mascalzone, non possiamo fare niente.   16) Se il ristorante è caro, ci andiamo lo stesso? — No, se il ristorante è caro, non ci andiamo.   17) Se tua moglie ti ama, sei contento? — No, se mia moglie mi ama, non sono contento.   18) Se il capufficio arriva tardi, arriviamo tardi anche noi? — No, se il capufficio arriva tardi, non arriviamo tardi anche noi.

Lezione 17, pagina 92
1) Conosco Giovanna.   2) Conosci (conosce, conoscete) Londra?   3) Sai (sa, sapete) guidare?   4) Sai (sa, sapete) la risposta?   5) Conosci (. . .) sua moglie?   6) Conosci quel negozio?   7) Conosci la sua famiglia?   8) Sai la lezione?   9) Conoscono i suoi parenti?   10) Sa l'italiano?

Lezione 17, pagina 93
1) It's not what you think.   2) It isn't what I mean.   3) I don't understand what you want.   4) I know what he/she'll tell you.   5) Do you know what interests him?

Lezione 17, pagina 93
1) Sa ciò che vuole mangiare?   2) Non sono sicuro(a) di ciò che pensa.   3) Sappiamo ciò che dobbiamo fare.   4) E' ciò che mi preoccupa.   5) E' ciò che mi interessa.

Lezione 18, pagina 96
1) E' la più alta della famiglia.   2) Non è ricco come mio fratello.   3) E' il peggior capufficio della ditta.   4) Sono al verde come Lei (te).   5) E' una bellissima ragazza.

Lezione 18, pagina 96
1) la migliore   2) la più povera   3) la più cara   4) il più vicino   5) la più lunga   6) il migliore   7) il peggiore   8) il più noioso.

Lezione 18, pagina 96
1) Questa ragazza è più seria di me.   2) Questa spiaggia è più bella di quella.   3) Il primo piano è più pulito del pianterreno.   4) Il fornaio è più vicino del macellaio.   5) Il tuo anello è più caro del mio braccialetto.   6) Sua moglie è più brutta della tua.   7) Questa lezione è più interessante dell'altra.   8) Il suo nuovo romanzo è migliore del primo.   9) Sua figlia è più carina della moglie.   10) Questa somma è più importante di quella della settimana scorsa.

Lezione 18, pagina 97

tall: più alto di, meno alto di, alto come, il più alto, il meno alto, molto alto, altissimo — *long:* più lungo di, meno lungo di, lungo come, il più lungo, il meno lungo, molto lungo, lunghissimo — *bad:* peggiore di, meno cattivo di, cattivo come, il peggiore, il meno cattivo, molto cattivo, pessimo — *hot:* più caldo di, meno caldo di, caldo come, il più caldo, il meno caldo, molto caldo, caldissimo — *strong:* più forte di, meno forte di, forte come, il più forte, il meno forte, molto forte, fortissimo — *sad:* più triste di, meno triste di, triste come, il più triste, il meno triste, molto triste, tristissimo — *heavy:* più pesante di, meno pesante di, pesante come, il più pesante, il meno pesante, molto pesante, pesantissimo — *deep:* più profondo di, meno profondo di, profondo come, il più profondo, il meno profondo, molto profondo, profondissimo — *weak:* più debole di, meno debole di, debole come, il più debole, il meno debole, molto debole, debolissimo — *dangerous:* più pericoloso di, meno pericoloso di, pericoloso come, il più pericoloso, il meno pericoloso, molto pericoloso, pericolosissimo — *difficult:* più difficile di, meno difficile di, difficile come, il più difficile, il meno difficile, molto difficile, difficilissimo — *expensive:* più caro di, meno caro di, caro come, il più caro, il meno caro, molto caro, carissimo — *careful:* più attento di, meno attento di, attento come, il più attento, il meno attento, molto attento, attentissimo — *intelligent:* più intelligente di, meno intelligente di, intelligente come, il più intelligente, il meno intelligente, molto intelligente, intelligentissimo — *polite:* più cortese di, meno cortese di, cortese come, il più cortese, il meno cortese, molto cortese, cortesissimo — *fair:* più giusto di, meno giusto di, giusto come, il più giusto, il meno giusto, molto giusto, giustissimo — *shitty:* più schifoso di, meno schifoso di, schifoso come, il più schifoso, il meno schifoso, molto schifoso, schifosissimo — *old:* più vecchio di, meno vecchio di, vecchio come, il più vecchio, il meno vecchio, molto vecchio, vecchissimo — *good:* migliore di, meno buono di, buono come, il migliore, il meno buono, molto buono, ottimo — *stupid:* più stupido di, meno stupido di, stupido come, il più stupido, il meno stupido, molto stupido, stupidissimo — *crowded:* più affollato di, meno affollato di, affollato come, il più affollato, il meno affollato, molto affollato, affollatissimo — *hard:* più duro di, meno duro di, duro come, il più duro, il meno duro, molto duro, durissimo.

Lezione 18, pagina 97

1) Il nostro viaggio è interessante come il tuo (il Suo, il vostro) — Il nostro viaggio è più interessante del tuo (del Suo, del vostro). 2) Le mie scarpe sono a buon mercato come le loro. — Le mie scarpe sono più a buon mercato delle loro. 3) I tuoi (Suoi, vostri) gioielli sono belli come quelli di lei. — I tuoi (Suoi, vostri) gioielli sono più belli dei suoi. 4) Questo libro vale poco come quello. — Questo libro vale meno di quello. 5) Il tuo (Suo, vostro) passatempo favorito è noioso come il mio. — Il tuo (Suo, vostro)

passatempo favorito è più noioso del mio. 6) Questa lezione è facile come l'ultima. – Questa lezione è più facile dell'ultima. 7) Il tuo (Suo, vostro) portafoglio è pieno come il mio. – Il tuo (Suo, vostro) portafoglio è più pieno del mio. 8) La mia doccia è calda come quella di Giovanna. – La mia doccia è più calda di quella di Giovanna. 9) Questo ristorante è affollato come l'altro. – Questo ristorante è più affollato dell'altro. 10) La mia stanza è transcurata come la tua (Sua, vostra). – La mia stanza è più trascurata della tua (Sua, vostra). 11) Queste montagne sono alte come il cielo. – Queste montagne sono più alte del cielo. 12) Il mio vestito è corto come il tuo (Suo, vostro). – Il mio vestito è più corto del tuo (Suo, vostro). 13) E' pigro come suo padre. – E' più pigro di suo padre. 14) Sono benestanti come i loro genitori. – Sono più benestanti dei loro genitori. 15) I professori sono poveri come gli studenti. – I professori sono più poveri degli studenti.

Lezione 18, pagina 98
tristemente – duramente – bene – male – seriamente – facilmente – lungamente – cortesemente – frequentemente – dolcemente – profondamente – stancamente – follemente – lentamente – rapidamente – prontamente – felicemente – seccamente – raramente – grandemente – stupidamente – intelligentemente – caramente – improvvisamente – probabilmente – difficilmente – pesantemente – fortemente.

Lezione 19, pagina 101
1) E' a sinistra. 2) Ho dormito due ore. 3) Ho divorziato due anni fa. 4) Abbiamo cominciato le lezioni d'italiano il mese scorso. 5) Ha (hai, avete mangiato molto stamattina? 6) Mi ha telefonato due ore fa. 7) Ho parlato per due ore ieri. 8) Ho avuto bambini solo quattro anni fa. 9) Hanno finito la lezione ieri sera. 10) Ha lasciato l'ufficio alle dieci.

Lezione 19, pagina 102
1) Non abbiamo visitato il museo. 2) Non ho dimenticato il tuo nome. 3) Non trovo che hai avuto torto. 4) Non ho amato molto quel tipo. 5) Non ha venduto la macchina a mia cugina. 6) Non ti abbiamo aspettato per mangiare. 7) Non abbiamo mangiato senza pane. 8) Non è ciò che ho visto. 9) Non hanno guardato la televisione ieri sera. 10) Oggi non abbiamo mangiato spaghetti alla bolognese.

Lezione 19, pagina 102
1) Ha avuto (hai avuto, avete avuto) male ai denti la settimana scorsa? – No, non ho (abbiamo) avuto male ai denti la settimana scorsa. 2) Ha (hai, avete) starnutato poco fa? – No, non ho (abbiamo) starnutato poco fa. 3) Ha (hai, avete) avuto mal di gola due settimane fa? – No, non ho (abbiamo) avuto mal di gola due settimane fa. 4) Ha riposato dopo il lavoro ieri? – No, non ha riposato dopo il lavoro ieri. 5) Ha (hai, avete) portato solo i libri? – No,

non ho (abbiamo) portato solo i libri. 6) Ha (hai, avete) dovuto pagare? — No, non ho (abbiamo) dovuto pagare. 7) Ha (hai, avete) avuto paura dei cani? — No, non ho (abbiamo) avuto paura dei cani. 8) Ha (hai, avete) avuto una bella giornata? — No, non ho (abbiamo) avuto una bella giornata.

Lezione 19, pagina 103
— sperare, sperato — dormire, dormito — guardare, guardato — potere, potuto — dovere, dovuto — mangiare, mangiato — comprare, comprato — volere, voluto — sapere, saputo — conoscere, conosciuto — capire, capito — preferire, preferito — proibire, proibito — guidare, guidato — aspettare, aspettato — trovare, trovato — ricevere, ricevuto — sentire, sentito — completare, completato — tenere, tenuto — chiamare, chiamato — gettare, gettato — seguire, seguito — riconoscere, riconosciuto — ripetere, ripetuto — dare, dato — parlare, parlato — provare, provato.

Lezione 19, pagina 104
1) Non ho mai preso la metropolitana. 2) Ha già speso tutto il denaro? 3) Che cosa ha (hai, avete) fatto ieri sera? 4) Le hanno (ti hanno, vi hanno) detto ciò ieri? 5) Ha (hai, avete) finito la lezione? 6) Ha (hai, avete) sentito che cosa ha detto? 7) Ha (hai, avete) scritto il suo indirizzo? 8) Ha dovuto farlo una settimana fa? 9) Hanno avuto tempo i turisti di vedere un museo stamattina? 10) Le (ti, vi) hanno mandato i libri a tempo?

Lezione 19, pagina 104
1) Gli alunni non hanno risposto alle domande. 2) Non mi hai fatto un bel regalo. 3) Il bambino non ha pianto molto durante la notte. 4) Non hanno bevuto troppo vino. 5) Non ho letto il libro e non ho visto la commedia. 6) Non abbiamo offerto il pranzo a tutti.

Lezione 20, pagina 109
1) We've never been to Chicago. 2) I haven't been to New York for a long time. 3) He went out with her last night. 4) The accident happened during the night. 5) He was born in Rio de Janeiro. 6) She died last year. 7) I've never fallen down. 8) We returned home after work. 9) She went upstairs. 10) I wonder if you have ever been to the States.

Lezione 20, pagina 109
1) Sei (è) mai stato(a) (siete mai stati(e) al cinema con lui? 2) Hai (ha, avete) mai visto un film di prima qualità? 3) E' caduta e si è rotta un braccio. 4) E'italiana ma malgrado ciò è nata a Nuova York. 5) Perchè è venuto(a) (siete venuti(e) a trovarmi solo una volta? 6) Il marito e la moglie sono morti insieme. 7) Non è tornato a casa oggi. 8) Sono andato(a) spesso alla spiaggia. 9) Non siamo mai stati(e) in Cina. 10) Sono andato(a) solo una volta allo zoo. 11) E' nata in Europa. 12) Dove è (sei) nato(a)? — Sono nato(a) a Roma.

Lezione 21, pagina 111
1) I've just finished writing a letter.   2) We've just finished drinking coffee.
3) She just went upstairs.   4) He/she's going to go out.   5) The plane's going
to take off.   6) That poor woman's going to die.

Lezione 21, pagina 111
1) Ho appena finito di leggere il libro.   2) Giovanna è appena partita.   3) Si
decida!   4) Hanno appena comprato un nuovo appartamento.   5) E'
appena uscito.   6) Sta per uscire.   7) Abbiamo appena finito di fare le
valigie.   8) Inganna suo marito.

Lezione 21, pagina 113
1) Do you want some more wine?   2) She isn't sick any more.   3) We often
talk to each other.   4) I don't want any more bread. Do you want some
more?   5) We write to each other a lot during the year.   6) Do you still
plan to divorce?   7) Do you want something else?   8) They love each other
very much.   9) Some more water, please!   10) Do you still have problems
with the boss?   11) Do you plan to ask your father for more dough?
12) Do you like coffee? – No, I don't like it.   13) Do you like Italian ice-
creams? – Yes, I like them very much.   14) Italian is spoken here.

Lezione 21, pagina 113
1) Si amano ancora.   2) Abitano ancora a Nuova York?   3) Lei vuole (tu
vuoi, voi volete) sempre fare un viaggio con me?   4) Si parlano spesso.
5) E' ancora preoccupata per la salute dei bambini?   6) Vuole (vuoi) ancora del
pane? – No, non ne voglio più, grazie.   7) Prende (prendi) ancora medicine
per il mal di gola?   8) Fa ancora male?   9) Le piacciono (ti piacciono) le
carote? – Sì, mi piacciono.   10) Si mangia molto pesce in Italia.

Lezione 21, pagina 114
1) Noi lavoriamo da due ore, ma lui ha lavorato solo un'ora.   2) Stanno
mangiando da mezzogiorno.   Hanno già mangiato tutto il pollo.
3) Prendiamo lezioni d'italiano da due anni. Abbiamo preso cinquanta
lezioni l'anno scorso.   4) E' stato(a) (sei stato(a) a Nuova York? – Sì, ci
sono andato(a) l'anno scorso.   5) Dorme da dieci ore. Ha dormito dieci ore
anche la notte scorsa.   6) Stai (sta, state) guardando la televisione da un'ora.
L'hai (l'ha, l'avete) guardata tutto il giorno ieri.   7) Vivono a Roma da
cinque anni. Prima sono vissuti (hanno abitato) a Parigi per un anno.   8) I
bambini giocano da due ore. Hanno giocato con i loro compagni anche ieri
per due ore.   9) Lavora per questa ditta da dodici anni. Ha lavorato per
l'altra solo due anni.   10) Stanno litigando da mezz'ora. Hanno litigato tutto
il giorno ieri.

Lezione 22, pagina 118

1) Pietro è venuto quando noi mangiavamo. 2) Tu leggevi un libro quando io sono venuto. 3) Giovanni parlava col direttore quando io sono entrato nell'ufficio. 4) Alle otto Maria è partita mentre noi lavoravamo ancora. 5) Le segretarie parlavano quando il direttore è entrato nella stanza. 6) Quando io sono uscito, pioveva. 7) Quando tu mi hai telefonato, io facevo il bagno. 8) Tu avevi un'aria triste quando ti ho incontrato ieri.

Lezione 22, pagina 119

1) Piangeva (piangevi, piangevate) quando sono entrato(a)? 2) Che cosa faceva (facevi, facevate) quando ho telefonato? 3) Bevevano vino mentre noi guardavamo la televisione. 4) Lei leggeva mentre lui parlava col capufficio. 5) Festeggiavamo il mio compleanno quando ciò è successo. 6) Che cosa diceva (dicevi, dicevate) quando lei è entrata? 7) Io lavoravo mentre Lei giocava (tu giocavi, voi giocavate) con i bambini. 8) Ho fatto quell'esperimento quando lavoravo per lui.

Lezione 22, pagina 119

1) What were you doing yesterday while I was sleeping? 2) I was eating when you came. 3) I was answering the questions while the other pupils were listening. 4) The kids were watching TV while their parents were reading. 5) We were drinking while you were working. 6) When you called, I was taking a shower. 7) I was taking a bath when you came in the bathroom. 8) He (she) was coming to see us when the accident happened.

Lezione 23, pagina 124

1) If you had the money, would you buy a new apartment? — Se hai i soldi, compri un nuovo appartamento? 2) If you could, would you help me? — Se Lei può, mi aiuta? 3) If the tourists had the time, would they see the museums? — Se i turisti hanno tempo, vanno a vedere i musei? 4) If the play were a flop, would we go to see it all the same? — Se la commedia è un fiasco, andiamo a vederla lo stesso? 5) If you didn't understand, would you tell me? — Se Lei non capisce, me lo dice? 6) If his company was successful, the boss would be satisfied. — Se la ditta ha successo, il padrone è contento. 7) If you got divorced, would you be unhappy? — Se tu divorzi, sei infelice? 8) If it rained, we would take an umbrella. — Se piove, prendiamo un ombrello. 9) If we had to do it, we would do it. — Se dobbiamo farlo, lo facciamo. 10) If the weather were bad, we wouldn't go for a walk. — Se fa brutto tempo, non facciamo la passeggiata. 11) If we were hungry, we would finish yesterday night's meat. — Se abbiamo fame, finiamo la carne di ieri sera. 12) If she couldn't come, would you come alone? — Se lei non può venire, tu vieni solo?

Lezione 23, pagina 124

1) Se quel libro Le appartenesse, me lo presterebbe? (Se quel libro ti appartenesse, me lo presteresti? Se quel libro vi appartenesse, me lo prestereste?) — No, se quel libro mi appartenesse non glielo (te lo, ve lo) presterei. 2) Se Lei fosse in ritardo, mi telefonerebbe? (Se tu fossi in ritardo, mi telefoneresti, ecc.) — No, se fossi in ritardo, non Le telefonerei. 3) Se Lei fosse un turista, andrebbe a vedere il Museo d'Arte Moderna di Nuova York? — No, se fossi un turista, non andrei a vedere il Museo d'Arte Moderna di Nuova York. 4) Se fosse stanco, andrebbe a dormire nella mia camera? — No, se fossi stanco, non andrei a dormire nella Sua camera. 5) Se fossero ricchi, viaggerebbero? — No, se fossero ricchi non viaggerebbero. 6) Se dovessimo scegliere un dentista, sceglieremmo quello? — No, se dovessimo scegliere un dentista, non sceglieremmo quello. 7) Se fosse bocciato all'esame, continuerebbe a lavorare? — No, se fossi bocciato all'esame, non continuerei a lavorare. 8) Se dovessi scegliere un marito, sceglierei il Suo? — No, se dovessi scegliere un marito, non sceglierei il Suo. 9) Se non avessimo tanto denaro, potremmo andare a Parigi? — No, se non avessimo tanto denaro, non potremmo andare a Parigi. 10) Se potesse comprare quelle sigarette, me ne darebbe? — No, se potessi comprare quelle sigarette, non gliene darei. 11) Se lei trovasse un appartamento carino, lo comprerebbe? — No, se trovasse un appartamento carino, non lo comprerebbe. 12) Se quel vestito fosse in liquidazione, lo prenderei? — No, se quel vestito fosse in liquidazione, non lo prenderei. 13) Se piove, andiamo lo stesso? — No, se piove, non andiamo. 14) Se ci fosse il sole fuori, staremmo a casa? — No, se ci fosse il sole fuori, non staremmo a casa. 15) Se Lei lavora a orario ridotto, guadagna abbastanza denaro? — No, se lavoro a orario ridotto, non guadagno abbastanza denaro. 16) Se suo marito la critica continuamente, lo lascerà? — No, (anche) se suo marito la critica continuamente, non lo lascerà.

Lezione 24, pagina 129

1) Se non dovessi lavorare, giocherei col gatto. — Se non avessi dovuto lavorare, avrei giocato col gatto. 2) Se piovesse, non andremmo. — Se fosse piovuto, non saremmo andati. 3) Se Lei non mi imprestasse denaro, non potrei comprare una macchina. — Se Lei non mi avesse imprestato denaro, non avrei potuto comprare una macchina. 4) Se avessi tempo, cercherei un lavoro migliore. — Se avessi avuto tempo, avrei cercato un lavoro migliore. 5) Se volesse, andremmo al cinema. — Se avesse voluto, saremmo andati al cinema. 6) Se potessi scegliere, prenderei questo. — Se avessi potuto scegliere, avrei preso questo. 7) Se il museo fosse aperto, ci andremmo. — Se il museo fosse stato aperto, ci saremmo andati. 8) Se il telefono suonasse, non risponderei. — Se il telefono avesse suonato, non avrei risposto. 9) Se avessi i soldi, comprerei una casa in campagna. — Se avessi avuto i soldi, avrei comprato una casa in campagna. 10) Se Mario arrivasse oggi, sarei contento. — Se Mario fosse arrivato oggi, saresti stato contento.

Lezione 24, pagina 129

1) Se lavoro a orario ridotto, non ho abbastanza denaro. — Se lavorassi a orario ridotto, non avrei abbastanza denaro. — Se avessi lavorato a orario ridotto, non avrei avuto abbastanza denaro.   2) Se devo fare i piatti, mi aiuti (aiuta, aiutate)? — Se dovessi fare i piatti, mi aiuteresti (aiuterebbe, aiutereste)? — Se avessi dovuto fare i piatti, mi avresti (avrebbe, avreste) aiutato?   3) Se tutto va male, vado a letto. — Se tutto andasse male, andrei a letto. — Se tutto fosse andato male, sarei andato a letto.   4) Se non può scrivere, telefona. — Se non potesse scrivere, telefonerebbe. — Se non avesse potuto scrivere, avrebbe telefonato.   5) Se continua (continui, continuate) a urlare, riattacco. — Se tu continuassi (se Lei continuasse, se voi continuaste) a urlare, riattaccherei. — Se tu avessi continuato (se Lei avesse continuato, se voi aveste continuato) a urlare, avrei riattaccato.   6) Se mi deludi (delude, deludete) ancora, ti lascio (La lascio, vi lascio). — Se tu mi deludessi (se Lei mi deludesse, se voi mi deludeste) ancora, ti (La, vi) lascerei. — Se tu mi avessi deluso (se Lei mi avesse deluso, se voi mi aveste deluso) ancora, ti (La, vi) avrei lasciato.   7) Se guadagna molto denaro, lo sposo. — Se guadagnasse molto denaro, lo sposerei. — Se avesse guadagnato molto denaro, lo avrei sposato.   8) Se hai (ha, avete) mal di testa, puoi (può, potete) riposare. — Se avessi (avesse, aveste) mal di testa, potresti (potrebbe, potreste) riposare. — Se avessi (avesse, aveste) avuto mal di testa, avresti (avrebbe, avreste) potuto riposare.   9) Se sei gentile (= buono, buona), non ti sculaccio. — Se tu fossi gentile, non ti sculaccerei. — Se tu fossi stato(a) gentile, non ti avrei sculacciato(a).   10) Se decidi (decide, decidete) di andare, devi (deve, dovete) dirmelo. — Se tu decidessi (se Lei decidesse, se voi decideste) di andare, dovresti (dovrebbe, dovreste) dirmelo. — Se tu avessi deciso (se Lei avesse deciso, se voi aveste deciso) di andare, avresti (avrebbe, avreste) dovuto dirmelo.   11) Se menti (mente, mentite) ancora, sono stufo. — Se tu mentissi (se Lei mentisse, se voi mentiste) ancora, sarei stufo. — Se tu avessi mentito (se Lei avesse mentito, se voi aveste mentito) ancora, sarei stato stufo.   12) Se vuoi (vuole, volete) prendere l'aereo, devi (deve, dovete) fare le valigie ora. — Se tu volessi (se Lei volesse, se voi voleste) prendere l'aereo, dovresti (dovrebbe, dovreste) fare le valigie ora.

Lezione 25, pagina 132

1) Diceva che avrebbe fatto subito le valigie.   2) Ti ho detto che saresti partito domenica.   3) Ha scritto che sarebbe venuto la settimana prossima.
4) Sapevamo già che saremmo stati bocciati all'esame.   5) Sapevo che un giorno o l'altro sarebbe tornato a casa.   6) Sapevamo che con questo libro avremmo parlato presto e bene l'italiano.   7) Ti ho detto che saresti andato in Italia per le vacanze.   8) Hanno scritto che sarebbero passati da Roma in settembre.   9) Mi sono reso conto che non avrei parlato italiano dopo pochi giorni.   10) Ha avuto la faccia tosta di dire che avrebbe pagato più tardi.
11) Stavano litigando per sapere chi non avrebbe fatto i lavori di casa.
12) Non si rendeva conto che se non fosse uscito alle otto avrebbe perso il

treno. 13) Andavano sempre d'accordo quando si trattava di decidere quale film avrebbero guardato alla televisione. 14) Quel rompiscatole ha detto che avrebbe aspettato anche due ore per parlare con Lei.

Lezione 25, pagina 132

1) So che verrà. 2) Diciamo che andremo al cinema. 3) Lo scrittore pensa che il suo libro sarà il migliore dell'anno. 4) Mi dice che gli piacerà lavorare a orario ridotto. 5) Si rende conto che il fatto di scrivere questo libro gli prenderà troppo tempo. 6) So che non sarai capace di farlo. 7) Mi rendo conto che quello scocciatore non partirà subito. 8) Leggiamo sul giornale che il tempo sarà pessimo. 9) Dicono che faranno sciopero. 10) Il medico dice che morrà. 11) Il bandito non pensa che sarà arrestato sul luogo della rapina. 12) Quella carogna dice che accetterà con piacere una bustarella.

Lezione 25, pagina 133

1) Sapevo che ci avresti (avrebbe, avreste) aiutati. 2) Sapevo che non saresti stato (che non sarebbe stato, che non sareste stati) soddisfatto (soddisfatti). 3) Ha detto che avrebbe saputo guidare a Natale. 4) Sapevo che avresti (avrebbe, avreste) litigato con mia madre. 5) Pensavo che avrei potuto farlo. 6) Pensavamo tutti che i prezzi sarebbero scesi. 7) Il candidato pensava che avrebbero votato per lui. 8) Sapevo che saresti stato (che sarebbe stato, che sareste stati) fortunato (fortunati). 9) Ha detto che sarebbe arrivato a tempo. 10) Non pensavo che avrebbe brontolato sulla decisione. 11) Pensavamo che avresti (avrebbe, avreste) potuto scrivere. 12) Non ti sei reso conto che avrei potuto aiutarti? (non si è reso conto che avrei potuto aiutarLa? non vi siete resi conto che avrei potuto aiutarvi?).

Lezione 25, pagina 133

1) No, non pensavo che avresti telefonato prima delle otto. 2) No, non sapevamo che oggi avreste fatto sciopero. 3) No, non abbiamo pensato che il bandito avrebbe tirato. 4) No, non immaginavo che quel tipo avrebbe voluto una bustarella. 5) No, non pensavo che oggi sarebbe piovuto. 6) No, non Le ho detto che avrei finito quel lavoro per martedì. 7) No, non sapevo che mi avrebbe amata pazzamente. 8) No, non pensavo che mi sarei trovata nei guai. 9) No, non immaginavo che mio marito mi avrebbe ingannata. 10) No, non sapevano che il padre li avrebbe puniti. 11) No, non ho pensato che avrebbe potuto aiutarmi. 12) No, la mia segretaria ieri non ha detto che avrebbe subito scritto e spedito la lettera.

Lezione 26, pagina 136

1) Diceva che aveva visto una tigre allo zoo. 2) Ero sicuro che lo avevo già visto (di averlo già visto) prima. 3) Quando è venuto avevamo già mangiato. 4) Ha detto che aveva divorziato perchè l'aveva ingannata. 5) Quando ha rifiutato questo posto, ne aveva già accettato un'altro. 6) Non gli credeva più, perchè non le aveva sempre detto la verità. 7) Aveva paura perchè

qualcuno lo aveva seguito. 8) Mi ha detto che aveva trovato (di aver trovato) una dieta formidabile. 9) Era già uscito quando ho telefonato. 10) Desiderava sapere che cosa era successo tra loro.

Lezione 26, pagina 137

1) Ha detto che ti aveva aspettato tutto il giorno. 2) Ha detto che era venuto invano. 3) Ha detto che aveva preso l'aereo. 4) Ha scoperto tardi che sua moglie l'aveva ingannato. 5) Mi sono reso conto che il signor Bianchi aveva fatto uno sbaglio quando ho verificato il libro dei conti. 6) Quando sono arrivata, essi avevano già affittato la casa. 7) Avevi finito i compiti quando sono entrato? 8) Avete detto che avevate già visto il film? 9) Perchè avete detto che avevate perso la grana? 10) Non avete pensato che quel tipo aveva fatto il poliziotto quando era giovane. 11) Ti ho detto che avevo perso la borsetta e che ne avevo comprata un'altra? 12) Maria ti ha detto che era venuta in bicicletta? 13) L'artista era morto quando i suoi dipinti sono diventati celebri. 14) Perchè non mi hai detto che tuo marito ti aveva mentito? 15) Perchè sua moglie gli ha detto che era partita? 16) Quando ti ho telefonato avevamo finito di mangiare. 17) Il ladro correva perchè aveva visto i poliziotti. 18) Il commerciante era soddisfatto perchè aveva guadagnato molto denaro. 19) Gli studenti erano contenti perchè le vacanze erano cominciate. 20) Non ho mangiato il pompelmo perchè avevo già mangiato una mela e due pesche. 21) Ha cominciato una dieta perchè era ingrassato troppo. 22) Quando la polizia lo ha arrestato, il bandito aveva tirato già due volte. 23) Quando il proprietario è arrivato, il ladro aveva rubato i gioielli e il denaro. 24) Quando ho visto quel film ci ho messo un'ora a scoprire chi aveva pagato il sicario per uccidere il testimone.

Lezione 26, pagina 138

1) Fra poco diventerà buio più presto. 2) Può ripetere per favore? Non ho capito. 3) Se non chiudi il becco, ti farai sgridare! 4) Siete arrivati ieri o stamattina? 5) Quando va in Italia, può procurarmi un po' di vino italiano? 6) Dove si è procurato questa bella giacca? 7) Potrebbe spiegarmelo? Non lo capisco. 8) Penso che dovresti tentare di avere (conseguire) il diploma quest'anno.

Lezione 27, pagina 140

1) Sono stanco ma voglio lo stesso andar fuori a pranzare. 2) La inganna, tuttavia lei lo ama. 3) Piove, ma voglio lo stesso fare un po' di spese. 4) I don't want to do the housework but still I do it. 5) I'm tired of moving, but I accepted this new job all the same. 6) She's ill but she still works hard.

Lezione 27, pagina 141

1) E' uscito senza pagare. 2) Invece di fumare, dovrebbe uscire a fare una passeggiata. 3) E' partito senza aver mangiato. 4) Prima di andare al cinema mangerò un panino. 5) Dopo aver telefonato, è andato a letto. 6) E' uscita

senza parlargli. 7) Ha superato l'esame senza studiare. 8) I banditi sono fuggiti senza rubare niente. 9) Invece di discutere dovremmo decidere cosa fare. 10) Dopo avere letto questo libro scriverò una lettera a mio padre. 11) Senza dire niente lo ha colpito. 12) Invece di mangiare ora, vuole andare a farle visita all'ospedale? 13) Grazie per essere venuto. 14) Ero già dimagrita molto prima di incontrarlo. 15) Invece di lavorare stava leggendo un giornale. 16) Non vedo l'ora di finire questo dannato libro.

Lezione 27, pagina 142

1) L'uomo di cui Le parlavo è il mio migliore amico. 2) La donna il cui l'amico è francese è molto provocante. 3) L'uomo a cui penso non è ancora venuto. 4) Mi può dare il denaro di cui ho bisogno? 5) Mi piacerebbe il genere di caffè a cui sono abituato. 6) E' il tipo di uomo di cui ho bisogno. 7) E' ciò di cui Le sto parlando. 8) L'uomo di cui conosco il fratello verrà da Lei (da te, da voi) domani. 9) L'anno in cui sono nato è stato un anno buono per il vino. 10) La casa in cui vivo appartiene a mio padre. 11) Il ponte su cui siamo è a senso unico. 12) La stanza in cui sono è molto fredda. 13) La sedia su cui siedi (siede, sedete) è vecchissima. 14) Il letto su cui sei è mio.

Lezione 27, pagina 143

1) Ha già mangiato. 2) Ha già finito il suo lavoro? 3) Hanno già telefonato? — No, non ancora. 4) L'ho già fatto. 5) Non ha ancora risposto. 6) Dorme già? — No, non ancora.

Lezione 27, pagina 143

1) Non ha ancora telefonato. 2) Non ha ancora trovato una nuova fidanzata. 3) Non hai ancora comprato un'Alfa Romeo? 4) Non abbiamo ancora dato un esame. 5) Non siete ancora andati a vedere l'Aida? 6) Non ho ancora visto questo film.

Lezione 28, pagina 145

1) Devi (deve, dovete) andare oggi. 2) Era tenuta a dirti (dirLe, dirvi) la verità. 3) Deve essere partito (sarà partito). 4) Devi (deve) essere stanco (dovete essere stanchi) — Sarai (sarà) stanco (sarete stanchi). 5) Siamo tenuti a lavorare così tardi? 6) Non eri (era) tenuto (non eravate tenuti) ad invitarlo. 7) Non dovevo dirti (dirLe, dirvi) la verità. 8) Devono non aver capito (non avranno capito).

Lezione 28, pagina 145

1) The journalist had to write an article about the new candidate. 2) Why didn't he come? He must be in Rome. 3) I haven't seen him for a long time, he must be in prison again. 4) I didn't have to go yesterday. 5) The streets are wet. It must have rained.

Lezione 28, pagina 146
1) Avrebbe (avresti, avreste) dovuto comprare più verdura. 2) Dovrebbe telefonarle. 3) Non avrebbe (avresti, avreste) mai dovuto dire ciò. 4) Perchè dovrei scrivergli? 5) Non penso che dovrebbe (dovresti, dovreste) scrivere ora, ma avrebbe (avresti, avreste) dovuto scrivere la settimana scorsa.
6) Perché i bambini non avrebbero dovuto mangiare alle cinque? 7) Non avrebbe dovuto mentire. 8) Ha ragione. Avremmo dovuto dirglielo. (Hai ragione. Avremmo dovuto dirtelo. — Avete ragione. Avremmo dovuto dirvelo.)

Lezione 28, pagina 146
1) He should have listened to you. 2) You should have waited for the bus.
3) You shouldn't be afraid of the dark. 4) I should have bought that painting. 5) They shouldn't have given him a bribe. 6) What on earth should we have done? 7) I don't think you should go. 8) You're supposed to know it.

Lezione 28, pagina 148
1) Close the window, John! 2) Don't open the door, Mary! 3) Send a card to your mother, David, send it today! 4) Children, finish your homework quickly! 5) Antony and Mark, don't touch my books! 6) Peter, take a pen and write to your father at once!

Lezione 28, pagina 148
1) Fuma (non fumare) una sigaretta Nazionale! 2) Guarda (non guardare) dalla finestra la gente che passa! 3) Lavora (non lavorare) tutta la notte!
4) Bevi (non bere) un altro caffè! 5) Scendi (non scendere) al pianterreno!
6) Compra (non comprare) una bottiglia di vino buono!

Lezione 28, pagina 148
1) Finite (non finite) questo lavoro per stasera! 2) Andate (non andate) alla piscina! 3) Fate (non fate) attenzione a quello che dice Marco! 4) Dite (non dite) quello che pensate! 5) Bevete (non bevete) una Coca Cola dopo aver nuotato! 6) Pulite (non pulite) la cucina dopo aver mangiato!

Lezione 28, pagina 150
1) Please come here, Mrs Smith! 2) Open the door, Miss Brown! 3) Don't close the window, Mr Peters! 4) Listen carefully to what I'm saying, Mr White! 5) You haven't yet paid your hotel bill, Sir? Pay it now, please!
6) Go now to do your shopping, if you want to. The shops are still open.
7) Drink another glass of wine! 8) Come into this room, ladies and gentlemen, and admire this painting by Tintoretto! 9) Give me those black shoes which are in the window! 10) Here they are, Sir, come and try them on! 11) Mr Brown, tell your tenant not to make so much noise at night time, please! 12) Change from gas to oil, it costs less!

Lezione 28, pagina 150
1) Mi scusi, signora! 2) Mi ascolti, signore! 3) Cameriere, mi porti uno scotch! 4) Telefonami stasera, tesoro! 5) Porta questo libro a tua madre, giovanotto! 6) Dovrebbe bere un po' d'acqua, signore! 7) Dovrebbe subaffittare una parte della Sua casa, signora Smith! 8) Mi scusi, signore, può dirmi dov'è la posta? — Prenda la prima via a destra a poi la seconda a sinistra. — Grazie mille.

Lezione 29, pagina 152
1) The boss was so angry that he went out shouting. 2) You talk so much! 3) He eats so much that he's gaining a lot of weight! 4) She's so tired she's going to stay in bed. 5) We laughed so much! 6) They had so much work yesterday that they left the office at 10 p.m.

Lezione 29, pagina 152
1) E' così testarda che non ti (La, vi) ascolterà. 2) E' così sincera che fa male. 3) Sono così ricchi (ricche)! 4) Ha bevuto tanto caffè che non poteva dormire. 5) Siamo così infelici che dovremmo divorziare. 6) Fa così freddo fuori che resterò a casa.

Lezione 29, pagina 153
1) Sto mangiando e stavo mangiando quando hai (ha, avete) telefonato. 2) Stavano avendo una lezione d'italiano quando è arrivato. 3) Stavamo leggendo quando tuo (Suo, vostro) fratello ha acceso la televisone. 4) Stavamo venendo a trovarti (trovarLa, trovarvi) quando abbiamo incontrato tua (Sua, vostra) suocera.

Lezione 29, pagina 153
1) Sì, ne ho. — No, non ne ho. 2) Sì, ne parlavamo bene. — No, non ne parlavamo bene. 3) Sì, ne abbiamo molta. — No, non ne abbiamo molta. 4) Sì, ne ha bisogno. — No, non ne ha bisogno. 5) Sì, ne parlano molto. — No, non ne parlano molto. 6) Sì, ne vendiamo molti. — No, non ne vendiamo molti. 7) Sì, gliene regalo qualche volta. — No, non gliene offro mai. 8) Sì, ne hanno due. — No, non ne hanno due.

Lezione 29, pagina 154
1) Ci sono vissuto un anno. 2) Ci andiamo subito? 3) Ci è andato con me.

Lezione 29, pagina 155
1) C'era molta neve in inverno? 2) Ci sarà molto lavoro da fare? 3) C'erano molti bambini che giocavano nel parco. 4) C'erano problemi con l'ultima lezione? 5) C'erano solo quattro persone nel ristorante. 6) C'erano molti passeggeri contenti del viaggio. 7) Ci sarà folla nella casa. 8) Ci sono sempre molti turisti a Roma.

Lezione 29, pagina 155
1) Ti ho detto (Le ho detto, vi ho detto) di non lavorare troppo. 2) Mi ha avvertito di non andare. 3) Mi hai promesso di non lasciarmi. 4) Ha scritto di non aspettarla. 5) Gli ho chiesto di non telefonare.

Lezione 29, pagina 155
1) Questa è la ragione per cui vuole andare all'estero. 2) Questa è la ragione per cui mi va bene. 3) Sono deluso, e questa è la ragione per cui parto.
4) Non [lo] so e questa è la ragione per cui sto menando il cane per l'aia.
5) Non sono sicuro e questa è la ragione per cui non so rispondere. 6) Siamo poveri e questa è la ragione per cui abbiamo bisogno di denaro. 7) E' un cretino e questa è la ragione per cui divorzio.

Lezione 30, pagina 159
1) Do you often make mistakes? — No, non mi sbaglio spesso. 2) Do you remember your last holidays? — No, non me ne ricordo. 3) Is Smith your name? — No, non mi chiamo Smith. 4) Do you give a darn about what I say? — No, non ce ne infischiamo. 5) Did you get married in church? — No, non ci siamo sposati in chiesa. 6) Do they get up early every day? — No, non si alzano presto tutti i giorni. 7) Does the child usually go to sleep late? — No, il bambino di solito non si addormenta tardi. 8) Don't you feel well? — No, non mi sento bene. 9) Did Tony and Mary get engaged yesterday? — No, non si sono fidanzati ieri. 10) Have you made up your mind or not? — No, non ci siamo decisi. 11) Did his (her) parents get very angry? — No, non si sono arrabbiati molto. 12) Do you get undressed in front of your husband? — No, non mi spoglio davanti a mio marito.

Lezione 30, pagina 159
1) Mi lavo e mi vesto per il ricevimento. 2) Ci domandiamo perchè gli ha (hai, avete) detto di non venire. 3) Si sposano domani. 4) Stasera voglio divertirmi.
5) Mi sbaglio sempre. 6) Si rende conto (ti rendi conto, vi rendete conto) di ciò che dice (dici, dite)? 7) Non mi ricordo di lui. 8) Si lamenta sempre.
— Di che cosa si lamenta? 9) Non so decidermi. 10) Mi infischio di tutto.
11) Spicciati! (spicciatevi! Si spicci!) 12) Mi sono rasato mentre lei si cambiava. 13) Se si decidesse non dovremmo più preoccuparci. 14) Se ci sposassimo ora, divorzieremmo presto. 15) Si abituerà (ti abituerai, vi abituerete) a questo dentifricio. 16) Non tutti i sogni si avverano. 17) I nostri vicini non si vergognano di rubare fiori dal nostro giardino. 18) Si scusi! (scusati! scusatevi!) 19) Mi sono perso quando tornavo dalla stazione.
20) Mi domando se la mia traduzione è esatta.

Lezione 31, pagina 161
1) tu stesso. 2) noi stessi. 3) voi stessi. 4) egli stesso. 5) essi stessi.
6) io stesso. 7) noi stessi. 8) io stesso. 9) Lei stesso.

Lezione 31, pagina 163

1) Mi sono domandato se sarebbe venuto.   2) Non si è reso conto di ciò che ha detto.   3) Mio nonno si è abituato a non fumare più.   4) Ti sei burlato troppo spesso di me.   5) Ti sei ricordato della nostra prima notte assieme?   6) Donatella si è lavata e si è vestita in un quarto d'ora.   7) Si è spicciato per uscire con te.   8) Non ci siamo lamentati di niente.   9) Mi sono sempre divertito quando sono uscito con voi.   10) La vecchia signora si è sempre seduta dietro il conducente.   11) Gli operai si sono resi conto che sarebbero stati licenziati.   12) Il commesso si è ricordato di quel cliente.

Lezione 31, pagina 163

1) Ci siamo sempre alzati tardi durante le vacanze ed ora ci alziamo presto per lavorare.   2) Non mi sono sbagliato ieri e non mi sbaglio ora.   3) Ci siamo divertiti ieri sera.   Ci divertiamo sempre.   4) Mi sono spicciato ma tu (Lei) non ti sei reso conto (non si è reso conto) che volevo vederti (vederLa) prima.   5) Lui non si decide mai abbastanza presto.   Tu ti sei già deciso?   6) Ti sei burlato (si è burlato, vi siete burlati) di me ieri. Sono stufo di te (di Lei, di voi).   7) Si è sposata di nuovo. Mi domando se si ricorda di tutti i suoi mariti.   8) Quasi tutti si interessavano alla conversazione.   9) Dovresti vergognarti (dovrebbe vergognarsi, dovreste vergognarvi) di prendere sul serio il suo pettegolezzo.   10) Non so abituarmi alla nuova macchina.   11) Mi sono tagliato quando ho tentato di radermi rapidamente.   12) Se mi fossi spicciato, non sarei arrivato in ritardo.

Lezione 31, pagina 167

1) ci siamo addormentati   2) hai fatto, farò   3) guarda   4) siete andati   5) leggeva, dormivo   6) litigano   7) sei stato   8) siete   9) guidava, è successo   10) sono sposati   11) dorme/dormiva/ha dormito   12) ha arrestato, aveva rubato   13) pensavo, avevi finito   14) studiamo   15) avete visto   16) sono andato   17) facevi, sono entrato   18) è   19) cominciamo/cominceremo   20) ho potuto, potrò   21) tento   22) aveva cucinato, sei tornato   23) ha riparato, funzionava   24) ci siamo lavati, ci laviamo   25) si ricordava, aveva detto, hai incontrato   26) dici   27) ho insegnato   28) sono divorziati, siete divorziati.

Lezione 32, pagina 168

1) Se posso, vado con lui. — Se potessi, andrei con lui. — Se avessi potuto, sarei andato con lui.   2) Se si amano/si amassero/si fossero amati, perchè non si sposano/non si sposerebbero/non si sarebbero sposati?   3) Se mi prendi/prendessi/avessi preso in giro, ti lascio/lascerei/avrei lasciato.   4) Se non dobbiamo/dovessimo/avessimo dovuto fare il lavoro noi stessi, facciamo/faremmo/avremmo fatto una passeggiata.   5) Se non studia [literally = se non lavora] /studiasse/avesse studiato, non supera/non supererebbe/non avrebbe superato l'esame.   6) Se saranno ricchi l'anno prossimo, compreranno una nuova casa. [the second and third form of IF aren't possible here].   7) Se possiamo/potessimo/avessimo potuto aiutare, telefoniamo/telefoneremmo/avremmo telefonato.   8) Se vuole (vuoi, volete)/volesse (volessi, voleste)/

avesse voluto (avessi voluto, aveste voluto) vendere la macchina, la compro/
comprerei/avrei comprata io. 9) Se è/fosse/fosse stato un cretino, sua moglie
non l'amerà/non l'amerebbe/non l'avrebbe amato più. 10) Se Sua (tua, vostra)
sorella prenderà/prenderebbe/avesse preso la pillola, non sarà/non sarebbe/
non sarebbe stata incinta. 11) Se portiamo/portassimo/avessimo portato i
cappotti in tintoria [literally: dal tintore], costa/costerebbe/sarebbe costato
caro. 12) Se gli operai fanno/facessero/avessero fatto sciopero, i sindacati
sono/sarebbero/sarebbero stati contenti. 13) Se c'è/ci fosse/ci fosse stata
un'altra guerra, siamo/saremmo/saremmo stati tutti uccisi. 14) Se tu
continui/continuassi/avessi continuato [a fare] fesserie, ti lascio/lascerei/
avrei lasciato. 15) Se non facciamo/facessimo/avessimo fatto una passeggiata,
grido/griderei/avrei gridato. 16) Se vuole (vuoi, volete)/volesse (volessi,
voleste)/avesse voluto (avessi voluto, aveste voluto) fare un viaggio, vengo/
verrei/sarei venuto con Lei (te, voi). 17) Se il suo amante non potrà più/non
potesse più/non avesse più potuto scopare, sarà/sarebbe/sarebbe stata delusa.
18) Se la pubblicità commerciale è/fosse/fosse stata brutta [literally: cattiva],
non è/non sarebbe/non sarebbe stata una novità [literally: nulla di nuovo].
19) Se i politicanti non prenderanno/non prendessero/non avessero preso
bustarelle, sarà/sarebbe/sarebbe stata [una cosa] sorprendente. 20) Se
dobbiamo/dovessimo/avessimo dovuto pagare presto le tasse, siamo/saremo
/saremmo stati nei guai. 21) Se i soldati si rifiuteranno/si rifiutassero/si
fossero rifiutati di partire per la guerra, il mondo sarà/sarebbe/sarebbe stato
finalmente felice. 22) Se non prendiamo/non prenderemo/non prendessimo
(non avessimo preso l'autostrada, il viaggio è/sarà/sarebbe/sarebbe stato più
lungo. 23) Se la sua politica è/fosse/fosse stata così stupida, non votiamo/
non voteremmo/non avremmo votato per lui. 24) Se devo/dovessi/avessi
dovuto dimagrire, tento/tenterei/avrei tentato. 25) Se non devo/non dovessi
/non avessi dovuto fare i lavori di casa, gioco/giocherei/avrei giocato con i
bambini. 26) Se non riesce (riesci, riuscite)/non riuscisse (riuscissi, riusciste)/
non fosse riuscito (fossi riuscito, foste riusciti), L'aiuto (ti aiuto, vi aiuto)/La
(ti, vi) aiuterei/L'avrei aiutata (ti avrei aiutato, vi avrei aiutati). 27) Se
aumenteranno/aumentassero/avessero aumentato i prezzi, perderanno/
perderebbero/avrebbero perso un sacco di soldi. 28) Se i poliziotti potranno/
potessero/avessero potuto prendere il malvivente, lo metteranno/lo
metterebbero/l'avrebbero messo in prigione.

Lezione 32, pagina 169
1) Sta cucinando il pasto da stamattina. 2) Lui diceva tante fesserie che lei
è uscita. 3) Lui sussurrava mentre io parlavo a voce alta. 4) Il braccio mi
ha fatto male tutto il giorno. 5) Ora mi lavo e mi vesto per uscire. 6) E'
vissuta dieci anni a Nuova York quando era giovane ed ora vive a Roma da
due anni. 7) Si rende conto (ti rendi conto, vi rendete conto) quanto sono
stupidi! 8) Non mi ricordavo il suo nome. 9) La pubblicità commerciale
era così brutta [literally: cattiva] ieri che ho spento la televisione.
10) Vendono al minuto da Natale. 11) Fabbrichiamo computers da molto

tempo. 12) Ho bisogno di sapere se può (puoi, potete) venire. 13) Devo dirLe (dirti, dirvi) qualche cosa d'importante. 14) Avrebbe (avresti, avreste) dovuto riparare la macchina ieri. Non ascolta (non ascolti, non ascoltate) mai quando Le (ti, vi) dico che dovrebbe (dovresti, dovreste) ripararla. 15) Non ho dovuto farlo per oggi. Devo farlo per domani. 16) Stavano avviando l'affare quando i poliziotti sono entrati. 17) Non deve (devi, dovete) lavare questo maglione. 18) Non sono abituato a mangiare il cibo italiano. 19) Avrebbe (avresti, avreste) dovuto telefonarmi per dire che era (eri, eravate) nei guai. 20) Non sapeva che cosa fare, così gli ho detto di andare dal capufficio. 21) Se Lei fosse (tu) fossi suo amico, sarebbe (saresti) abituato al fatto che beve tanto. 22) Come sei tonto! Non avresti dovuto credergli! 23) Non lo sopportavo, e non capisco perchè va matta per lui. 24) Ha (hai) ascoltato la loro stupida conversazione? 25) Stava per andare in pensione quando sua moglie si è ammalata. 26) Non sono tenuto ad aiutarLa (aiutarti, aiutarvi) poichè Lei non mi ha aiutato (tu non mi hai aiutato, voi non mi avete aiutato) quando ne avevo bisogno.

Lezione 32, pagina 170
1) Sono fidanzati da Natale. Pensa (pensi, pensate) che si sposeranno presto?
2) Io ridevo mentre Lei mi prendeva (tu mi prendevi, voi mi prenderate) in giro.
3) Dovrebbe (dovresti, dovreste) farle un regalo per il compleanno, e avrebbe (avresti, avreste) dovuto fargliene uno l'anno scorso. 4) Sto tentando da due ore di avere la comunicazione con quel dannato tipo. 5) Non [me] l'aspettavo, ma non mi sorprende. 6) Non vedo nessuno e non sento niente. 7) Ho poca grana. Puoi imprestarmene un po'? 8) La nostra ditta fornisce computers alla fabbrica da molti anni. 9) Non ha capito niente. Non capisce mai niente. 10) Stavo divorziando quando lo ho incontrato. 11) Inganna la moglie da quando si sono sposati [literally: dal matrimonio]. 12) Deve (devi, dovete) ricuperare [il tempo perso], se non vuole (vuoi, volete) restare troppo indietro. 13) I malviventi stavano celebrando il furto quando i poliziotti sono entrati. 14) Non avrebbe (avresti, avreste) dovuto prendere quelle droghe. 15) Non posso aiutarLa (aiutarti, aiutarvi). Sono troppo stanco. 16) Picchia la moglie da quando è nato il bambino. 17) Da quanto tempo è incinta? 18) La gamba mi fa male dall'incidente. 19) La (ti, vi) disturbo se fumo mentre mangia (mangi, mangiate)? 20) Ho dovuto lasciare una grossa mancia. Anche Lei avrebbe dovuto (tu avresti dovuto, voi avreste dovuto) lasciar[ne] una. 21) Non potrei rimanere [literally: restare] onesto nella politica. Lei [lo] potrebbbe (tu [lo] potresti, voi [lo] potreste)? 22) La malavita à così potente [literally: forte] che abbiamo tutti paura. 23) Da quanto tempo siete sposati? 24) Sapevi che faceva all'amore con la segretaria mentre eri in viaggio? 25) Avrebbe (avresti, avreste) dovuto abituarsi (abituarti, abituarvi) ai suoi scherzi molto tempo fa. 26) Non deve (devi, dovete) portare il sapone. 27) Paghiamo forti tasse e ci roviniamo nello stesso tempo. 28) Avrebbe (avresti, avreste) dovuto dirmi prima che non sarebbe (non saresti) venuto (non sareste venuti).

Danger in the Dark . . .

. . . I ran, and it seemed like a mile to the edge of the pond, though it was just past the summer house. But down there at the end of the yard the dark was thick and different—I guess it was the fog that formed over the water. Not a bit of light came from anywhere, so I could barely see the pond. There was a wet, dank smell, and suddenly I thought about all of Edgar Allan Poe's tarns. That pond would have made a great tarn. Without any trouble at all, I could imagine dripping, decaying skeletons rising out of it. . . .

Was that a movement of some kind, over there where the edge of the pond had once caved in?

Was it—Miranda?

Even though she was afraid of the pond, as Eddie said, it might be that ghosts *had* to return and haunt the place where they died, whether they wanted to or not.

There was something moving, down there in the dark. . . .

Wylly Folk St. John

The Ghost Next Door

AN ARCHWAY PAPERBACK
Published by POCKET BOOKS • NEW YORK

An Archway Paperback published by
POCKET BOOKS, a Simon & Schuster division of
GULF & WESTERN CORPORATION
1230 Avenue of the Americas, New York, N.Y. 10020

Text copyright © 1971 by Wylly Folk St. John
Illustrations copyright © 1971 by Trina Schart Hyman

Published by arrangement with Harper & Row, Publishers, Inc.
Library of Congress Catalog Card Number: 71-157896

ISBN: 0-671-44290-2

First Pocket Books printing September, 1972

15   14   13   12   11   10   9

AN ARCHWAY PAPERBACK and colophon are trademarks
of Simon & Schuster.

Printed in the U.S.A.

IL 7+

This book, with love, is for
the real Lindsey and Eddie and Kirk
and Tammy and Sherry. *And Miranda.*

CONTENTS

1

SHE USED TO
LIVE HERE

I might never have gotten involved with the ghost next door if it hadn't been for Eddie and Kirk, my kid brothers. I don't know why I should feel responsible for those two, but I do. As my best friend Tammy says, blood is thicker than plasma. Her father, Dr. David Greenfield, is a professor at the medical college, so Tammy ought to know—even if he is a psychiatrist instead of a regular doctor.

Tammy and I are both going-on-thirteen, and we'd really be blondes if only our mothers would let us have a color rinse. Eddie's only nine, and Kirk's just six. We don't want them hanging around with us, but sometimes they do anyway.

We live on the edge of a small city in Georgia named Georgetown because George Washington visited here once. Our side of the block has just three houses. The Morrows—that's us—live in the middle one, between the old Alston place and the Greenfields'. We all have great big yards—everybody has around here—and the Greenfields have a tennis court, and Miss Judith Alston has a fish pond way off in the back, past her summer house.

The pond is deep out in the middle—and that's where Miss Judith's little niece Miranda got drowned, a long time ago. Ever since that time, Miss Judith has lived by herself. She's a tall, old-maid lady who believes in ESP and spiritualism and all that stuff, but she likes children—once she gets used to them—especially girls like us. For awhile after Miranda died Miss Judith couldn't stand the sight of a child, I heard Mama say once, because it hurt too much. Seeing any living child made her remember that Miranda wasn't. But that accident happened before I was born.

After we got to know Miss Judith pretty well, she showed Tammy and me the child's picture, which she kept on her piano. It was a tinted photo —Miranda's eyes looked kind of brown-green and her hair was dark brown and sort of floppy. She was only ten. Her chin was pointed and her cheeks were thin. Miss Judith said she was "a faery child," with "a pixie face."

Miss Judith told us how she tried to get in touch with Miranda through a spiritualist group she had joined a few months before—the Georgetown chapter of the American Psychic Society—but she'd had no luck.

"You believe in that stuff, Miss Judith?"

2

"Well, we don't really know, do we, Lindsey?" she said, sort of wistfully. "If there's the slightest possibility—well, there's no harm in trying—"

I don't believe in it myself, and neither does Tammy, but we didn't tell her that.

Miss Judith was sitting on the piano bench, and the fingers of one hand absent-mindedly picked out a hesitating little tune. Her house is an old-fashioned one with high ceilings, and the notes echoed and seemed to come back from somewhere, very softly.

"What's that you're playing, Miss Judith?" Tammy asked.

She stopped, but the echo went on for a minute. "Was I?" Miss Judith looked at her right hand as if it belonged to somebody else. "Yes, I guess I was. It's a piece called *The Dance of the Fireflies*. Miranda used to practice it over and over. She was going to play it in the recital—that summer."

I knew it wasn't polite to ask questions, but I was dying to know, and she seemed to be in a good mood, so I dared. "Miss Judith, how did Miranda happen to be living with you instead of with her own father and mother?" I had already asked Mama, but she said she'd have to tell me all about it when I got older. Tammy's folks moved here only five years ago, so she couldn't find out either. At least they said they didn't know. When

3

grown-ups say they don't know, you never can be sure whether it's the truth or not.

But Miss Judith told us. "Why, Lindsey, her father and mother were divorced, and she was supposed to live with her father. He is my younger brother, and they lived here in the old family home for several years, while he was connected with that space-research project across the river. He was working for the government, you know, so he had to be away a lot. Especially that spring."

"Yes'm," I said. "I know Dr. Alston is a very famous scientist—my Dad told us that he's a nuclear energy expert. But we've never met him."

"He never has been back," Miss Judith said, and her voice was sad. "He asked for a transfer to Houston. He couldn't bear to be here without Miranda, you see. There were so many things to remind him. And I . . ."

She sounded as if she were about to cry, so I hurried to say, "Her picture's nice, Miss Judith, and I bet she would have been great in the recital." And I almost thought I heard the music echoing again. But then I've been told I have a vivid imagination.

"Yes," Miss Judith said, blinking her eyes, and not crying after all. "She was very artistic—and sensitive. Her own mother was interested in psychic things; that's why I thought we might get some-

5

thing from The Other Side—it's really why I joined the Psychic Society.

"Miranda would have been some kind of creative artist when she grew up, I'm sure. She used to like to help me make unusual things. She would say, 'We're good makers, aren't we?'"

"What did you make?" Tammy asked with interest.

"Well, let's see. We made strange-colored flowers —did you know a daisy will turn green if you put it in green food coloring and leave it awhile to draw the color up its stem? We made a blue rose out of a white one, too. And Queen Anne's lace— that was the prettiest of all, when we turned it all sorts of colors."

"That's neat. I'd like to try it," Tammy said. "Mother's got some food coloring, and the Queen Anne's lace is about to bloom right now."

"Be sure to cut the stem above the joint, or through the joint," Miss Judith warned, "or it'll be hard for the color to get through—and once we made a birdbath out of pretty-colored bits of broken glass and china, set like a mosaic pattern into cement. I wonder what became of that birdbath. And—oh, yes—the cement owl. I never did find the cement owl." She began to laugh a little, the kind of laugh that's nearly crying. "I haven't thought of that owl for a long time," she went on. "Miranda wanted to make an owl, she said, 'with love in its

6

eyes.' So we did. But she hid it somewhere—and it's still hidden. That was so many years ago! I wish I could find it."

"How did she make love show in its eyes?"

"I'll tell you," Miss Judith said, standing up, so we knew it was time to go, "if you can find the owl for me. It's somewhere out in the yard. She said she discovered the right place for it, out there, a secret place. She was teasing—she said she was going to show me, as a surprise on my birthday, but—well, you girls might look for it, when you have some spare time. But be careful about snakes. Pledge cuts the grass in the front yard all right, but he hasn't weeded the edges of the yard or down there in the back for a long time. He has so many yards to take care of, I'm lucky, I guess, that he even cuts the grass in the front for me."

"Yes'm," I said. "We'll look for the owl, because I sure want to know how you made it show love in its eyes."

"Well, I'll tell you this much." Miss Judith was almost smiling again as she went to the door with us. "We used clear amber glass marbles. She called it 'the owl with the golden eyes.'"

We hunted for the owl a long time, that summer, but we never found it. Now it was another summer, and we were surprised when we were visiting Miss Judith one day to see that the picture of Miranda wasn't on the piano.

Miss Judith saw us looking puzzled and said, "I was intending to ask you girls—please don't mention Miranda while my brother and his family are here. They're coming for a visit. It's the first time since—"

"We won't," I said. "But why?"

"It is a strange request," Miss Judith agreed in her formal way. "Of course my brother's second wife knows he was married before, but he never could bring himself to tell her and their child, Sherry, about Miranda. Miranda's death hurt him so much. He blamed himself for leaving her, just as I blamed myself for . . . It hurt him so much that he has tried not to think about it ever since, tried to put it out of his mind entirely. And maybe he succeeded; maybe it's a kind of emotional block. Do you know what that is?"

"No'm," I said, but Tammy said "Yes'm," because she reads her father's psychiatry and medical books, and she told me about emotional blocks later. It's like having a blank space where you used to be able to think about something before your feelings got all mixed up.

"Anyway," Miss Judith said, "he can't bear to talk about Miranda, so it's best not to mention her. If you told Sherry, she'd be asking questions. And Dr. Alston might go to pieces if he had to explain about Miranda now, after all these years, when he's only just been able to bring himself to visit his old home again."

"Okay, Miss Judith, we understand," I said, and Tammy nodded. "How old is Sherry?"

"Why," Miss Judith said, as if she were counting it up and it surprised her, because that was the age Miranda had been, "I believe she must be— ten." Too young for us.

But not for my kid brothers. Eddie and Kirk went over to Miss Judith's right after Dr. and Mrs. William Alston and Sherry got there. The boys were invited to stay and make friends with Sherry, and they did. From then on, those two were always hanging around with Sherry.

She seemed like a nice little girl, Tammy and I agreed when we met her. But I wondered how Miss Judith—or Dr. Alston either—could bear it; she looked exactly like Miranda in the picture. The same pale, heart-shaped face and dark hair and greenish eyes and pointed chin. She was skinny and wore droopy shorts, but when you're ten you have to wear what your mother buys for you, and lots of mothers don't like to buy tight shorts— they've got a thing about pants being "comfortable."

It was several days before we really began to wonder about Sherry. Miss Judith and Mrs. Alston were sitting on the terrace under the big magnolia tree. Tammy and I were tired of playing records in my room, so we went over to talk to them. Eddie and Kirk had gone to the dentist with Mama—Eddie needs braces the worst way, and Kirk's second front tooth was coming in crooked—so for once they weren't around. Miss Judith asked us to sit down and gave us each a glass of lemonade. It tasted wonderful. Tall frosted glasses of lemonade are the greatest on a hot day.

"Where's Sherry?" Tammy asked, not really caring, just being polite.

"Oh, she's around somewhere," her mother said. She called, "Sherry! Come in, please—you've got company."

"Oh, don't bother her, if she's out playing," Tammy said, in her older-girl voice, and I giggled, because after all she was only two years older than Sherry. She was trying on her adult manners.

Sherry came prancing up on a make-believe horse and hitched it elaborately at the other end of the terrace. I thought—she must be retarded or something. Even Eddie has given up riding horses that aren't there.

Miss Judith thought so too. "Isn't she a little old for that sort of thing?" she asked Sherry's mother.

"Oh, she's just reminding me that a real horse is what she wants more than anything in the world," Mrs. Alston said, laughing. "She lets us know, every chance she gets. And if I'm not careful, her father will give it to her. He gives in to her too much for her own good. He's so sensible about

most things—I can't understand why he's so indul-
gent with Sherry."

"I wish she liked me," Miss Judith murmured.
"I wish she would just come and put her arms
around me or kiss me or something, the way—"

"The way what?" Mrs. Alston asked.

"The way some children do. They usually like
me." She smiled at Tammy and me, and we smiled
back, to let her know we understood.

"Oh, Sherry likes you," Mrs. Alston told Miss
Judith. "She's just engrossed in a game she's playing, that's all. In a little while she'll be all over
you—you'll see."

"That old whip—I wonder where she found
that?" Miss Judith said, and she looked agitated.
Sherry had a whip in her hand, the kind we used
to get at carnivals, with red and black braided
around the handle. But it was so old you could
hardly see the color anymore. "What kind of a
game is it?"

"Oh, she's a typical only child. She made up an
imaginary playmate, that's all. The child psycholo-
gists call it compensation. She hasn't any brothers
or sisters; so she makes up a companion to play
with. That's why she doesn't need you—or me—
right now."

"She has Eddie and Kirk," I said. "Eddie had
an imaginary thing once. He called it Bird Dog.
It was an invisible dog that could fly like a bird.

11

But Eddie was a lot smaller than Sherry then. And when Kirk got big enough to play with him, Eddie let Bird Dog go."

"It is a bit odd," Mrs. Alston agreed, "that she should just now be finding this imaginary child, when she has some real playmates next door. The way she talks, sometimes I think she believes this little girl is real."

Sherry looked back toward the thickest shrubbery, where a child could be hiding, and said over her shoulder as she came toward us, " 'Bye. See you tomorrow. Eddie and Kirk will be back then."

Miss Judith poured her a glass of lemonade, Tammy and I said "Hi," and Mrs. Alston said in that sickening voice grown-ups use when they try to pretend along with a child, "Where does your little friend live, honey?"

Sherry didn't have any make-believe at all in her voice. She took a sip of the lemonade, said "Hello," sort of shyly in the direction of Tammy and me, and answered matter-of-factly, "I don't know. She says she doesn't have any real home right now. Her father got a divorce from her mother. He got custody-of-the-child, but—what's custody-of-the-child, Mom?"

"It means she is supposed to live with her father, dear."

Miss Judith held out a hand to Sherry, but Sherry came over and sat on the coping next to me,

12

nstead. "Did you ever have a horse? Did Eddie?"
she asked. "I want a horse of my own."

"No," I told her. "And I don't think I want one.
It would be a lot of trouble to take care of."

"I'd love taking care of a horse."

Miss Judith said to Sherry, "What have you been
playing, dear?"

She drew marks with the whip on the ground.
"Oh, nothing. Just playing. In our Hideout."

That word did something to Miss Judith. She
gasped, "Hideout!" and dropped her lemonade
glass. It broke on the pretty, mossy old bricks that
paved the terrace, and wasted every bit of the
lemonade.

Mrs. Alston said, "What's the matter, Judith?
Are you sick? You look as if you'd seen a ghost."

Right then something like a cold finger began
to move up my spine, though it was a hot day.

Miss Judith said to Sherry, trying to speak calmly,
"You mean, under the fig tree?" and it sounded
as if she already knew.

Sherry said impatiently, "Of course. You know
how the branches come down almost to the ground
and the big leaves make a Hideout."

"Why do you call it that, Sherry?" Miss Judith
was holding her hands together so tight the knuckles
were white.

"Why, because that's what it is. Our Hideout.
We haven't let Eddie and Kirk in on it yet, but we

13

might tomorrow." She had a bland, innocent look on her face, as if she were putting somebody on, and I thought it was Miss Judith.

Poor Miss Judith didn't even try to pick up the broken glass. Tammy started to do it, but I was frozen by what was going on between Sherry and her aunt.

Miss Judith said urgently, "Sherry. Do you—does she—have a black horse tied outside the Hideout? A black horse named Nightmare?"

"Why, Aunt Judith! How did you know?" Sherry said delightedly. She went over to Miss Judith then and leaned against her shoulder, smiling up at her confidingly. The cold finger went on up my neck and made my hair prickle. "Mom," Sherry said, looking across at Mrs. Alston, "can't I please have a black horse named Nightmare for my birthday?" Her bangs were too long and she looked like a witch-child, glancing up from under them.

"What's this all about?" Mrs. Alston asked Miss Judith.

"Nothing." Miss Judith tried to pass it off, but Sherry knew. She knew something. "I'm just playing Sherry's game with her."

"Well, that's the way to win her over, all right; play games with her," Mrs. Alston said.

"Sherry," Miss Judith said, very quietly. "Sherry, what's your little friend's name?"

"I don't know, Aunt Judith. She hasn't told me her name yet."

"Where did you find that old whip, child? It's all right—you can have it—but where did you find it?"

"Oh, she knew where it was. She knows where everything is, Aunt Judith. She used to live here."

2

SOMETHING IN
MISS JUDITH'S ROOM

Miss Judith has plenty of self-control—I'll say that for her. She just closed her hands tighter. After a minute she said, "Excuse me, please," and got up and went in the house. So of course Tammy and I left.

Back in my room, we lay across the bed on our stomachs with our feet in the air, the way we usually do, and talked. "Do you think she really plays with Miranda?" I asked.

"Of course not." Tammy didn't believe in ghosts, and neither did I—but I wanted to. I'd have given anything to see a ghost.

"Then how come she knew—?"

"I don't know, but I think it might have something to do with that bunch of psychic nuts Miss Judith fools around with—the ones who have séances."

"Why do you think that?"

"I don't know," Tammy said again, thoughtfully.

"Except I saw that president or whatever he is, of the club—you know, old Mr. Carson Farrar—talking to Sherry yesterday."

"Well, he lives just across the street. He's a public relations man and I guess kids are some of the public. He talks to us sometimes, too."

"I know, but we get away from him as soon as we can."

"Right," I said. Dad told me public relations men are supposed to make everybody like some special things or companies or people, but I've never even liked Mr. Farrar himself. And it isn't because of the séances, either. It's because of last summer.

Mr. Farrar has office hours whenever he wants to; so he has time to run the Little League in this neighborhood. He kept promising Eddie that he could play in a game, and even gave him a uniform. Eddie kept going out there to practice every afternoon, and picked up the bats after the others hit the ball. The last game of all, when Eddie was so sure Mr. Farrar was going to keep his promise and let him play at least once, our whole family went out there to the field behind the clubhouse because Eddie wanted us to see him hit a home run.

But he didn't get to play at all. Mr. Farrar doesn't seem to have any feelings. He didn't even give Eddie a reason. Just said, "Too bad, Eddie. Maybe next year." He hasn't any kids of his own

—that's why he has time to belong to so many things. If he had kids maybe he'd have known enough to keep his promise, or else not make it. You just don't disappoint a little kid.

Dad told Eddie we have to be good sports about things like that, but Eddie didn't go out for Little League this summer, and I don't blame him.

Mrs. Farrar is okay, though. Even if she does go to the séances too.

"Do you suppose Mr. Farrar told Sherry about Miranda?" I asked.

"Well, Mother says the Farrars have lived here on this street since the year one; he'd have known Miranda was drowned. Sherry wouldn't have known unless somebody told her."

"But he couldn't possibly have known where Miranda hid that old whip that Sherry found. And I doubt that Miranda ever told Mr. Farrar about the Hideout or Nightmare. So it looks as if Sherry has got to be in communication with her, as they say at the séances."

"How do you know what they say?"

"I've been reading up on psychic societies."

We have lots of old books about all kinds of things—they used to belong to my grandparents. We also have a big encyclopedia in twenty volumes that a man sold Mama once, but we don't mention that very often.

"Tell me more," Tammy said admiringly.

18

"Well, nobody who has any feelings at all is ever going to remind Miranda's family about her getting drowned. It would be cruel. I don't believe even Mr. Farrar would be mean enough to fake anything like that at a séance to fool Miss Judith. So what was he doing talking to Sherry?"

"Maybe he ought to be appointed a Stranger for life," Tammy said. "One of those Strangers kids aren't supposed to talk to. We could warn her against him."

"Wouldn't do any good now. She's already met him, and knows he's a neighbor; even a dimwit like Sherry would catch on he's not really a Stranger."

"She's not actually a dimwit," Tammy objected. "She might be very bright. A genius. Sometimes they're hard to tell apart, Daddy says."

"Well, I'll ask Eddie what Mr. Farrar and Sherry were talking about."

As soon as he got back from the dentist's, Eddie showed us his new braces, and then remembered he had to feed his rabbits; so we went out in the yard with him and Kirk. The rabbits are named Brer Rabbit and Mrs. Brer, but Eddie got stubborn and wouldn't name the babies Flopsy and Mopsy and Cottontail and Peter as I suggested. He calls them One and Two and Three and Four, because he says there are going to be so many he doesn't want the names to ever run out, and numbers don't. Mark, the boy who gave the rabbits to Eddie because his mother got tired of so many of them, told Eddie to expect some baby rabbits every six weeks.

Eddie is looking forward to having a whole bunch of rabbits, but Mama isn't. And Dad makes Eddie clean out the cages every single day, or else they'll stink. The father rabbit has to be kept in a separate cage when the babies are little, or he'll kill them.

Eddie said he had no idea what Mr. Farrar was talking to Sherry about, but that Sherry had found the whip under the edge of the summer house, in a hiding place that somebody had dug out behind the foundation—which was about to cave in. Sherry fell into the hole—that was how she found the whip. "She found a bunch of other things, too," he said.

"Such as?"

"Oh, some bricks, and an old pot and spoon, and some nickels and dimes and pennies in a baking powder can—we spent those when the ice cream man came around—and some old beat-up books in a tin box, and a rubber ball that wouldn't bounce. And a lot of other old stuff."

"Did she find a cement owl with golden eyes?" I asked excitedly.

"Heck, no. What do you mean, owl with gold eyes? Owls have black eyes—I think."

"Miss Judith told us about a cement owl that got lost," Tammy explained in her talking-down-to-little-brothers voice. She hasn't got any little brothers, or she wouldn't think she could get away with that. "It had yellow glass marbles for eyes. We just wondered if Sherry had found it."

"Oh, you just wondered," Eddie mimicked. "Well, if she had, I wouldn't tell you about it." But I knew Sherry hadn't, from the way Eddie looked.

I gave Tammy the high sign and we started to leave Eddie and Kirk to the rabbits. "Don't forget their fresh water," I reminded him.

"They're my rabbits," Eddie said. "As long as they drink it, who cares if it's fresh or not? Maybe rabbits like old water best. Water doesn't wear out, since you know so much."

"I know they'll die if you don't give them fresh water every day," I said.

"Kirk's supposed to change the water anyhow," Eddie said. "I told him I'd give him Five and Six if he would."

"Kirk's too little to have all that responsibility. And besides, Five and Six aren't even born yet."

"I am not either too little," Kirk said. He was getting the water pans out as Tammy and I left.

Tammy had to go home for supper, but she said she'd call me later to see if I had dug any more out of Eddie.

I was trying to get Eddie to talk about Sherry at supper, but somehow the conversation got off the subject. It was when Eddie said, "I don't want any cauliflower," and Mama said, "Why?" and Eddie said, "Because a head of cauliflower looks like somebody's brains." Well, it actually does, when you come to think about it.

Dad said, "Where did you see somebody's brains?" and Eddie said, "In Dr. Greenfield's garbage can," and Mama said, "Excuse me," and left the table in a hurry. She's going to have a baby in January, and her stomach gets upset at the least little thing.

"What were you doing in Dr. Greenfield's gar-

bage can?" Dad said, which didn't seem to me to be the most important thing to find out right then, but Eddie cleared it up when he called after Mama, "You don't have to throw up, Mama. It wasn't real brains." He told Dad, "It was a model of brains that Dr. Greenfield used for teaching students at the college. He bought a new model, so I asked him if I could have it and he said yes. I stuck it in my closet. Maybe I better tell Mama where it is, just in case."

"That would be a good idea," Dad said. "But you aren't supposed to go scrounging around in the neighbors' garbage cans, Eddie."

"They don't mind," Eddie said. "They throw away some real good stuff sometimes."

Mama came back and said sternly, "Leave the garbage cans alone after this, Eddie!" So he didn't tell her what he found in Mr. Farrar's. It was a mouse that wasn't quite dead. Mr. Farrar lets his cat, Old Smokey, play with the mice he catches, until they're nearly dead, and sometimes he doesn't bother to put them out of their misery when he throws them in the garbage can. I just can't help not liking Mr. Farrar. Eddie put that mouse out of its misery, though, very humanely, and gave it a nice funeral.

After supper I tried to bribe Eddie to tell me more about what he and Kirk did when they were over at the Alstons' playing with Sherry, but he clammed up. I had to report "no luck" when Tammy called.

She had some real news. "Guess what?" she said. "A real live medium is coming to stay with the Farrars next week—a famous one, Daddy says. She's going to talk to the Psychic Society, and they're going to have a séance—at our house!"

"But your folks don't belong to the Society," I said. "I never thought your dad would have anything to do with ghosts."

"Silly, he's going to try to prove there's nothing to it. He says if they can show him any scientific evidence of survival after death, he wants to see it. He says he has an open mind on parapsychology and psychic phenomena, but he's extremely skeptical. Those were his very words, Lindsey."

"So how come they're going to let him show them up?"

"Well, he's sort of got Mr. Farrar in a corner, offering to have the séance at our house so there couldn't be any suggestion of fakery, he said, so the whole thing would be done in a scientific manner. This lady medium is coming next week and we'll get to see her in the flesh—Daddy says in lots of flesh. I guess she must be pretty fat."

"Hey, did your dad tell you all this, or did you—?"

"I listened," Tammy admitted. Well, there are times when you have to eavesdrop or you'll never

now anything about anyone. "But he did talk
out it some at supper too," she added.

"What's the medium's name?" I felt kind of
xcited myself, at the idea of seeing a real live
edium, after what I had read about séances and
ediums in those old books.

"Her name's Dame Pythia Wilks, and she's
rom England, where they have a lot more psychic
ocieties than we do here. And there are witches'
ovens and all that kind of stuff, Daddy says. A
oven is a bunch of witches that get together every
ow and then, like a club meeting, and sing hymns
ackwards and put spells on people they don't like,
nd such junk."

When I went over to Tammy's next day, she
aid we'd ask her father some more about Dame
ythia. He was at home because it was one of his
esearch days instead of a teaching day.

Dr. Greenfield said she had a control named
Kleeman who, when he was alive, was supposed to
ave been a World War II German soldier who
earned his English in an American prisoner-of-
var camp.

"What's a control?" Tammy asked.

"A medium," he said, looking at us over the top
of his glasses, "can't talk directly to her audience.
She's supposed to be in a trance. Her body is theo-
retically taken over by the spirit of the control—in

25

this case, Kleeman—who then communicates me
sages from the dead in the spirit world to the pe
ple who are in the room."

I already knew that, but Tammy looked doul
ful.

Dr. Greenfield went on, "If my guess is rigl
Dame Pythia lives on publicity. Her reputati
depends on her communications being apparent
true, things people who are present at a séance c
recognize because of some trivial detail they thi
nobody knows about except the dead person."

"But fake mediums find out ahead of tin
everything they can," I said, "about all the peop
who are going to be at the séance. And the peop
are fooled into thinking it's their dead relatives—

"Well, Lindsey, you seem to know a bit abo
fraudulent mediums," Dr. Greenfield said, smilin

"I've been doing research," I told him. "C
course, Dame Pythia might not be. Fraudulent,
mean. She and Kleeman might be okay."

"That's what we'd like to find out, isn't it?" D
Greenfield said. "Because apparently she's coun
ing on a lot of publicity here. You see, Dr. Alsto
is a very famous man, and if she could convinc
him that she can put him in touch with Mirand
—well, it would mean top publicity for Dam
Pythia Wilks all over the English-speaking world.

"You mean she'd actually try to—oh, poor Mis
Judith!" I said, horrified. "That's the cruelest thin

26

ever heard of. And it's just like Mr. Farrar. I
bet it was his idea. He probably told Dame Pythia
about Miranda just so she'd come here."

"Why do you say that, Lindsey?" Dr. Greenfield asked. He looked at me like a psychiatrist,
which he is.

"Because Mr. Farrar does things like—well, he
doesn't mind if kids suffer. Or mice."

"Hmmmm." Dr. Greenfield's eyebrows went up.
"Of course, some of these psychic characters have
hypnotized themselves into believing that they're
doing the living a favor by putting them in touch
with their dead loved ones. Maybe even that they're
giving the grieving survivors some comfort.

"But I happen to have heard rumors that Mr.
Farrar is helping Dame Pythia write a book about
her communications from the dead. So I'm even
more skeptical in this case than usual. Naturally
they'd both want all the publicity they can get, to
make it a best seller, and I'm curious to see how far
they'll go to get it."

"I bet that Mr. Farrar was talking to Sherry
just to get some background on the family for
Dame Pythia to use," Tammy said.

It was a good guess, but I thought she was
wrong. "He probably knows more about Miranda
than Sherry does. He was here when it happened,
remember?"

"But he doesn't know as much about Dr. Alston

27

as Sherry does," Tammy pointed out. "Maybe he doesn't even know what kind of a doctor Dr Alston is. I don't. He's not a doctor like you Daddy."

"No—he's a Ph.D. A Doctor of Philosophy. His specialty is physics," Dr. Greenfield said.

"Even though Sherry may not know who Miranda is, exactly," I said, "she does know about the whip and the horse named Nightmare and the Hideout. She might tell Mr. Farrar about those— if he were clever about it."

Dr. Greenfield wanted to know what I meant, so we told him about Miss Judith and Sherry's imaginary playmate. "Do you believe in ghosts, Dr. Greenfield?" I asked him.

"In a way I do," he said seriously. "The dead do come back to haunt the living—but only in their minds. In their memories. In their dreams. In their guilts. It doesn't seem likely, though, that Sherry could be troubled by Miranda, that way. She didn't have any knowledge of Miranda when she came here?"

"Miss Judith said Dr. Alston never told Mrs. Alston or Sherry about Miranda. And she asked us not to mention her, so of course we didn't."

Dr. Greenfield said thoughtfully, "I'd like to talk to that little girl."

"Are the Alstons coming to the séance?" Tammy asked.

"Not Sherry." Dr. Greenfield laughed. "Miss
Alston will be here, of course, since she belongs to
the group. And she will try to get Dr. Alston to
come, Mr. Farrar said. Mrs. Alston will be away
that weekend with her college roommate in Atlanta."

"Daddy—may we come?" Tammy begged. "Lind-
ey and I—we'd be quiet as—"

"No," Dr. Greenfield said definitely. "I'm sorry,
Tammy—this isn't a thing for children to get mixed
up in. And you two keep it quiet—don't tell your
friends, understand?"

We understood, and we didn't talk to anybody
about it. But we laid our plans to be there just the
same, even without permission.

I was going to spend the night with Tammy,
when they had the séance. Mama said I could,
and Mrs. Greenfield agreed, as usual. I guess she
thought it would keep Tammy up in her room and
out of the way, if I were spending the night—we
usually play records up there till after midnight.
Little did she know. Those records drop automatically; they're long-playing ones and you can put
on twelve at a time; she'd think we were playing
records.

The downstairs hall closet at Tammy's house
backs right up to the living room. It was built in
after the house was already finished, when somebody decided they needed another closet. So it has
only the one wall, a thin panel of knotty pine, be-

29

tween. When Tammy and I tried it out the nex
day while both her parents were away, there wa
plenty of room for us, as well as a lot of hats and
raincoats.

And not only that—those knotty pine board
had knots that were easy to dig out with Dr.
Greenfield's chisel, to make holes we could see
through. They wouldn't be noticed at all from the
living room, because that wall wasn't in direct
light and the holes looked just like the other knots.

But we had to wait nearly a whole week.

To keep ourselves occupied, we concentrated
on looking for the cement owl.

"Let's start in Miss Judith's summer house, because that's where Sherry found the whip," Tammy
said. "Let's go ask Miss Judith if we can. Dr.
Alston's gone out—his car's not in the drive. So
we won't be disturbing his thinking." Mrs. Greenfield had told her never to bother Dr. Alston.

Mrs. Alston let us in, and said Sherry was out
playing with Eddie and Kirk somewhere. When
we said we hadn't come to see Sherry, only to ask
Miss Judith something, Sherry's mother said, "She
just went up to her room," and called from the
foot of the stairs, "Judith! Lindsey and Tammy
want to speak to you a minute."

Miss Judith called down from the hall above,
"Let them come up," and we heard her opening
the door to go into her room as we started upstairs.

Then we heard Miss Judith scream.

It was a dreadful scream, as if she were frightened to death.

We ran up the stairs as fast as we could.

3

THE MYSTERY OF
THE BLUE ROSE

Miss Judith was lying on the floor, white and still and crumpled.

"Is she dead?" Tammy asked, her voice quavering.

I grabbed the hand-mirror from the dressing-table and held it under her nose, and it fogged a tiny bit. "No. She's only fainted."

Mrs. Alston arrived then and dashed back to get the ammonia; when she brought it we left the first-aid to her while we looked around to see what could have frightened Miss Judith.

The room looked perfectly normal. There were flowers in the vases, and the bed was made up. Her antique furniture looked real solid. There wasn't anything supernatural about the atmosphere. No sudden cold surrounded us. No dog bristled and growled at nothing. Miss Judith doesn't even have a dog.

But I heard what sounded like a door closing.

Maybe a door that wasn't there? A door that had been boarded up, long ago?

On the other hand, it might just have been somebody else in the house, innocently closing some other room's door. Nothing abnormal about that. Only there wasn't supposed to be anyone else in the house. Could Sherry have come back, without anybody noticing?

Then I saw what had made Miss Judith faint.

The flower in the bud vase on her bedside table was a bright blue rose.

Miss Judith was sitting up now, gasping from the liberal dose of ammonia. Mrs. Alston helped her to the rocking chair. "What in the world is the matter, Judith?" she asked. "Was it an intruder—or—?"

Miss Judith wasn't about to let on about the blue rose. But we knew she was thinking that Miranda's ghost had put it there.

"I—I don't know," she said at last, in a queer voice. "Where's William? I've got to talk to him—"

"You remember. He's gone across the river to see the people he knows at that laboratory where he used to work. He might even stay overnight. Do you want a doctor? Maybe Dr. Greenfield is at home."

"No, he's at the college," Tammy said. "This is one of his teaching days."

"I don't need a doctor," Miss Judith said, and

now some of the color had come back to her face.
"A doctor couldn't help me any."

I wished Mrs. Alston would go away so I could
ask Miss Judith if she really thought Miranda's
ghost had brought her a rose. And Mrs. Alston did
go away. I wonder if I have some extraordinary
power, to influence other people's actions just by
wishing? No, or it would work on Eddie and Kirk
too—they're the ones I do most of my wishing
about.

On her way out, Mrs. Alston said, "I'm going
to call and see if I can get William to come home.
I'm worried about you, Judith—you've been so
strange lately." And she went downstairs to the
telephone in the study and shut the door so Miss
Judith wouldn't hear what she told Dr. Alston.

I went and picked up the blue rose. It was a
real rose, just as real as one out of the garden—
except that a fine tracing of all the many tiny veins
on the petals brought an odd blue color to them
that no natural rose ever had. It even smelled like
a rose.

Miss Judith said faintly, "It's a rose like we used
to make, Miranda and I, with the food coloring—"

I stuck my finger into the vase and took it out
stained blue. "There's even food coloring in the
vase," I said. "Miss Judith, did you ever tell anybody—except Tammy and me—about how you and
Miranda made the flowers?"

"I don't think so," Miss Judith murmured. "But," she went on thoughtfully, "William knew about it at the time. I can remember Miranda showing him some green daisies once."

"You didn't tell Sherry, for instance?" I asked Miss Judith. "Tammy and I didn't tell anybody, of course."

"Why, no, Lindsey. I never thought of—you see, Sherry isn't—well, I just can't bear the idea of any other child taking Miranda's special place, doing Miranda's special things. Sherry has her own place in my heart. But it even hurts to let her have Miranda's room. Of course I had to—there wasn't another suitable room for the child. But I couldn't have her doing the things Miranda did with me, like coloring the flowers. I'm going to teach Sherry to knit, though."

"Don't tell her anything, Miss Judith," I cautioned earnestly. "She talks to Mr. Farrar, and—well, it would be better for Dr. Greenfield's scientific investigation of that séance if Mr. Farrar didn't know a thing about Miranda."

"You girls know about the séance?" Grown-ups amaze so easy.

"Yes, but they won't let us come."

Miss Judith said, "It really would be evidential, if Dame Pythia or her control could tell me something only Miranda and I knew—"

"In the books there's one theory," I told her,

"that it's done by thought transference, instead of communicating with dead people. So try not to even think about whatever it is that only you and Miranda knew, Miss Judith. Dame Pythia might be able to do mental telepathy and read your mind, even if she can't actually get through to The Other Side. Dr. Greenfield wants scientific evidence. The whole set-up might be phony—just to get publicity, and because Dame Pythia makes a good living out of those people who believe in her. Or it just might be real. Then you'd know for sure."

"Yes," Miss Judith said.

"We came over to ask you," Tammy said, "if we could search in your summer house for the owl. We didn't look there very hard, before."

"The owl? Oh, yes," Miss Judith said, still sounding far away. "Yes, do look for it. I wish you could find it." She seemed to come back to real things. "Be careful, though—that old well curb in the summer house has probably rotted, and if you fell into the well I'd never forgive myself. So don't go near the edge of the well, you hear?"

"Yes'm," we said. At our age, we do know better than to fall in a well.

Mrs. Alston came back then, so we felt it was all right to leave Miss Judith.

The summer house's openwork lattices were all overgrown with weeds and vines, mostly honeysuckle, which was blooming. The little cream-

colored trumpets smelled so sweet you could shut
your eyes and think you were in Heaven. I guess in
olden times when lots of Alstons lived in the house,
they sat out there on summer evenings watching
the fireflies, and the gardener kept the honeysuckle
trimmed and the brick floor swept, and when they
wanted a drink of cold water somebody drew up
a bucketful from the well. But now the bricks
were mossy and green and crumbling, and the
vines tripped you up, and the old wicker chairs
were falling apart. And Tammy and I were careful
to watch out for snakes.

It was sort of sad out there, as if the ghosts of
all the dead Alstons were watching us and wishing the summer house was like it used to be. I bet
they played croquet, too, on the lawn in front of
it, and the ladies' skirts were long and touched
the grass.

We found the hidey-hole where Sherry had gotten the whip and stuff, and we dug it out further,
but there wasn't anything else in that spot. Just as
we were giving up we heard noises outside, and
there were Sherry and Eddie and Kirk.

"What are you doing?" Eddie wanted to know.

"Yep, what are you doing?" Kirk echoed. He
usually did.

"Nothing." We made it a rule to tell them as
little as possible about our activities.

"I know what they're doing," Sherry said. "They're

looking for the owl with the golden eyes. Aren't you?" she asked Tammy. "It's not here. I already looked."

"We looked, too," Eddie said.

"Yep," Kirk said.

I asked her, "Where did you look?"

"Doncha wish you knew?" Eddie said.

"Doncha?" said Kirk.

And Sherry said, "She didn't tell me where she hid it."

"You mean the kid you said used to live here?" I was careful not to give away anything that she hadn't already revealed.

Sherry nodded. She moved over toward the edge of the well, with Eddie and Kirk behind her.

"Don't!" I said. "Don't go close to the edge. The curb is crumbly!"

"Oh, it's all right," Sherry said. "She said it was okay. She plays right by the well. You know I wouldn't let Eddie and Kirk get hurt."

I grabbed her arm and pulled her back. "You better stay away from that well. And, Eddie and Kirk, that's an order." That's what Dad always says when he really means it.

Sherry looked at me from under those long bangs of hers as if she was trying to decide whether or not to jump in the well just to spite me. Then she shrugged and skipped away, saying to the boys, "Let's go see if she's in the Hideout."

When they had gone I asked Tammy, "What do you think? Is she putting us on?"

"Hard to tell," Tammy said. "She's got the boys wrapped around her little finger, all right. They believe everything she says."

"I wonder if she was born with six fingers? I've heard if you're born with six fingers on each hand it means you can see things other people can't. Or is that if you were born with a caul? Maybe the six fingers are for witch babies. She could be a changeling. Sometimes she looks like a witch's child instead of Mrs. Alston's."

We agreed that probably Sherry was born with a caul as well as six fingers on each hand.

"Let's ask Miss Judith," Tammy said.

"Okay, but not right now. I don't think we ought to bother Miss Judith any more today, do you? She was so shook up about the flower. Tammy, how are we going to solve the mystery of that blue rose?"

"Well, it wasn't a ghost rose, that's for sure."

"Maybe Miranda's ghost went into the kitchen and got the food coloring and fixed the rose."

"Maybe Sherry went into the kitchen and got it." Tammy was just as skeptical as Dr. Greenfield was.

"But why would Sherry want to scare Miss Judith like that?"

"She might be just a mischievous kid," Tammy

40

surmised. "Or, as Daddy would probably say, she might be trying to get some attention for herself."

"But Miss Judith didn't tell Sherry about the flowers they used to dye. If it's Miranda who's come back, now, she already knows—and she might have done it because she loves Miss Judith still, and wanted to give her a flower like they made a long time ago. Not to scare her. Or—she might have told Sherry how they did it—and maybe Sherry fixed a blue rose because she thought it would make Miss Judith love her the way she did Miranda. It's sort of sad, if Sherry's feeling left out because she found out about how they loved Miranda—and Miranda's feeling left out because Sherry's here in her place."

"Lindsey, you sound as if you really believe in Miranda's ghost. Like you think she's really around here and Sherry really sees her."

"I don't know whether I believe it or not," I admitted. "But there are lots of things even scientists haven't found out about yet. Ghosts might be one of them. Well, I don't think we're going to find the cement owl here, do you?"

"The next most likely place she might have buried it is the Hideout," Tammy said.

"But they're playing there."

"Well, tomorrow we'll ask Miss Judith if we can dig around that fig tree."

I don't especially like hard digging. "Why don't

41

we get Eddie and Kirk and Sherry to do the digging?" I suggested. "If we tell them we've figured out that it's buried in a certain spot, like treasure, they'd dig to China."

"You could be right. We'll let them do the hard work."

They weren't in the Hideout, though, and when we went hunting for them all over the yard we couldn't find them. Once we thought we heard them giggling behind the shrubbery beside the terrace, but nobody was there when we looked. Not even a transparent Miranda.

It was nearly dark when we came around the house and found them playing on the terrace, throwing a dirty old ball back and forth. They hadn't been there five minutes before.

"Where've you been? We were looking for you," I said.

"Nowhere." That way Sherry had of looking up slantways was catching; Eddie was doing it too, now, and of course Kirk copied everything Eddie did. "Just playing. She knew where this ball was, of course," Sherry said vaguely.

"Yep," Kirk said.

"Look, Sherry." I got in front of her to look her straight in the eyes, and the ball Kirk threw hit me in the back and rolled off into the shrubbery. "Don't you know her name yet?"

She smiled at me and ran after the ball. "Oh,

42

sure, I know her name now. C'mon, Eddie and Kirk!" and they ran away across the lawn. Elusive —I think that's the word for her. Or is it evasive? I'll have to look it up.

That night I cornered Eddie in the boys' room and offered him my old chemistry set if he'd tell me the name of Sherry's imaginary friend, but he wouldn't.

"I don't know what her name is," he admitted at last. "Sherry knows, though. She hasn't told us yet."

"Eddie, you don't ever see this—this kid, do you?"

"No. She's in—invisible. You know, like Bird Dog. But Sherry sees her. I used to see Bird Dog, but the rest of you couldn't. Remember?"

"I remember all right," I said sternly. "I remember you *said* you saw him. Eddie, you're too old to believe in that stuff now. Sherry's just putting you on."

"No, she's not. Sherry really does know her. Or else how could she find things her friend used to play with when she lived there?"

"Oh, Sherry just happened to find them. Anybody might happen to. They'd been lying around all those years when no children were there to be curious, that's all. If Sherry really talks to her and gets answers, how come she can't find the cement owl with the golden eyes? Why doesn't Mir—that invisible kid—tell her where she hid that?"

"I bet she will tomorrow," Eddie said hopefully, "and then if I find out her name you'll give me the chemistry set."

"Yep," Kirk said sleepily from his bunk.

"Tammy and I thought the owl might be buried under the fig tree," I said casually. "In the Hideout. You know, when Sherry's friend was playing buried treasure, all those years ago."

"It might!" Eddie said, taking the bait. "I'll tell Sherry. We'll dig all around there, tomorrow."

And we'll watch you, I thought.

"Good idea. You do have pretty good ideas sometimes, Eddie."

I gave him the chemistry set anyway; I didn't have any use for it and I needed the space in the closet. " 'Night, Eddie. 'Night, Kirk."

Then I saw what he had taken out of his pocket and put with the little bottles in the chemistry set, and I gasped.

"Eddie! Where did you get that?"

"Get what?"

"That bottle you just added to the chemistry set."

"Oh, that? I found it. Well, I—you won't tell? Mama'd kill me. Well, I got it out of the Alstons' garbage can."

It was a little square bottle that blue food coloring comes in. There was some of it still around the sides.

I grabbed it. "I'll bring it back," I promised. "I've got to show it to Miss Judith—" and I ran out before he could object.

I slipped out the back door because Mama might have thought it was too late to go visiting, and hurried over to the Alstons'. They were sitting on the front porch. Dr. Alston wasn't back yet, I guessed, because his car wasn't in the drive, and Sherry was just starting to go to bed.

I probably should have broken the news more gently, but I was so excited I just burst out, "Look, Miss Judith, what Eddie found in your garbage can!" and I held out the blue bottle. "Somebody," I panted, "knew about the food coloring and all—"

The porch light was on, and she could see what it was. It shook her up, all right. She put her hand up to her heart, and I for one wished Dr. Alston would hurry up and come back. She needed somebody to talk to, and she couldn't tell Mrs. Alston what was the matter.

Sherry laughed, and it was a thin silvery sound. She whirled around and around in her nightgown, and I thought about elves and fairies and changelings. "Oh, did you find it?" she asked Miss Judith. "Did you find—the blue rose?"

"Child—Sherry—did you—?"

"I made it for you," she said, and her voice was innocent.

"You made it?"

"She told me how."

I shivered. So did Miss Judith—or she was trembling, anyhow.

Sherry whirled over and kissed her mother, then went and kissed Miss Judith's cheek. " 'Night, Mom, 'Night, Aunt Judith."

Miss Judith said in a queer half-choked voice, "She? Who? *Who*, Sherry?"

Mrs. Alston said indulgently, "Don't you know your little friend's name yet, Sherry?"

Sherry was at the screen door now, ready to go upstairs. She was holding the screen half open, letting all the candleflies get inside, but Miss Judith didn't tell her to shut the door. She just held her breath and waited for Sherry to answer.

"Sure," Sherry said at last, impishly. "Of course I know her name."

"What is it, then?" Mrs. Alston didn't really care; she was just making conversation. But Miss Judith leaned forward, clasping her hands together as if she were saying grace, only tighter.

There was a long pause, and then Sherry said directly to Miss Judith, "Her name's Miranda, Aunt Judith. *You* know."

"That's a pretty name," Mrs. Alston said.

46

Miss Judith said faintly, "Did you—ever—hear it before, Sherry?"

Maybe she was thinking some of us who knew about Miranda had let it slip, but Sherry smiled dreamily, her eyes half closed. "No. I don't think I ever heard it before. Aunt Judith—" Her voice trailed off sleepily, "don't you remember her—Miranda?"

"No! No!" Miss Judith said hysterically. "Of course—it's impossible—you made her up—" That Sherry was enough to give anybody hysterics, especially her relatives.

The screen door slammed, and Sherry and the candleflies were inside. But I didn't hear her running up the stairs. She slipped away silently, like a ghost.

Dr. Alston's car turned in the drive. "There's her father now," Mrs. Alston said. "He can go and tuck her in, Judith. Maybe he can calm down that wild imagination of hers. Let's go to bed, too. You can talk to William in the morning."

Miss Judith had recovered that special dignity of hers. "Yes," she said. "Goodnight, Olivia. Goodnight, Lindsey. Thank you for bringing me the little bottle."

"Eddie wants it for his chemistry set," I said. "May I have it for him?"

"Of course." Miss Judith even smiled a little.

"Goodnight," I said to them both.

Mrs. Alston murmured, "Miranda! What a name to make up."

I saw Miss Judith give a start, and in a minute I realized that she heard something. Something besides the name Miranda. Because I heard it too. I know I did.

It was the hesitant, tinkly sound of soft, single piano notes, very faint and faraway.

Miss Judith almost ran into the house, and the screen slammed behind her. She'll catch whoever's at the piano, I thought. Mrs. Alston looked after her, shaking her head worriedly.

"Didn't you hear anything, Mrs. Alston?" I said.

"Only some music, maybe a radio playing, Lindsey. Probably in Dr. Alston's car, you know, out on the drive."

A radio. Well—possibly.

Or it could have been Sherry fingering that piano, I told myself as I went back home. I had heard she used to study music. But I bet if it was Sherry, she had dashed up the back stairs and was in bed with her eyes shut by the time Miss Judith got to the piano.

I still felt shivery, though. A radio—why would a pianist play that particular tune—and with one finger?

But then, how would Sherry know Miranda used to play *The Dance of the Fireflies?*

4

A LONESOME
LITTLE GHOST

Tammy and I might not have overheard Miss Judith and Dr. Alston talking next day, if we hadn't happened to find out where Sherry and the boys had been hiding while we were looking for them, the afternoon before. It was a place Sherry had heard about from Miranda, Eddie told me later. After Sherry shocked Miss Judith with the name, she didn't mind the boys knowing it, too.

I met Tammy at the back hedge as usual, because we had planned to search every inch of the Alstons' yard for the cement owl, that morning. The kids were already digging around the fig tree on the other side of the house, and we meant to keep an eye on them, too.

Tammy said mysteriously, "I think I know where they were yesterday afternoon, Lin. It's a great hiding place, too."

"And just wait till I tell you about last night!" I said.

"What happened?"

We sat down on Miss Judith's marble garden bench and I told Tammy about the blue coloring bottle and Sherry making the rose, and telling Miranda's name, and then the eerie music. Tammy said, "I bet it was just the radio, though. That's what they call coincidence, you know."

"It was no coincidence, Tam. It was no radio. Why, there was even a wrong note, like when a kid makes a mistake in practicing, and goes back and strikes the right one. And besides, it gave me goosebumps. And I'm getting them again, just talking about it."

"Maybe you ought to have a physical."

"Don't you ever have goosebumps when you think about Miranda?"

"No. Not really. I kind of pretend to myself that I think she's a ghost, sometimes, because it would be so great if it were really true about ghosts. But no, I guess I'm a—whatever it is Daddy is."

"Skeptic. Well, I'm halfway between," I said honestly. "Now tell me where they were hiding, and how you found out."

"Come on, I'll show you. First let's look on the other side, and be sure they're still digging."

They were. The big leaves of the fig tree made a good screen, but we could see activity behind them. Tammy said, "They won't be able to see us; the house is between. Come on."

She led the way around to the other side of Miss Judith's house. "You don't see it?"

"No. Nothing but lawn and trees and a lot of overgrown shrubbery over toward our place, and her day lilies are beginning to bloom."

"And her magnolias," Tammy said significantly. There was an enormous old magnolia tree shading the terrace close to the house, some of the limbs touching it. The leaves were long and thick and green, and a few of the big white cup-shaped flowers showed up among them.

"I get it!" I said. "You mean, they were up in the tree hidden behind the leaves."

"Right," Tammy said. "I saw Sherry coming down from it earlier this morning. I don't think she saw me, though. I was sort of behind the hedge. It was before Eddie and Kirk came over."

"It looks easy to climb—it would have to be, for Kirk to get up there. The limbs are almost like a ladder on both sides. Let's go up."

I went first, and we both had reached the first-floor level of Miss Judith's house—it's high off the ground with a basement underneath, where the kitchen used to be when there were lots of servants —when we heard her voice. But she wasn't talking to us.

I put my finger on my lips, and Tammy nodded. We both held our breaths and kept very still, and I'm ashamed to say we listened. Miss Judith was

talking to Sherry's father in the study that used to be Miss Judith's father's. He was a minister and needed a study. I guess it was Dr. Alston's study, too, when he lived there.

The first thing I heard was Miss Judith saying, "I put away all the photos. And nobody has told her. But she knows. William, she knows about Miranda!"

Dr. Alston's voice said, "And Olivia? Does Olivia know?"

"Not yet. She thinks Miranda is a playmate that Sherry imagines. And I don't know—I can't be sure whether Sherry knows just who Miranda is— was. But, William, she knows things you and I never told her—how to color the flowers—and she found the whip you bought Miranda at the carnival that time—and she knows about Nightmare and the Hideout under the fig tree."

Dr. Alston's voice was a little husky. "There must be an explanation. Somebody must have told her. I should have told her, and Olivia, a long time ago. But at first I couldn't. Then it seemed too late. They wouldn't understand. It's hardly a rational thing, this crazy grief I still feel. Especially here, where Miranda was."

"Nobody knew," Miss Judith's voice said, "about Nightmare and the Hideout. Except Miranda. And you and I."

I could tell Miss Judith was crying, even before

Dr. Alston said, "Don't cry, Judith. Here, take my handkerchief—"

After a pause he said, "You gave her Miranda's room. Was there anything there? Anything that might have told Sherry—?"

"Miranda herself might have been there—"

I had the cold shivers, hearing that, even though the summer sun was shining hot outside the dim green place where we hid in the leaves. The magnolia flowers smelled sweet, but it was kind of decayed-sweet. And when I glanced at Tammy, she wasn't looking so awfully skeptical just then, either. When a squirrel scurried down from the top of the tree and passed us, we nearly fell off the limb.

Dr. Alston said slowly, sadly, "In that room? You know Miranda is—not anywhere, Judith. Not there. Not here. Not anywhere."

"William, we don't know. Suppose—just suppose it's true that spirits can come back. Maybe she wasn't disturbed until Sherry seemed to have taken her place here. Maybe Miranda thinks we've forgotten her. And maybe she wants us reminded that she was our little girl, too. I'll never forgive myself —when Sherry said Miranda's name and asked if I remembered her, I said no! Because you hadn't told Olivia, I thought it'd be best for her to think Sherry made her up. I denied Miranda, William.

I denied she'd ever existed. I shouldn't have done that. She has to haunt me, now."

"Judith, that Psychic Society isn't good for you. There's no need for you to feel so guilty about a white lie like that. I hope you'll drop out of the society and join a garden club or something wholesome."

"William, I've been wanting to ask you about the society. Mr. Farrar invited Dame Pythia Wilks to come here, and she accepted. She's the famous trance medium from England, you know. The séance will be held at Dr. Greenfield's house, because he wants it to be as scientific as possible, with no chance of fraud. He wants to investigate psychic phenomena and try to prove it's trickery. But he might get convinced. Anyway, I want you to come with me to that séance. It's next weekend, when Olivia will be gone to visit her friend in Atlanta. Maybe Dame Pythia will get through to Miranda for us."

"Why would a famous trance medium come here? There can't be much money in it for her," Dr. Alston said.

"She's giving a lecture in Atlanta, and Mr. Farrar persuaded her somehow to come over here for one night. It's not too far, and I'm sure the Society will put up an honorarium for her. A good many of the officers are very well off, you know. Besides being president of our branch, Mr. Farrar belongs to the National Psychic Society too, and met Dame Pythia in New York at their convention last year. You'll go with me to the séance, won't you, William? And if—if Miranda's there, we won't deny her again."

Dr. Alston said, "Well, I'll tell you what, Judith. I'll make a deal with you. I'll go—if you'll agree to give up the Psychic Society. I mean, when something happens there to convince me that it's a fraud, then you'll quit it completely."

"All right," Miss Judith agreed. "That's fair enough, William. If there's nothing evidential enough to prove Miranda's with us, then I'll stop having anything at all to do with the Society. Because if anything is ever going to come through from Miranda, this would surely be the time."

"Well, don't think about it until then," Dr. Alston said. "Please, Judith. I'm worried about you. I'm certain Miranda's at rest, not playing with Sherry, and I want you to be certain too."

"Do you suppose Sherry could have overheard us mention Miranda?" Miss Judith asked. "You know, we did talk about her the second day after you came, when Olivia was upstairs and we were here in the study. If Sherry was where she could hear us, and realized who Miranda was—"

Tammy and I nodded at each other. We knew where Sherry was, all right, when she overheard them. But it left lots of things still unexplained.

"That might be it." Dr. Alston sounded relieved. "She might have subconsciously remembered the name, and used it for her imaginary friend."

"But we didn't mention any details that Sherry somehow knows. Only her name."

"Now stop worrying about it, Judith. You've agreed to let the whole thing rest on how that séance turns out. Make us some coffee, will you? You always made the best coffee. I wish you'd teach Olivia how."

As their voices faded away Tammy and I got down from the tree in a hurry, before anybody could see us.

"Poor Miss Judith," Tammy said as we went to see how the digging was coming along. "How disappointed she's going to be after that séance."

"I wonder," I said. "There are two other possibilities, Tam. One is, that something 'evidential' will happen—it means, I guess, evidence that points to the truth. The other is, that Mr. Farrar will *make* some evidence show up. And that would be worse for Miss Judith than if nothing at all happened. He might be able to do it if he pumped Sherry enough. Or if he remembers enough about Miranda."

"Did it ever occur to you, Lin," Tammy said, "that this may be a case of dual personality? Sherry and Miranda might be the same. I don't mean the real Miranda; I mean the one Sherry made up. Or pretends about. Or sees. Or whatever. Sometimes the good and bad sides of a person split—and Sherry does have a way of blaming Miranda for things like going near that old well. Sometimes a little kid will make up an imaginary playmate who does all the bad things that he himself really does. Maybe Sherry is setting up Miranda to take the blame for anything she doesn't want to be blamed for."

"She's too old for that."

"No—dual personalities can be in grown-ups, too. Don't you remember that movie, *The Three Faces of Eve,* that we saw on TV? That was a case of triple personality."

"Maybe, Tam—but I still think Sherry's found out somehow about who the real Miranda was, and is simply jealous because Miranda was first and she thinks they loved her more. So she's trying everything she can, good and bad, to get their attention. Seeing Miranda is one way to do it."

Tammy said, "I don't see what Sherry's got to be jealous about. She's alive, she's here, and from what I hear she gets everything she wants from her father. How can she think he doesn't love her as much?"

"She can tell. He's just giving her things to make up for not giving them to Miranda. I bet she senses that everything her father does for her somehow goes back to his feeling about Miranda. It would make anybody feel bad."

We had come to the Hideout now, and Tammy said, "Found it yet?"

Sherry looked up slantways from under her bangs and admitted, "No. But we will!"

Tammy and I would have liked to find the owl with the golden eyes before Miss Judith's birthday, which we had discovered was the following week. We wanted to show her where it was hidden, as a birthday surprise, the way Miranda had planned. She hadn't had time to do it; maybe that was why her spirit couldn't rest. Unfinished business. If we could do this for Miranda, maybe she could be at peace, and the haunting would be finished. That's the way I figured it, anyhow. Tammy just thought it would be fun to find it and surprise Miss Judith, and find out how they had put love in its eyes.

"C'mon," Sherry said to Eddie and Kirk, and they dropped their tools and followed her as if they'd been hypnotized. She really had them with her, all right.

"It's kind of funny," Tammy said, as we looked around where they'd been digging, "that Sherry doesn't simply say Miranda told her where the owl is, and bring it out."

"Maybe Miranda doesn't want Sherry to be the one to find the owl. It would spoil her birthday surprise for Miss Judith. Maybe she's jealous of Sherry."

"There you go again. Talking like that ghost is real, Lin."

"She's real as long as somebody thinks she is. It gives me a queer feeling when I think about having so much power in my mind. I can keep Miranda alive—I, Lindsey—if I find the owl I can *be* Miranda for a minute and give Miss Judith her birthday surprise, and then lay Miranda's spirit to rest."

"Now you're giving me the shivers," Tammy complained. "There's nothing here, anyhow. They dug pretty well everywhere, and pretty deep."

"Not quite down to China, but deep enough," I conceded. "Well, where do we look next?"

"She told Miss Judith it was somewhere in the yard," Tammy said thoughtfully. "There's a kind of dense thicket in that back corner where the hedge goes over into your yard. Pledge never gets in there to cut grass or trim it or anything. But when Miranda lived here it wasn't like that. She could have gotten in there easy, and put the cement owl in a little niche or something in that fieldstone wall that goes across the back behind the hedge."

"That's a good place." I gave Tammy credit. It was just the sort of place Miranda might have chosen. She might even have taken one of the loose rocks out of the wall and made the niche. "Let's look at every inch of that wall. She could have made a niche anyplace along it, and things could have grown up in front of it."

"Don't let the kids see what we're doing," Tammy said.

But before we could hack a way through the briars with Pledge's scythe that we got out of Miss Judith's woodhouse, there was Sherry, closely backed up by Eddie and Kirk. "We found a snake in there yesterday," she said innocently.

"Yep," Kirk said.

"Aw, it was probably just an earthworm," Tammy said. "They look like snakes sometimes, the big ones do."

"No. It was a snake, a poisonous snake. Miranda said so. But she said for us to pick it up if we wanted to. She said we shouldn't be afraid of snakes."

"You didn't pick it up, though?"

"No," Sherry said. "I would've except I don't like snakes that much. Eddie tried to pick it up but it got away."

"Eddie!" I was acting like a big sister again. "Don't you ever touch anything that wiggles, you hear me? Or Kirk either. It could kill you! You'd die in horrible agony if it ever happened to be a poisonous snake instead of a worm!"

"It's okay—" Sherry danced away, singing the words, with Kirk and Eddie playing follow-the-

61

leader behind her. "Miranda likes snakes, and worms too—" They were all singing it at the tops of their voices as they skipped out of sight around the corner of the house.

Something about that whole thing was worrying me, and finally I realized what it was. I turned to Tammy. I don't know what I'd do without Tammy to talk things over with. We hardly ever agree about anything, but we sure do get our ideas lined up better when we have to defend them against each other's objections. "Tammy. You know what all this sounds like? It sounds like Miranda is trying to get those kids into danger. Remember she said it was all right for them to go near the well? And now she wants them to pick up snakes."

"Nobody proved it was Miranda. It's Sherry who said Miranda said that." Tammy always put her finger on the right objection. "Proves my theory about Sherry wanting somebody to blame for anything wrong she does."

"Sherry wouldn't want to get herself or the kids in real danger. But Miranda—"

"Miranda wasn't a wicked child," Tammy reminded me. "She was just a poor little kid who didn't have her mother to go to—and she fell in the pond when the edge caved in at the deep part, and she couldn't swim. She wasn't mean or anything."

"Eddie and Kirk can't swim either. I wonder if

Sherry can?" I glanced over toward the Hideout, and almost thought I could see something move behind the leaves—some transparent shadow of an elfish child, a lonely child whose mother wasn't around, who had only her aunt. Poor little Miranda. "Well, listen, Tammy, suppose she isn't wicked or mean, but just lonesome. A lonesome little ghost whose father won't acknowledge that he once had a little girl named Miranda? Maybe she doesn't want to hurt them, but only to get them over on the other side. She might want playmates she could keep forever—wherever it is she has to spend forever—and they have to die to be like her—"

"Do shut up, Lindsey!" Tammy looked a little bit scared. "You're giving me goose pimples again. And I don't even believe in all that. Sherry's just trying to see how far she can go toward danger without actually doing anything really dangerous. She wouldn't let the kids get hurt. She's just teasing you because you let her see that it shakes you up. Don't pay any attention to her and she'll drop it."

"Just the same, I'm going to order Eddie and Kirk not to go near that pond, with or without Sherry. I think they're in danger. From one or the other—Sherry or Miranda."

"It's lunch time," Tammy said, shrugging. "You can tell them when you go to lunch. We'll finish examining the wall this afternoon. I do think it's

63

a great place to look. That niche idea is the best one we've had yet."

We each went home to eat. I cornered Eddie and Kirk in the bathroom—Mama told me to see that they washed their hands because they had been playing with earthworms, though they assured her it was snakes. "You two stay away from the pond," I said, "and that's an order!"

"Don't worry, we aren't going near that old pond," Eddie said. "Not never."

"Why, that's fine, but how come you decided that?"

"Because," Eddie said.

"Yep, because," Kirk said. His hands were filthy, and I had to help him scrub them. Eddie was wiping his on the towel, but some dirt still showed besides what he left there.

"Because Miranda's afraid of the pond, that's why. It's the only thing she's afraid of, Sherry says."

5

DANGER AT
MIDNIGHT

Well, it was more likely, Tammy and I decided,
that Sherry had been told to stay away from that
pond. I would've told her to, if I'd been her parents
or her aunt. But of course she wouldn't want Eddie
and Kirk to know she couldn't do everything around
there that she wanted to. That would've spoiled
her image, for them.

Tammy and I checked every inch of the wall,
that afternoon, and found several places, where
stones were missing, that could once have been
niches for an owl with golden eyes. But there was
no owl. It was a real disappointment.

Eddie and Kirk and Sherry stuck around for
awhile, watching us hack away the briars and even
helping a little. When we got to the corner of the
lot, where the side street leads over to the shopping
centre, we saw Mr. Carson Farrar.

Of course, he had to stop and ask what we were
doing, being nosey like he is, and of course Kirk

had to tell him, being too little to know that the less you say to Mr. Carson Farrar the better "Lookin' for the cement owl with golden eyes that M'randa hid."

I told Kirk Mama wanted him and Eddie, but it was no use. They spilled all the details they knew, and even something we didn't know, that Miranda must have told them through Sherry. They said that Miss Judith and Miranda made the owl by putting wet cement in a plastic bag and shaping it like an owl, then made finger holes for the eyes and drew lines for the wings and claws through the plastic into the wet cement; they let it dry in the plastic, and then peeled the plastic off after it was dry. If Miranda could tell Sherry all that, it really was funny that she wouldn't tell her where it was hidden. But then, we figured, Sherry might know where it was and just wasn't saying. You can't tell about that kid.

Mr. Farrar said he hoped we'd find the cement owl, but of course he didn't really hope so.

Eddie said, "Maybe you could make one in your workshop, Mr. Farrar."

"Yep," Kirk said.

"What would I want to make a thing like that for?" Mr. Farrar shook his head, and went on home. I was glad to see him go, because we still had a bit more of the wall to check.

But we didn't find the cement owl. It was a

whole afternoon wasted. Well, we hadn't much else to do, anyway.

I don't know whether to blame Sherry or not for what happened that night. I do know, though, that it wouldn't have happened—at least not that night—if Mrs. Brer hadn't decided to have her babies, and Eddie and Kirk hadn't sneaked out in the middle of the night to help deliver them.

When I got up to get a drink of water and saw their closed door, I knew right away that was where they were. Usually they leave their door, as well as all the other doors they go through, wide open. There had to be a reason for that closed door— they weren't in their room, and didn't want anybody to know it.

Naturally, I looked in. I remembered that at supper Eddie had said Mrs. Brer was acting funny, and he looked speculatively at Mama, and Dad said, "That's enough, Eddie." Because a gentleman doesn't think about a pregnant lady and a pregnant rabbit in the same category like that. Even if they are both mammals.

I didn't know how long Eddie and Kirk had been gone, or how long it takes a rabbit to have babies, but I thought I ought to go look, and get them back to bed before they got into trouble for being out. And I was curious, too, about Mrs. Brer and exactly how rabbits have babies.

My clock said ten minutes to midnight. I slipped into my shorts and shirt, and hurried down to the back yard. I looked for Dad's flashlight, on the shelf in the pantry, but it was gone. So I knew Kirk and Eddie had it. I went back upstairs for my own flashlight. It was a dark night, and I wished Tammy had been spending the night with me, so I'd have somebody along when I went out there. I felt as if Miranda might be over there in Miss Judith's yard in the dark, sitting on that phantom horse Night-mare, watching me across the hedge. It was a hot night, but I shivered.

Well, Eddie and Kirk weren't at the cage. They had been there, though—Eddie had had enough sense to move Brer into the other cage. The first family of young was huddled in the corner of Mrs. Brer's cage. She was hiding way back in the straw, and there were funny little almost-not noises.

I flashed the light into the cage, but I couldn't see much; Mrs. Brer had dug deep into the straw. I wondered about the baby rabbits; I thought Five and Six at least might have come by now, if not Seven and Eight. It was strange that Kirk wasn't right there, dying to see his two.

Where could the kids be? I felt danger all over me, in every goosebump.

Everything was too still—like before a thunderstorm—hot and still and dark. The way it is just before the wind picks up and starts blowing the rees around and some big drops come down and he clouds hit together and the lightning looks like a bare white tree branch with twigs forking out.

I stood there by the cage and held my breath, and there wasn't a sound anywhere, except Mrs. Brer scuffling in the straw. I called softly, "Eddie— Kirk—" but I didn't want to wake Mama and Dad and get the boys in trouble. I flashed the light around, but couldn't see any sign of them. They must have gone over to Alstons' yard, I thought— that little witch Sherry was probably flitting around on her broom and had enticed them over there at midnight to do something mysterious. And they'd go anywhere Sherry said. They aren't scared of the dark, either.

But I was, a little, at this point. Did I dare go over there? It shouldn't have been any different than any other night, and I'd been out at night lots of times. But somehow it felt different. Maybe because it was late. And still. There weren't even any cars going past on the street; it would have been comforting to see a couple of headlights come around the corner. Anyhow, I felt more alone than I'd ever felt in my life.

But just because I was scared, I had to do it. To show myself that being scared is normal and you get over it if you're brave enough to face up to it. Only, I didn't quite know what I was scared of. But I thought it might be Miranda's ghost.

I went cautiously across our yard, and the grass felt damp and dewy, and I realized I hadn't put on any shoes. My feet didn't make any noise on the grass, but when I went through the hole in the hedge, the dead bits crackled loud as pistol shots.

There in front of me was the Hideout.

The big fig leaves drooped around it, and when I flashed my light they looked flat and black-green. Did I dare look inside that cave of darkness? Maybe it was only Eddie and Kirk and Sherry hiding in there, waiting to jump out at me. But suppose it was Miranda in there—holding a cement owl with golden eyes? Not the real one—a ghost owl with spooky eyes—an owl you could see through?

Then I thought—and it was a curiously comforting thought—about the fact that the real owl had love in its eyes. Sherry didn't seem to know about that. And Miranda couldn't be so bad, if she wanted it to have love in its eyes.

So I pushed the drooping branches aside, and slipped into the Hideout. The leaves fell back behind me with a soft rustle, like a heavy curtain. I noticed in panic that my flashlight was getting dimmer—the batteries were old. This was the worst possible time for them to give out. In the thin light before the batteries went dead I could see that nobody was in the Hideout but me.

Unless—was that Miranda behind the shadow of the tree's big trunk? I almost thought I could see

a transparent movement, a wisp of dark hair, and a white something that would be a pixie face. But I knew it was my imagination.

Then my light went out and I stood in the dark, rooted to the ground with plain terror.

I swallowed hard, and said out loud, "Love in its eyes—" as if that could make a difference. It was the first thing that came into my head, and I latched onto it. And suddenly I felt less scared. I wasn't exactly relaxed, but at least I wasn't rigid.

On impulse, I spoke to Miranda, just as if she were there. "Miranda—what is it you want?"

There wasn't a sound. Which doesn't prove she wasn't there.

Well, anyhow, I knew that Eddie and Kirk weren't. I parted the branches again and left the Hideout and walked across Miss Judith's yard, just as if I felt as brave as I wished I did.

Across the street, I could see lights at the Farrars'. Probably they were having a secret meeting of the Psychic Society's inner sanctum, to organize things for the séance. Usually, according to the books about proceedings of such societies, they had somebody to tape-record everything the medium communicated, so they could study it later and check out everything the control said. Nearly always, if they tried hard enough afterwards, somebody could remember a dead friend or relative whose initial was J or whatever, and who had something about automobiles in his past, and was taking medicine when he died, and vague things like that, which "checked."

Maybe the officers of the Psychic Society were at the Farrars' deciding how many of the members they'd let come to this very private séance. Dr. Greenfield had told Tammy that only about ten of them were going to know about it at all. And if it weren't kept a secret from the others, they'd be mad because they weren't invited. A Dame Pythia Wilks séance was the greatest thing that could ever happen in a Psychic Society, and the left-out members might tar and feather Mr. Farrar if it leaked out, Dr. Greenfield said. And that might be a real good idea, Tammy and I had agreed privately. We had never seen anybody tarred and feathered, but we couldn't think of a better one to start with than Mr. Farrar.

While I was standing there looking at the lights in the Farrars' house, I forgot to be so frightened. From this angle the Alstons' house seemed to be all dark, though I knew if Miss Judith happened to be over at the Farrars' the night-light would be on in her front hall. I thought I'd see if it was.

I slipped around to the front, and sure enough, there was a dim light showing through the glass in the door. I circled to the other side of the house, then, wondering if Eddie and Kirk were up in Sherry's room with her. They could have gotten into her window by climbing that magnolia tree, I thought when I stood under it, because her room was right over the study, and one of the big limbs of the tree actually touched the roof, which sloped only a little under Sherry's window. It was a house that had different levels of roofs, and her window was on the second floor. There was an attic window even higher up, above hers.

Sherry's room (she had taken us up there once) was real pretty, the way Miss Judith had fixed it up for Miranda. Only Sherry thought it was for her. Or did she? Sometimes I felt sure all Sherry's tricks were just sort of desperate bids for Miss

Judith's love—and then again I was doubtful. But —that blue rose. Could either of them think Miss Judith would *like* it?

There I was, thinking about Miranda again, and the eerie feeling came back. Miranda had climbed this very same magnolia tree—maybe she had used it to get in and out of her window, if she wanted to slip out and not let them know she was gone.

The old magnolia tree must have been pretty big even when Miranda lived in that room up there. Some of its branches were higher than the rooftop now—they'd reached beyond her window, even then.

Kirk and Eddie could have climbed up there— only it would have been silly to do that, when Sherry could've just come down and let them in the door. And since there wasn't any light in Sherry's room, I concluded they must be somewhere else.

Then a thought struck me that turned me cold. The pond! What if they had gone down to the pond? I had only Eddie's word for it that Miranda didn't want them to—and Sherry might decide to take them down there anyway. I had told Dad he should teach Eddie and Kirk to swim, and he laughed and said, "Why not you, too?" I told him it wasn't so necessary for me. Now I saw that it could be necessary. If one of them was drowning, I couldn't save him.

I ran, and it seemed like a mile to the edge of

the pond, though it was just past the summer house. But down there at the end of the yard the dark was thick and different—I guess it was the fog that formed over the water. Not a bit of light came from anywhere, so I could barely see the pond. There was a wet, dank smell, and suddenly I thought about all of Edgar Allan Poe's tarns. That pond would have made a great tarn. Without any trouble at all, I could imagine dripping, decaying skeletons rising out of it. I was still clutching the useless flashlight; it seemed better to have something to hold onto even if it was only that.

Was that a movement of some kind, over there where the edge of the pond had once caved in?

Was it—Miranda?

Even though she was afraid of the pond, as Eddie said, it might be that ghosts *had* to return and haunt the place where they died, whether they wanted to or not.

There was something moving, down there in the dark.

Maybe it's only a water moccasin, I thought. That shows you how scared I was, thinking hopefully of a water moccasin instead of a ghost.

I whispered, "Eddie? Kirk? Are you there? Answer me!" and then wondered why I was whispering. I said it out loud, and my voice sounded so strange —the croak of it frightened me as much as if it had been somebody else's weird voice. "Eddie! Kirk!"

If they had been there, they had already drowned, I thought, shuddering. All three of them might be floating out there with weeds in their hair like Ophelia, and couldn't answer.

And then the storm broke. All of a sudden there were huge drops of rain pelting me, and lightning coming and going made the pond show up and then disappear, a great shining black flat blob; and then nothing but dark space again. But I saw with great thankfulness that there were no bodies floating on it with weeds in their hair.

Then I heard the terrified screams.

6

THE SECRET
PLACE

The frightened, wild screaming seemed to come from somewhere behind me, from the Alston house. I whirled around, and saw a light come on outside their back door, and Dr. Alston rushing out, tying a robe on over his pajamas. He had heard it too. It wasn't just my imagination.

I ran toward him, and we met nearly in front of the summer house. Just about that time there was another yell from inside the summer house. I recognized Eddie's voice.

"It's Eddie," I panted, and Dr. Alston ran inside with me behind him. Eddie's flashlight pointed toward the old well. He was crying, "Kirk's in there! Kirk fell in!"

Sherry was leaning over the well curb, and for a moment I had a mean thought—is she pushing him down or trying to get him out? But Dr. Alston grabbed her and pushed her back and leaned over, himself. We could hear Kirk hollering now too.

Dr. Alston said, "Hand me that flashlight." Eddie did.

Dr. Alston flashed the light down into the well, holding on with his other hand to the strongest edge he could find. "Hang onto the chain, Kirk!" he commanded. "Don't let go. I'll get you out. Just hold on!"

Kirk was scared to death. He was sobbing out loud, but I was proud of him—he caught his breath and said, "Yes, sir," before he started screaming again.

"The rest of you stay way back from the well!" Dr. Alston said sternly, and I thought maybe Sherry was in for it, this time. But Dr. Alston was too busy rescuing Kirk to even wonder why we were all out there.

The well had water in it; we could hear Kirk splashing whenever he had to stop crying to breathe. But we didn't know whether it was deep enough to drown him. I thought of water moccasins and shivered. There were probably all sorts of terrible things down there. Even skeletons.

Dr. Alston was testing the edge, trying to find a firm place to lean while he reached for Kirk. The chain that had held the well bucket looked so rusty I was afraid it would break if he tried to pull Kirk up by it. He evidently thought so too, because he told me, "Lindsey, will you go to the garage and

the woodshed and see if there's some strong rope there?"

"Yes, sir!" I said. "But my flashlight batteries are dead. How can I find the rope in the dark?"

"I'm afraid I'll need the flashlight here, in case the chain should break before you get back," Dr. Alston said. "Maybe the light from the back door will help some. Wait a minute—take these matches —and be careful with them. Hurry now!"

I took the matches and ran for the garage. I couldn't see any rope there. But in the woodshed there was a rope coiled up and hanging on a nail. It looked pretty old, but it was thick. It looked long enough, too—though of course I had no idea how deep the old well was. I was so nervous I dropped a match and had to stop to be sure the flame was out. I lit another, grabbed the rope off the nail, and started back toward the summer house. The rain had stopped.

Just then Mrs. Alston came out of the back door in her nightgown, saying, "What's going on? William! Sherry's not in her room!" And Miss Judith came around the corner of the house—probably from the Farrars' where the meeting had broken up—saying, "What's the matter?"

I hollered to them, "Kirk's in the old well!" and rushed on with the rope.

Dr. Alston kept saying, "Hang on, boy!" while he tied the rope to a tree just outside the summer

ouse and knotted a loop in the other end of it
that would slip tight when pulled. He lowered it
to Kirk. "Can you hang on with one hand and
get the rope over your shoulders and under your
arms?"

"No, sir," Kirk sobbed. "I'll fall and drown!"
He was so scared, poor kid. So was I, but I said,
"Dr. Alston, how about tying me to the end of the
rope and letting me down there so I can tie the
rope on Kirk? Or maybe he can just hold onto my
neck while you pull us both up—"

Dr. Alston said, "You're a brave girl, Lindsey.
But I think I'd better tie the rope around myself
and go down there after him. I believe I can climb
back out by pulling myself up with it, and using
the rocks at the sides of the well to put my feet on."
He saw Mrs. Alston and Miss Judith then, and
said, "Get my flashlight from the car, please, Olivia,
and if you have one, Judith, do get it, too. I'll
need more light." He had drawn the loop up and
was tying it around his waist.

"Is there time to call somebody to help?" Miss
Judith said.

"No—Kirk might lose his hold, and we don't
know how deep the water is," Dr. Alston said.
"Hurry with the lights. After you bring me those
you can phone for help."

He had climbed back up, with Kirk hanging
onto his neck, before the Rescue Squad got there,

and all the excitement was over without even wak
ing up the neighborhood. But it surprised me when
Sherry started crying. I had never seen her cry
before. She ran and hugged Kirk and then just
stood there holding onto him till he twisted away
from her—I think it scared him more than falling
into the well, to see Sherry cry.

"What were you children doing out here this
time of night?" Dr. Alston asked Sherry, but he
didn't sound very angry—only as if he thought he
had to.

"It was a dare. She dared us to look down in the
well at midnight," Sherry sobbed.

"Who dared you? Not Lindsey?" Dr. Alston
looked shocked.

"No, sir," I said emphatically. "I missed the boys
and came to look for them, before Mama and Dad
could find out they were gone. I was afraid they
might have wandered down to the—" And then I
stopped, not quite wanting to mention the pond.

"Who dared you, Sherry?"

Sherry looked so defenseless, standing there in
front of us with her arm crooked over her face, that
I couldn't help feeling sorry for her. But then she
said, "Miranda—it was Miranda—" and I felt hard-
hearted again when I saw how shook up Dr. Alston
and Miss Judith both looked. Of course Sherry's
mother still thought Miranda was just her imaginary playmate. So she told Sherry she didn't want

hear any more about Miranda—that she needn't blame her naughtiness on a make-believe child any more, because they wouldn't stand for it. Sherry didn't argue, but Dr. Alston said kind of wearily, "Oh, now, Olivia, let's not be harsh."

When he said that, Sherry started crying even harder, and Dr. Alston tried to take her in his arms, but she wouldn't let him. She was fighting him and sobbing, "You don't care about *me*—you don't—" and Mrs. Alston had to almost carry her into the house. So I guess she wasn't punished after all, and maybe that was all right, because she probably didn't really mean any harm.

Mama and Dad had slept right through the excitement. So did the Greenfields. I told Tammy all about it the next day. "And I brought Eddie and Kirk home, and Mrs. Brer had Five and Six and Seven and Eight and Nine. Eddie ran ahead and looked. Kirk wasn't caring much about rabbits right then. He didn't want me to tell Mama and Dad about the well, so now he has to do anything I tell him to for the next three weeks. But Dr. Alston might let on to them."

"Well, I'd like to see Five and Six and Seven and Eight and Nine," Tammy said. I've never seen any rabbits that new." So we went and inspected them, and then went over and watched the workmen filling up and boarding over the old well. Dr.

Alston must have been really scared, to get them out there so quick.

We asked the workman who was down in the well (it wasn't really very full of water, after all) if he saw anything down there like a small lump of cement shaped like an owl with yellow glass eyes, but he didn't.

We went around to the side yard, then, and Miss Judith came out about that time, and asked if Kirk was all right. I said, "Yes, ma'am, but I'm surprised to find my hair hasn't turned white over night, from the shock."

She said she thought she had a few more gray hairs that morning. Tammy said, "I wish I hadn' missed all the excitement."

"Never mind, there's bound to be some more," I told her. "Here comes Mr. Farrar. I think I'll ask him if we can come to the séance, just to see what he'll say. Mrs. Farrar must have the car again; he's walking home from the hardware store."

"How do you deduce that?"

"He's carrying a kind of heavy-looking brown paper sack with Greene Hardware Company printed on it." We both went off into giggles, and even Miss Judith was smiling when Mr. Farrar came along the sidewalk abreast of us.

I thought I'd start the conversation casually and then lead into the real question. "What're you mak-

84

ing in your workshop now, Mr. Farrar? The flower-pots you made for Mrs. Farrar look great."

"Nothing." He really meant it was none of my business.

I composed my face to look serious. "Mr. Farrar, Tammy and I are very much interested in spiritualism, and we would like to be at the séance when you have it at her house. And I'm sure I'm psychic —I was born with two cauls, you see."

"Two cauls!" Mr. Farrar gasped, and Tammy nearly exploded trying to keep from laughing out loud. Maybe he actually believed it for a minute. It was all I could do to keep from saying I'd been born with eight fingers on each hand, too. "Maybe you are a sensitive, Lindsey, and sometime we'll have to explore that possibility. But not this time. It's possible to have only a very few serious psychic investigators at this meeting."

"Well, I'll be there anyway," I said solemnly, "if I should happen to die before Friday. You can count on me to get in touch with you through Kleeman."

"Lindsey—hush!" Miss Judith said. "You aren't going to die before Friday, child."

"Maybe I will," I said. "Tammy, too. We'd do anything to get to the séance. Do suicides ever Come Through?" I don't know how I managed to keep a straight face. Tammy just hid hers in her hands.

"Maybe she is clairvoyant," Mr. Farrar said to Miss Judith. "Do you have some kind of premonition, Lindsey?"

"I don't know what that is," I said innocently. "All I know is, I had a kind of mental picture—in technicolor—of me lying in a coffin. I could even feel how narrow it was. And there were flowers—pale pink carnations, I think—and music. Was that a premonition, Mr. Farrar?"

"Good heavens, child," was all he said to me. But he said to Miss Judith, "There *is* some evidence to prove clairvoyance. Dr. Rhine, you know—"

"She's joking, Mr. Farrar," Miss Judith said. "It's not a very funny joke, but you know how children are."

Mr. Farrar shook his head and went on across the street to his own house, and I called after him, "Please be sure to tell Kleeman I'll be there Friday night if I can, Mr. Farrar."

"Lindsey, you shouldn't!" Miss Judith said, shocked.

"I know it, Miss Judith," I said, after Tammy and I had recovered from laughing ourselves into a coughing spell. "I'm sorry, but I do hate Mr. Farrar, and it's fun putting him on."

"I wish you wouldn't joke about such things," Miss Judith said sadly, and then I really was sorry, and I tried to tell her I wouldn't have hurt her feelings for the world. She forgave me, but I could

ll she still felt sad. "Well," she told us, "I have
o go and straighten up Miranda's—I mean Sherry's
—room, while she's out playing with Eddie and
Kirk."

"They're looking at the new rabbits," Tammy told
er. "You want us to go with you, Miss Judith?
o you won't be lonely in Miranda's room?"

"Why, yes, if you want to, Tammy. That might
e a good idea. You may turn out to know as much
sychology as your father, some day. I'll admit I
ather dread being in there, without Miranda." Or
with Miranda, I couldn't help thinking.

Of course it wasn't kindness on Tammy's part—
we had been dying to get into Miranda's room again.
There might be clues there, clues to where the
cement owl was hidden, or to where Sherry was
getting all the stuff she knew about Miranda. Or
we might be able to feel the eerie presence, if
there really was a ghost child living there too.

We followed Miss Judith up the stairs, eagerly.
The room she had fixed for Miranda was all pink
and white, like strawberry ice cream and whipped
cream, or like those mountain laurel flowers we
saw once up in the hills.

"Some of the furniture in here was my mother's
when she was a girl," Miss Judith said. "The rose-
wood desk was, and that little rocking chair she
used for a sewing chair. And then they were mine,
when I was growing up."

"It's lovely," I said. "I wish I had real antiques in my room."

Miss Judith opened the desk—it had a top that folded down on hinges—to show us the inside. There were lots of pigeonholes, and a little drawer in the middle. "There's a secret place behind this drawer," she said. "Well, not so very secret—it's just a deeper space behind the drawer than it really needs, which doesn't show unless you take the drawer all the way out. I loved hiding things there when I was a child. So did Miranda. I haven't showed it to Sherry, yet."

But before she could take out the drawer for us to see behind it, she noticed something lying flat on the polished surface under the pigeonholes. "Why—she found these, too!" she exclaimed.

"What is it?" Tammy said.

There were two books lying there, an ABC book with colored pictures, and *A Child's Garden of Verses* by Robert Louis Stevenson. "These weren't here," Miss Judith said with that strange tone in her voice that I was getting used to, "before Sherry came. I don't know where she found them. I haven't seen them since Miranda was here. She loved these two books—I never knew what became of them."

She opened the poetry book to the flyleaf, and I could see what was written there. "'For Miranda, with all my love, from Mother." I didn't have to look in the other one; I knew it said the same thing.

"Her mother gave them to her," Tammy said unnecessarily. "The lady who was interested in spiritualism."

"I wonder where Sherry found them—if Sherry found them—?" Miss Judith murmured.

"I know!" I said. "Remember, Tammy? Eddie said when they found the place that had been dug out in the summer house, when Sherry fell into it, there were some other things in it besides the old carnival whip. Some money in a baking-powder can, and some old beat-up books in a tin box. These must be the books. That was where Miranda hid her treasures."

"But not the cement owl," Tammy reminded me.

"Well, she probably had other hiding places."

"Did Eddie say how many books there were?" Miss Judith asked.

"No, he didn't. I can ask him. But I doubt if he'd remember. Eddie's not terribly interested in books right now. Unless they're about raising rabbits. Or comic books, of course. Did she have more books, Miss Judith?"

"I don't know," Miss Judith said. "She might have. She had a little diary—" She put the books carefully back in the desk, where she had found them. "That's right where she used to keep them," she almost whispered. I could tell she was thinking that maybe it was Miranda who put them there, not Sherry at all. "She used to sit here and write."

Tammy was getting impatient, and I was anxious, too, to see the secret place in Miranda's desk. "You were going to show us the secret place behind the drawer," I said gently.

"Oh, yes." Miss Judith came back from the past, almost. "This is the way it works." She started to take out the drawer.

"You said you never showed this to Sherry?" I asked, wondering if the child might have found something there, something she was using to mystify us. That diary, for instance.

"I never did, Lindsey. I didn't want Sherry to have the same experiences with me that Miranda had; so I didn't tell her about the secret place. We used to leave notes for each other there, Miranda and I." I remembered she had said something like that before, about not wanting to do the same things with the two of them.

"But Sherry might have found the secret place on her own."

Miss Judith took out the drawer and laid it on the desk's writing surface, shaking her head. "No, I don't think anyone would suspect there was a secret hole back there, do you?" she said. "Not unless there was some reason to take the drawer all the way out."

"Oh, kids always take things apart," I told her, knowing Eddie and Kirk.

We all leaned over and peered into the dark place where the drawer had been.

There was something in it.

"Look!" That was Tammy.

"What is it?" That was me.

Miss Judith turned white, then she steadied herself and said faintly, "I haven't looked in there for years, not since—"

Almost fearfully, while Tammy and I held our breaths, she put her trembling hand into the secret hole.

7

DAME PYTHIA
ARRIVES

The piece of paper was sort of scrappy, but only
slightly yellow. "Dear Aunt Judith," it said, "I love
you." It wasn't signed.

Had Miranda written it, long ago? Or—can
ghosts write?

Or had Sherry written it, just the other day? I
remembered the blue rose. Had Sherry wanted
Miss Judith to think it was Miranda's ghost who
had left the note there? At least, to think so at
first? Or had Sherry just been making another pitiful
attempt to make her aunt love her the way she
had Miranda? Maybe she honestly didn't realize
how it would make Miss Judith feel. And Sherry
had told her aunt she fixed the blue rose, as soon
as the subject came up. She might admit writing the
note, too, when she was asked. There was no need
to sign it, of course, when only one child with an
"Aunt Judith" was—supposedly—in the house.

Miss Judith's hands were shaky, and there were

tears in her eyes. She must think Miranda wrote it, I thought, feeling sad for her. "Miss Judith," I said softly, "does it look like Sherry's writing?"

"It must be Miranda's," she said faintly. "She must have written it all those years ago."

"But could it be Sherry's writing?" I kept at her, though I was sorry for her. "You're her Aunt Judith too. And the paper doesn't look too old."

"Old enough, though," Tammy said.

"I don't know," Miss Judith said. "I haven't seen much of Sherry's writing. And it's a long time since I saw Miranda's. I honestly can't tell which it is."

"Let's find Sherry and ask her," Tammy suggested.

Miss Judith went with us to the rabbit cages.

Eddie said, "I gave Seven to Sherry. But he has to stay with his mother until he's weaned."

Sherry said, sighing hopefully at her Aunt Judith, "I did want a horse, but I guess a rabbit's better than nothing."

"Yep," Kirk said.

"Well, if you don't want Seven—" Eddie said, a bit indignantly.

"Oh, I want him, all right. I'm going to name him Nightmare."

"He's not black."

"Well, there could be a sort of grayish Nightmare, couldn't there? Like a black-and-white dream instead of technicolor? And then if I ever do get a horse named Nightmare, I can change my bunny's name back to Seven."

"Well, okay," Eddie said a little doubtfully.

I broke into their silly yakety-yak to ask, casually, "Sherry, when did you write this note to your Aunt Judith?" I read in a psychology magazine that the way to find out if a child did anything isn't to say "Did you?" but "When did you?" I've been on my guard ever since.

"Oh, did you find it, Aunt Judith?" Sherry smiled affectionately at her aunt; you'd have sworn there was nothing tricky about her. Just like the time she admitted the blue rose was a surprise for poor Miss Judith. "I was wondering if you ever would. I wrote it two days ago, and I thought you'd never look in the secret place."

"How did you know about the desk?" Miss Judith asked, and it was pitiful, the way she looked at Sherry, pleading, "Dear, please tell me—"

"*You* know who," Sherry said. "Mom said not to mention her name anymore."

Miss Judith got very pale. "Don't look like that, Miss Judith," I said. "Sherry's probably just making it up. You know she was just fooling around the desk and happened to find the secret place."

"Yes, that's right; I just happened to find it, Aunt Judith," Sherry said, in that innocent-slippery tone of voice kids use when they want people to think they're telling a whopper even if it happens

94

to be the truth. It's a good way to tell the truth and still have all the advantages of lying. It was working right now, on Miss Judith. But *I* didn't believe Sherry found out from Miranda—she looked too much like a kitten playing with a dead bird.

"Well," Miss Judith said uncertainly, "it's a sweet note, Sherry, and—thank you, dear."

"Aunt Judith," Sherry said, looking up through her bangs in that weird way she had, "why didn't you tell me about the secret place in the desk? Or any of the other things you told Miranda?"

Well, that was a poser. I could tell Miss Judith didn't know what to say, because really there wasn't any good answer, even if Dr. Alston had left her free to tell, and he hadn't.

Miss Judith answered weakly, after awhile, with another question. "Who—do you think Miranda is, Sherry?"

Sherry flitted away, like an elfish imp, calling back over her shoulder. "Don't you know? Don't you know? She's my make-believe sister, that's who!"

Yes, any imaginative kid might have said it. Whether she knew the facts about Miranda or not. And whether Miranda was a real ghost or not.

Eddie latched the rabbit cage and he and Kirk hurried off after Sherry.

"Don't let her bug you, Miss Judith," Tammy said kindly.

"She's such a mysterious child," Miss Judith sighed. "If I believed in reincarnation, I might wonder if Miranda had been re-born as Sherry. They look so much alike. Sherry was born two years after Miranda died. So it would have been possible, if reincarnation is possible."

"But you don't believe in it?" I asked Miss Judith. "You mean the Psychic Society doesn't go in for reincarnation?"

"I don't know what to believe," Miss Judith said, sort of desperately.

"Well, one thing's for sure," I told her, "you can't believe Miranda is in communication with Sherry and still believe she's reincarnated in Sherry. It'll have to be one or the other, won't it? So I guess you have to decide which is the least weird, huh, Miss Judith? Or else not believe in any of it, and decide Sherry is making it all up, getting her knowledge about Miranda from something—or someone—we don't know about."

"I suppose so," Miss Judith murmured, but she sounded doubtful still. "Anyway, I'll know in a couple of days. The séance is Friday night. If nothing comes through from Miranda, with Dame Pythia and Kleeman trying, then I'll stop believing she's able to communicate."

She wanted so much to believe it that I wished it could be true. I hoped Dame Pythia and Kleeman were really in touch with The Other World. But

at the same time I was mad at Mr. Farrar for trying
to get publicity at the expense of Miss Judith's
feelings. I hoped something would happen at the
séance that would scare him to death—maybe
Tammy and I could think up something.

When Friday came, we were out front watching
for Dame Pythia to arrive at the Farrars'. We had
seen her picture in the Atlanta papers, and in *Time*
and *Life* magazines too, so we weren't surprised
at how fat she was. But we had no idea what a
funny color of pinkish-orange her hair would turn
out to be. And she wore blue stretch-pants that
were really stretched, and a kind of long tunic in
all sorts of psychedelic colors. While we were watching her get out of Mr. Farrar's car, Sherry and
Eddie and Kirk came around from the backyard,
and all five of us strolled across the street and
said "Hello" to both of them. Mr. Farrar said,
"Hello, children," very grudgingly, but Dame Pythia
said, holding out her hands like she was sleep-
walking, "Vibrations! Vibrations! There are sensi-
tives here!"

I said, "I was born with two cauls," just to see
what she'd say, and she grabbed me by my shoulders
and said, "Ah," just as if a doctor had told her
to say it while he held a little flat stick on her
tongue. She must have guessed I was putting her on
about the two cauls, because she didn't react beyond the "ah."

97

She looked at Sherry and Mr. Farrar said, "This is Sherry Alston, Dame Pythia," and Sherry said, "How do you do," quite nicely. Dame Pythia turned me loose and grabbed Sherry by the shoulders and looked deep into her eyes. Sherry squirmed, and Dame Pythia let her go and nodded significantly to Mr. Farrar. He said, "She's the little girl I was telling you about." I knew he had introduced Sherry instead of the rest of us because she was important to the plot. But we didn't like to be ignored. I said, "I'm Lindsey Morrow, and this is my friend Tammy Greenfield. You are going to her house for the séance tonight; her father is Dr. Greenfield. These are my brothers, Eddie and Kirk."

Dame Pythia didn't bother about manners; she latched onto Tammy and ignored the rest of us. "Tammy," she said, tasting the name as if it were raspberry syrup. "When is your birthday, child?"

"February fifth," Tammy said, and I nearly giggled, because it wasn't—that was Kirk's birthday. "I'm a child of Aquarius." She isn't; her birthday's in September, just about a month before mine. She was trying to see just how psychic Dame Pythia could be when somebody was putting her on. And Kirk helped by saying, "Yep."

"Ah," Dame Pythia said again. "Ethical, idealistic, a lover of truth—" and then I did giggle. "Uranus is the planet which rules Aquarians, the

99

planet of progress and of truth. And when were your father and mother born, Tammy?"

Of course Tammy knew Dame Pythia was pumping her for stuff to use that night, in case she decided to try anything on Dr. Greenfield. "Daddy's birthday is June twentieth," she said innocently, "and Mother's is August thirteenth." So I was sure they weren't. Well, I believe white lies are justified when you're trying to help somebody like Miss Judith by showing up a person who's trying to hurt her.

"Do you remember your grandma, dear?"

"Of course," Tammy said, wide-eyed. She bravely blinked back tears and wiped her eyes on the back of her hand. Both her grandmothers are still alive, but you'd never have guessed it. "I was six when she died. Her first name was May, just like my middle name." Well, I hadn't heard about that, but knowing Tammy, I was pretty sure she had just changed her grandma's name. And Tammy herself had never had a middle name at all, she told me a long time ago.

I wondered why Dame Pythia wasn't asking Sherry some questions, to help in fooling Dr. Alston and Miss Judith. I found out later why—she already knew enough about the Alstons. And of course she didn't care a hoot about me and Eddie and Kirk—our parents weren't going to be at the séance.

Tammy said, "Dame Pythia, could Lindsey and I please come to the séance? We're very interested in psychic things."

Sherry said quickly, "If you'll let me come, I'll bring Miranda." She was supposed to spend the night at our house, sleeping in my room while I was over at Tammy's, because her mother had gone to Atlanta, and her father and aunt might be very late getting home from the séance.

Mr. Farrar said crossly, "No. As I told you before, girls, the meeting isn't for children."

Dame Pythia said to him, "Perhaps she *is* in touch—"

But Mr. Farrar said curtly, "Impossible." So he *knew* there was nothing to it! It proved to me he didn't believe in any of it—not even in trance mediums—or he'd at least have thought *maybe* Sherry could communicate with Miranda through Dame Pythia.

Sherry ran off, calling back, "Then Miranda won't come! She'll stay with me! You won't hear from Miranda at your silly old séance!"

It really sounded as if she believed it. As if there really were a Miranda she was in communication with. She must have overheard some talk of the séance at home, and she may have even guessed by now who Miranda was. She'd have to be pretty stupid not to.

Kirk and Eddie ran after Sherry, and Tammy

and I went on to her house, giggling all the way down to our toes. When nobody was looking we inspected the hall closet, and it was all ready for our knothole view of the séance. The dug-out holes were still wide open, which goes to show that their maid, Theolia, doesn't dust behind those chairs very well, or she'd have noticed them. We could see nearly the whole room when the lights were on. At that moment Dr. Greenfield was moving the couch from his study into the middle of the room, for Dame Pythia to lie on, and we hoped it would hold up under the strain. He hoped so too, we heard him telling Mrs. Greenfield while they were setting up extra bridge chairs around it.

"There's just no chance for any trick stuff here," he went on, in a satisfied voice. "Sometimes, you know, they apparently materialize objects from The Other World—but we know they can't do it in our living room. They'd have to have wires rigged up, or magicians' apparatus or projection machines or something."

"I don't think," Mrs. Greenfield answered, "from what I've read, that Dame Pythia does any of what they call 'external manifestations.'" Her voice sounded as if she might be laughing to herself. "Perhaps she's too lazy to make the effort. I think she relies entirely on Kleeman and his extraordinary knowledge of the victim and his contact on The Other Side."

"You're right, but we want to rule out any possibility of trickery."

It was all very exciting. Tammy and I could hardly wait for eight o'clock that night, when everybody was supposed to meet. I was eating at the Greenfield's; they had fried chicken, which Theolia really knows how to cook—it's the greatest. But we were so excited we could hardly eat a thing except two drumsticks apiece, and some biscuits and honey, and apple pie and ice cream. Theolia is a genius at making apple pie, too. We didn't have a bit of room for the salad and green vegetables.

We got excused as soon as we finished the ice cream, and went up to Tammy's room, which is a corner one with a window at the front and one at the side—we had a great view in both directions. It was nearly eight, but still twilight. Cars kept coming until the street was lined with them. Somebody must have told some others, because more than ten people got out of the cars.

"Look," Tammy said. "Here comes Dame Pythia across the street with Mrs. Farrar."

"Wonder where Mr. Farrar is?" As president of the group, he certainly wouldn't be late for the séance.

Then I saw him. He was acting odd, furtive-like. He went out the back door of his house, and hurried on down the alley out of sight.

But in a few minutes Tammy said, "Here comes

Mr. Farrar now." He was coming from the direction of my house—or he could have gone beyond that to the Alstons', I thought. It was very peculiar, to say the least.

"Put on the records," I said. "The cars have stopped coming, and now that Mr. Farrar's here, the fun should begin."

Tammy put twelve records on, fairly loud, so they could be heard downstairs, but not loud enough for her mother to call and tell her to cut down the noise.

Then, holding our breaths and not making a sound, we crept down the stairs and shut ourselves into the hall closet. There was plenty of room, because since it was summer only raincoats were hanging there now.

What if Miranda were really able to "communicate" tonight—not through Dame Pythia and Kleeman, but in some other way? I felt chilly all of a sudden, in that stuffy, airless closet.

And Tammy—the girl who didn't believe in ghosts—whispered, "Lindsey, it's cold in here, isn't it?"

8

THE SEANCE

"I'm almost shivering," I whispered back. "How could it be cold in a stuffy closet on a hot night?"

"We've got to be imagining it," Tammy mumbled. "Let's take a look through the holes."

I spotted Dame Pythia at once. She was meeting all the members, and saying ordinary things to them, just as if she weren't a famous medium. Then Mr. Farrar said, "Well! Shall we get started?" Everybody found a chair and settled down, as close as they could decently get to the couch. Mrs. Farrar was fussing with the tape recorder, which was on a table at the end of the couch, where Dame Pythia's head would be. Mrs. Farrar must have been elected to get everything on tape, to check it out later.

Mr. Farrar made a little speech, about how lucky they were to have Dame Pythia with them, and thanked Dr. and Mrs. Greenfield for inviting the Society to have the séance at their house.

Dr. Greenfield said graciously, "We are most

interested. Now is there anything further we should do in preparation?"

"Well, we usually have only a dim light," Mr. Farrar said. "Discarnates seem to shun the brighter lights, and we want to attract as many of them as possible."

"Discarnates" was a new word to us, but I guessed it was another name for ghosts.

When Dr. Greenfield turned out all the lights but one, everybody stopped talking and looked at Dame Pythia. She was sitting on the edge of the couch, which made it sag.

"I have no idea," she said, "what we'll get to-night. Sometimes they come, from The Other Side, and then again they don't. If anything happens, it will happen because of you people, not because of me. It will be because there's someone Over There who wants to communicate with you. I can't bring them. Kleeman can't bring them. But if they come, Kleeman will put you in touch with them.

"Often what they say will seem trivial to you—but most conversations between the living are trivial, aren't they? Why should discarnates be different? And if the details seem not to be anything you can recognize, make a note of them and check it out later. You'll find there is often something in the conversation that will prove the entities on The Other Side still live, still remember the ones they loved while here.

"I will not be conscious, of course, of anything that happens while I am in the trance state; Kleeman takes over my body. Ask him any questions you wish. Remember, he can't bring anybody back; he can only describe the ones who are trying to get through to you. You will have to do the recognizing."

She tied a white silk scarf over her eyes, and stretched out on the couch, crossing her ankles. Then she seemed to fall asleep. There wasn't enough light for Tammy and me to see her too well, but enough to see her stomach in the psychedelic tunic rising and falling as she breathed.

There was a breathless hush, and I even heard the click as Mrs. Farrar turned on the tape recorder.

Then a man's heavy voice coming from Dame Pythia said, "Guten Abend. Goot eefning. I am Kleeman."

Nobody laughed. A lot of them said politely, "Good evening, Kleeman," just as if he were real. I was watching Miss Judith and Dr. Alston. Miss Judith had answered Kleeman, but neither Dr. Alston nor Dr. Greenfield spoke.

I won't try to do Kleeman's German accent—it sounded as if he were trying to clear his throat, and he turned sentences around so the last part came first. Once in a while, though, he forgot to use his accent. I wondered if any of the Society members noticed that. They were all too busy telling Kleeman the things he was fishing to find out.

"Someone there is here," he said, "trying to get across, someone whose name begins with J—"

"My brother Jack," one lady said eagerly. "Is it Jack?"

"Does anyone know a John?" Kleeman said. "I can't quite get it—it is something about an automobile accident—"

"I had a friend named Jim who was in an automobile accident," another lady said. "But I didn't know it killed him. Is it Jim? If it's Jim, ask him to tell me his dog's name. That would be something evidential."

"Ach, it is fading," Kleeman said regretfully. "Now comes a lady who was close to someone in this room."

Tammy nudged me, and we had a hard time keeping from exploding.

"Now a calendar I see—her first name has something to do with this calendar," Kleeman said solemnly. "The months are passing—one, two, three, four, five—here it stops."

"May!" one of the ladies cried. "Her name must have been May!"

Dr. Greenfield didn't say anything and neither did Mrs. Greenfield, which must have puzzled Dame Pythia considerably, since they were supposed to recognize her. Kleeman sounded disappointed. "This lady nobody recognizes?"

He changed the subject abruptly. "Comes now somebody named George. Does anybody know George?"

"If it's my great uncle George," a lady said hopefully, "he can tell me what kind of tree he planted at my house just before he died."

George didn't respond to that. Kleeman said, "Medicine it is about—too much medicine—he was a long time sick? Or maybe an overdose?"

"I don't know," the lady murmured uncertainly. "I'll check it out. Maybe it's evidential."

"Someone in the room," Kleeman said, "has a birthday in June?" Several people admitted it, but

Dr. Greenfield wasn't one of them. "Somebody comes for this gentleman—somebody with an M—" He wasn't going to give up on May, not knowing she wasn't really Dr. Greenfield's mother—whose name, I found out later, was Rebekah. Tammy and I smothered our giggles. One of the June ladies said, "I have a sister Mary—but she's still on the earth plane, as far as I know." She looked a little scared, as if May might have died in the past five minutes and this was how she was getting the news.

"A soldier comes," Kleeman went on. That was a pretty fair possibility—almost everybody knows of some soldier in the family who was killed in some war, and Kleeman hadn't said yet what kind of uniform the discarnate was wearing.

"What color is his hair?" Mrs. Farrar whispered. I remembered hearing Mama say that Mrs. Farrar's father had been killed in World War II, and I felt sorry for her. "If he has red hair, that would be evidential."

Kleeman was too cagey to make it red. "Not clear is his head. It might be a hat—or bandages—"

"He got a head wound!" Mrs. Farrar said. "Oh, it's Father! Oh, if only he could speak to me!" If she hadn't spoken up, I guess Kleeman would have put the bandage on the discarnate's leg or some other place, so somebody else would claim him.

Kleeman said, "He tells you he comes through as he died, so as to be recognized, but that Over

There is no pain felt. He has transcended his bodily ills. He says to tell you all is beautiful where he is, and do not be sad."

Mrs. Farrar murmured, "Thank you, Father— I'm so glad!" and I felt sorry for her again. Because she really is quite nice. It's just that we can't see how she can stand being married to Mr. Farrar. And somebody ought to explain to her about immortality so she wouldn't have to feed people like Dame Pythia in order not to have to worry about her poor father's soul, which is sure to be okay unless he was a murderer or something, and even then I'm not certain it wouldn't, because maybe it's not a murderer's fault if he's that way.

Kleeman brought in a few more very vague discarnates that some of the people thought might be evidential if they checked them out—one lady was going to ask her aunt if her mother had ever had a cat named Macbeth because if she had, that was surely her mother trying to get through.

And then Kleeman really got down to business. He began to sing, just a snatch of a Shakespeare song, and anything less like Ariel's voice would be hard to imagine. "—*doth suffer a sea-change into something rich and strange*—" he growled. I elbowed Tammy. We had *The Tempest* last year in English. "Miranda," she whispered back.

"Comes now a small child," Kleeman said. "Hovers near—trying to reach a lady in this room

—and a man. The name begins with N . . . or . . . I can't see clearly—it's misty there—no, it's M."

"Miranda!" Mrs. Farrar cried out, and then clapped her hand over her mouth. I can't believe she knew what they were up to. She reached over and patted Miss Judith's hand so kindly and sympathetically.

"Is it a—girl child?" Miss Judith asked faintly.

Dr. Alston on her other side said fiercely, "Wait, Judith! Don't say anything at all!"

Kleeman said solemnly, "I cannot tell. It is too cloudy there. But yes, she nods. You are both right. It is a little girl. She wants someone in this room to remember a—a little book, a little leather book—a present, a Christmas present—"

Mrs. Farrar said excitedly, "I remember! It *is* Miranda! I gave her a diary for Christmas—that last Christmas before—remember, Judith? I gave her the little blue leather diary. She told me she wrote in it every night."

Miss Judith said in a choked-with-tears voice, "I do remember. I thought of it when I found the other books in her desk, where she sat and wrote in the diary."

But Dr. Alston looked suspiciously at Mr. Farrar and said, "Do you remember it too, Mr. Farrar?" and Mr. Farrar said he didn't, but of course he did. That had to be how Kleeman found out.

I nudged Tammy and she whispered, "Sherry found it! That would explain lots of things." But did Miranda's ghost show Sherry where she hid the diary? Miss Judith hadn't found it in all those years.

Kleeman went on, "There is here someone who loved this child, who does not believe she comes back from The Other Side. For him she has this word which will mean nothing to any other person here. It is a strange word. I do not this word myself know. 'C-o-o-t.' Does it mean anything to anyone here?"

Dr. Alston gasped and leaped to his feet. "What *is* this?" he shouted. "Where did you get that?"

Kleeman was silent. Dame Pythia didn't stir.

"Do you know the word, Dr. Alston?" Mr. Farrar asked.

"William!" Miss Judith said. "Do you? Was it something you and Miranda knew? I never heard it myself. William, can it be—Miranda?"

"No!" Dr. Alston said firmly. "It's a pet name I called Miranda when she was a baby. You weren't living near us then, Judith. This is some kind of a trick. Miranda wouldn't have remembered the name; she was too small when I stopped using it."

"All is revealed when we get to The Other Side," Mr. Farrar said. "She would know it now. But nobody in this room knew it except you, Dr. Alston?"

Dr. Alston sat down again. "All right," he said grimly. "What else do you know?"

"She says," Kleeman grunted, "you to remind —something about a seashell with a name written on it and a silver knife with paint drippings from it —and an alligator's tooth."

Dr. Alston groaned, and put his head in his hands. Miss Judith said slowly, almost fearfully, "I remember you punished her once when I was there, when she was very small, for putting one of the good silver knives in a can of green paint. Oh, Miranda! My little Miranda! Is it you?"

It was clearly what they all thought "evidential." And Dr. Alston as clearly recognized the seashell and the alligator's tooth, too. Those weren't things that could happen to everybody, like automobile accidents.

I felt colder and colder.

Then Kleeman said, "The child tells about a bird. A bird—heavy—not to fly—made of something heavy—a bird with yellow eyes. An owl, that's it—"

Miss Judith gasped, "The owl! Oh, if she can tell me where to find the owl, that will really prove it's Miranda. Nobody knows where she hid it. She told me she didn't even write it down in her diary, because it was such a secret. Tell me, Miranda— you were going to tell me for my birthday, remember?"

Kleeman's voice said, "She is fading . . . she has to go . . . she must hurry to tell—she says to look under four bricks at the edge of—of the . . . Is there water? Lake or pond?"

"Yes!" Miss Judith said. "There's the pond. She might have been arranging those four bricks when she fell in! Oh, William, if it's there, if only it's there, we'll know!"

There was what the books call "an electric silence" in the room, while Dame Pythia's stomach rose and fell with her heavy breathing.

Then Tammy sneezed.

9

THE CLUE IN
THE DESK

Well, the sneeze didn't exactly break up the séance—I guess Kleeman was getting pretty tired of talking with that German accent anyhow. But Tammy's mother came looking for us when she heard the sneeze. Kleeman was saying, "Gute Nacht. Goot night," and everybody said, "Goodnight, Kleeman," and then Dame Pythia sat up heavily, creaking the couch, and said in her ordinary voice, "Did anything evidential happen?" As if she didn't know.

Then Mrs. Greenfield found us, and we had to go up to bed. We didn't even get any of the refreshments that we had planned to sneak upstairs before they got around to their coffee.

We had set Tammy's alarm clock for five, because we wanted to get up at daylight and go dig for the owl, and you couldn't very well do that in the dark. Even Miss Judith and Dr. Alston wouldn't be that foolish, we figured. But we were pretty sleepy, and could barely open our eyes, even with the alarm clock ringing its head off.

"Turn it off," Tammy mumbled. "Mother'll hear it."

"It's your clock," I said. But I did it, because it was on my side of the bed. I was more awake than Tammy; so it was my responsibility to get us up and not let us go back to sleep. "Come on, Tam," I said firmly. "On your feet. We've got to go and dig up the owl, remember? And then we'll know whether that was really Miranda who showed up last night."

She was pretty reluctant, but we both were wide awake after I washed my face and tried to wash hers and we had a scuffle over the washrag. Then we dressed in a hurry and tiptoed downstairs without waking her parents.

It was a foggy morning. Everything was so gray we could scarcely see. We went cautiously across my backyard—not making any noise because we didn't want the boys and Sherry to wake up and get in on the search—and stopped only a minute to say hello to Mrs. Brer and the babies. She was twitching her nose at us, and so was Brer over in his separate cage. We didn't stop to feed them— we were too excited about the cement owl. Just suppose we find it under those bricks, I thought— that means ghosts are real. My skin prickled.

We heard voices before we saw who was talking.

Dr. Alston and Miss Judith were just ahead of us, walking down to the pond—he was carrying a shovel. I pulled Tammy back, and she nodded. Maybe they oughtn't to know we were there. Maybe we ought to let them find the owl. After all, Miranda was their little ghost.

But we had to see what happened. So we followed, very quietly.

Dr. Alston was saying firmly, "Judith, we simply must keep this in mind: whatever it is at work here, it is not Miranda. Now you must stop believing it was Miranda. I am not convinced."

"You said you might be if anything evidential happened," she said plaintively, "and it did. You recognized things nobody knew but you—not even I knew about the pet name. I did know about the silver knife with the paint, and the seashell you brought her from the beach, and the alligator tooth she cut her teeth on, but Dame Pythia didn't. It's really evidential, William."

"Farrar remembered that his wife gave Miranda the diary. The medium used that for openers. And by the way, what became of the diary?"

"I've been trying to remember if I saw it, when I put her things away. I was still in shock then, you know. You said you didn't want to see any of them—and I didn't either. So I put all her clothes and toys and little things in a heavy pasteboard box and stored them in the attic. I can't remember

f I saw the diary then or not. I was just trying to
get through the task as well as I could, as quickly
as I could. It might be there."

"We'll look, after we find this cement owl under
these four mythical bricks."

"If the owl is there, William, you'll have to
admit we were really in touch with Miranda last
night," Miss Judith pleaded.

"If it is, I'll be very much surprised," Dr. Alston
said, as if he wasn't the least bit worried about
having to admit it.

But he had sounded a bit doubtful about those
other things, the things Miss Judith had called
'evidential." They weren't easy for any skeptic to
explain away.

Now they had reached the edge of the pond.
"We'll have to walk around it, I suppose," Dr.
Alston grumbled, "until we come to four bricks.
If we ever do."

"Be careful," Miss Judith said automatically.
Then she gave a little gasp. "Why, look, William!
There's some bricks! Old mossy ones. Four, if you
count nearly whole ones."

"And," Dr. Alston said with more excitement
than he had shown yet, "something was buried
under them. There's a hole. An empty hole. Dug
recently, not an old one."

Miss Judith was so disappointed she sat right

down on an old tree stump and started to cry. "Oh
William! Somebody took it. Now we'll never know."

Dr. Alston started digging in the empty hole,
but we could tell he didn't expect to find anything.
"No use," he said after awhile. "Somebody beat us
to it, all right. Now why would anybody—?"

"Nobody knew about it," Miss Judith wailed,
"except the people who were there last night, and
they all wanted us to get in touch with Miranda.
They all hoped it would check out and prove she
was really there. They wouldn't have stolen it."

"There's something very strange about this whole
thing," Dr. Alston said. "I'd like to talk to this
Dame Pythia when she's not in a trance."

"Oh, I'm afraid you can't, William. She was
catching an early plane. Mr. Farrar was going to
take her to the airport about four this morning.
He's probably back by now. She left her New York
address though, for you to get in touch with her
if you wanted her to try to communicate further
with Miranda. Do let her, William. She might
tell us who dug up the owl."

I could have made a pretty good guess at that
myself, if only there had been any way Sherry
could have known what went on at the séance.

"Well," Dr. Alston said, "come on, Judith. Let's
go and check the box in the attic, because if
there was a diary anywhere and Sherry found it,
some of the details she knew that bothered you

could be explained. The ones Dame Pythia knew, of course, are a little harder to account for."

"But Miranda told me she didn't write in the diary where she hid the owl with the golden eyes," Miss Judith reminded him, "because it was such a special secret. She wrote about how we made it, but not where she hid it."

"Let's look for the diary, anyway."

Tammy and I were already halfway up in the magnolia tree before they got as far as the summer house. We hoped they had left the attic windows open because of the heat, and sure enough, they had. We were snug and quiet in the branches next to that window long before Miss Judith and Dr. Alston had climbed the stairs. We could hear them open the door and fumble for the lights, and then we could hear them talking.

"Here's the box," Miss Judith said. "Why— William, it's been disturbed. It's not the way I left it, I'm sure. I always tape boxes shut a certain way. This one has had the tape broken and then stuck back together."

"It was so long ago, you might have done it yourself and then forgotten about it, if you found something else to put in after taping it. But it could have been Sherry, I guess. I'll ask her. If she says she didn't do it, what then? Judith, I confess I sometimes feel just—just helpless with Sherry.

It must be that I'm soft with her, because of Miranda. I let her get away with too much."

"I know how you feel," Miss Judith said. "I feel the same way. We ought to be firmer with her."

"Maybe Olivia can," Dr. Alston said.

"William, I tell you, we ought to tell Olivia about Miranda. Somehow I have a feeling that that's what Miranda wants—to be acknowledged. To have you tell Olivia and Sherry about your other little daughter. And have you carry her picture in your wallet along with Sherry's, and have me put her picture in the living room again. She might not be such a restless spirit, then."

"Now, Judith, you know Miranda is beyond wanting anything," Dr. Alston said sorrowfully. "Here, can you to bear to look through this box? I'll open it and we'll see if the diary is in it."

After a few minutes Miss Judith said, sounding as if she were crying, "I remember how she looked in that little flowered dress. Oh, William, I can't do it. Shut the box."

"There's no diary here," Dr. Alston said. "Did you look in the desk in her room—in the secret place in Mother's old desk?"

"Yes. There was only the note Sherry wrote, that nearly gave me heart failure. But of course, if Sherry found the diary, she hid it again. Very cleverly. We may never know whether she has been getting her knowledge from it, or from her 'make-believe sister.' "

"I'll try to make her tell me if she found the diary."

I could have told Sherry's father he wouldn't succeed. But he'd find that out. We saw the lights go out in the attic, and when we heard the door close, we rushed down out of the tree and went back to Tammy's for breakfast.

Dr. Greenfield was finishing his coffee, and he and Mrs. Greenfield had evidently decided to go easy on us for listening in on the séance the night before, because they smiled at us. Or maybe they were just finishing laughing. "Well, girls," he said, "after hearing the 'evidence,' do you have any more reason for believing the dead communicate with the living, than you had before?"

"Not exactly, sir," I said, "especially since Kleeman tried to fool you with some stuff Tammy told Dame Pythia about her grandma's name being May, and all that. But, Dr. Greenfield, somebody dug up the cement owl before we could check it out—before even Dr. Alston and Miss Judith could check it out." And while we ate about a dozen pancakes apiece we told him about the hole where the bricks had been.

"This is puzzling," he agreed. "If you find the answer, let me know."

"How about you, sir?" I asked. "Did you find

any evidence to prove anything about ghosts one way or the other? Do you think Miranda was there last night?"

"No," Dr. Greenfield said. "Candidly, Lindsey, I don't. But I'll be interested to hear what you girls turn up, about the explanation of all those 'evidential' bits that only Dr. Alston could have known about."

"If you were going to investigate it scientifically," I asked him, "how would you go about it?"

Dr. Greenfield lit his pipe and considered. "I suppose," he said thoughtfully, "assuming I believed the medium was a fraud, I'd try to find out where she could possibly have gotten the information which apparently no one but the victim knew."

Something had been bothering me in the back of my head, about that desk with the secret place in it, ever since Dr. Alston had mentioned it to Miss Judith, and it wasn't the diary or the note I was thinking about. Now, what Dr. Greenfield said somehow made things click into place. That "light bulb" you read about suddenly turned on, and I shouted, "Whee! I've got it! That's it! Tammy— Dr. Greenfield—I know now where Dame Pythia found out about the seashell and the alligator tooth and everything."

"Where?" Tammy demanded, but I said, "No time to explain now. We've got to hurry and catch Mr. Farrar before he leaves for his office. I've got to try my psychology trick on him and see if I'm right."

I grabbed Tammy and rushed her out, with her mouth still full of pancakes.

Dr. Greenfield said, "I think I'd better go with you." I didn't tell him not to, but I didn't wait for him, either.

10

THE OWL WITH
THE GOLDEN EYES

Mr. Farrar was just opening his garage when we got there, with Dr. Greenfield right behind us. Since it was a double garage, he had his workshop in there too, where he made things with all that stuff he was always getting from Greene's Hardware Store.

He was about to get into his car and drive off.

"Good morning, Mr. Farrar," I said.

"Morning." He wasn't too friendly, as usual.

"Did Dame Pythia catch the plane all right?" Dr. Greenfield said.

"Oh, she decided to stay another day and see if Dr. Alston wouldn't like to try another sitting. The results last night were spectacular—don't you agree, Dr. Greenfield?"

"I was—impressed," Dr. Greenfield said.

"I was, too, sir," I told Mr. Farrar innocently, "but we were wondering when you knew the first Mrs. Alston?"

He fell right in the trap, probably because he was impatient to get rid of me and get away.

"In New York. Why?"

"At the Psychic Society meeting, of course?" I said sweetly. "She was trying to get in touch with Miranda too? We knew from Miss Judith that Miranda's mother was interested in psychic things. Did she have a sitting with Dame Pythia? Did Kleeman tell her anything evidential?" I asked eagerly.

"Of course. But what's it to you, Lindsey? I'm in a hurry—if you'll excuse me, Dr. Greenfield," and he got into his car. Then he leaned across as he backed out, to say casually, "Oh, by the way, Doctor, have you heard if the Alstons found the owl?"

"It wasn't there," Dr. Greenfield said, watching him keenly. "They found the four bricks all right, but there was nothing under them."

"There had to be!" Mr. Farrar looked baffled.

"Why do you say that?" Dr. Greenfield asked interestedly. He didn't say someone else had taken the owl, and Tammy and I kept quiet. Anybody who was putting on Mr. Farrar had our blessing.

"Well—uh—Kleeman was so positive—and it was the one thing Miss Alston needed to convince her about her niece. Look, I really have got to get down to the office. We'll have another meeting tonight, if Dr. Alston wants to." And he drove off.

Dr. Greenfield strolled around the workshop part of the garage. "Hm. Copper sulphate. Wonder what he's been making."

"That's poison," Tammy said.

"I know, dear," her father said.

"Well?" I could hardly wait. "Don't you want to know, Tam, how I guessed about how Kleeman knew what to tell Dr. Alston?"

"Sure," Tammy said obligingly. "How'd you guess?"

"Well, after your father said what he did about finding out where Dame Pythia got the information that nobody could possibly know but the victim, it just came to me. It was simple. Who was the only other person who knew Miranda when she was a baby? And Miss Judith had said Miranda's mother was interested in psychic things. So naturally she might be trying to get in touch with her in The Other World, and might have met members of the Psychic Society at that convention in New York. And Mr. Farrar and Dame Pythia could have gone back and found out anything they wanted to know, by asking her questions while pretending to tell her things that came from Miranda. That was what I was trying to remember about the desk—it had the books in it, remember, that Miranda's mother had given her. Her mother was the clue to the whole thing."

"Dr. Alston will be glad to know there's a rational explanation," Dr. Greenfield said.

"But Miss Judith will be disappointed."

"And it was clever of you to get Mr. Farrar to admit he knew Miranda's mother, Lindsey."

"Any time," I said airily. "That trick always works. Even on Eddie."

"But," Tammy said, "the cement owl still isn't explained."

"It isn't even found."

We went back across the street. "I'd better check in at home," I said, "and let them know I'm still alive. And see what Sherry and Eddie and Kirk are up to. Want to come, Tammy?"

"Might as well."

"Shall I," said Dr. Greenfield, "tell the Alstons what you deduced, Lindsey? Or would you rather tell them yourself?"

"Oh, please, you tell them, sir. I hate to see how disappointed Miss Judith is going to be. But if only we could find the owl—you see, I have a theory, Dr. Greenfield, that maybe Miranda really is hanging around, although not bothering with Kleeman and Dame Pythia and Mr. Farrar. But maybe she stays close to Miss Judith, because she loves her. If I could come back after I die, I wouldn't haunt just any old strangers, and I wouldn't show up at séances like Dame Pythia's—I'd stick around close to the people I loved when I was alive. Maybe Miranda wants us to find the cement owl and show it to Miss Judith for her birthday, just like Miranda meant to do herself. And then maybe she could rest in peace."

"It's a fine theory," Dr. Greenfield said solemnly. "Let me know if you find anything to substantiate it. Well, I'll go tell the Alston's there's nothing to the 'evidential.'"

We saw the three kids down by the rabbit cages, and they turned around quickly when they saw us; so we knew they were up to something.

All at once I had an inspiration. Maybe the psychological trick would work in a slightly different form, on Sherry, too.

"Sherry," I said casually, "how did you know where to dig for the cement owl, last night?"

She opened her mouth to answer, and then caught herself and clammed up. But Eddie blurted out, "Miranda told her!"

"Yep," Kirk said.

So she did have it. Where had she hidden it? But—Miranda?

Sherry smiled confidingly then, glancing up from under those witch-bangs. "Yes. Of course. She told me where it was."

"You're putting us on," Tammy said flatly.

"Oh, no, Tammy. I wouldn't do that." Sherry was the picture of innocence.

"If you dug it up," I said, "where is it now?"

"Miranda doesn't want me to tell anybody. She wants me to wait and show it to Aunt Judith on her birthday."

Well, there it was. It still sounded as if Sherry really had been in communication with Miranda's ghost. And there was no real evidence that she had ever actually found Miranda's diary, although personally I felt absolutely certain she had. It was the only way she could have known most of the things she knew. But Miss Judith had said she was sure Miranda didn't tell in the diary where she had hidden the owl.

Sherry said, "I've got to go now."

Kirk and Eddie started to follow her, but I said sternly, "It's nearly lunch time. You two go inside and wash up," and they—for a wonder—obeyed me. But Sherry turned around and made a funny sign in the air with her arms, like crossing her heart in the air, and ended with her fingers on her lips, and Eddie and Kirk imitated it. I guess that meant they had sworn to keep her secrets. They kept looking at the rabbits and giggling; so I guessed the secrets had something to do with Brer and Mrs. Brer as well as with the cement owl.

I walked around to the front with Tammy as she was leaving, and we saw Dr. Alston and Dr. Greenfield come out of the Alstons' house, and Dr. Alston went striding over to the Farrars' looking furious—and then in a few minutes he came back and shook hands with Dr. Greenfield, and they each went on inside their own houses.

Tammy and I kept on watching the Farrars' to see what would happen, and sure enough, a taxi drove up and Dame Pythia rushed out of the house and got into it. That was the last we ever saw of Dame Pythia. Too bad. We don't get to see a medium perform her tricks every day. There never was a word of publicity in the papers about her giving a sitting for the famous scientist, Dr. Alston, either. She was an awful fake. But still, I'd like to see a true medium sometime—one of those who really are honestly psychic. I'd like to go to a séance that's for real, not phony.

After lunch Tammy came over, and we were walking out into the backyard when Eddie said for no good reason, "You girls mustn't bother Brer."

"Well, that's a new one," I said, and Tammy added, "Who's bothering your old rabbit?"

"Wait a minute," I said. "Why not, Eddie? Brer kind of likes to be taken out of his cage and petted. Not that I have time to pet any rabbits today."

Eddie—too late—saw that he had made me suspicious, and tried to change the subject. "I think I'll train Eight for a house-rabbit," he said quickly. "It ought to be pretty easy to housebreak a rabbit, huh, Lin? Easier than a puppy. Will you help me? Will you ask Mama to let me have Eight for

133

a house-rabbit, please, Lin?" When Eddie looks at you with those soulful blue eyes of his, it's hard not to promise him anything. But I resisted. If there's anything we don't need while Mama's pregnant, it's the job of housebreaking a rabbit.

"Never mind about Eight," I said. "It's Brer we were talking about. Why don't you want us to bother him?"

"Well, because he's a new father," Eddie said after thinking awhile. "New fathers get disturbed pretty easy. I wouldn't want him disturbed."

"Don't worry—we wouldn't think of disturbing him," I said, giving Tammy a significant pressure on the arm as we walked away around the corner of the house. "That is, not until they've gone over to the Alstons' and out of sight of the cages," I told her. "Then we'll see what it is they've got hidden in Brer's cage!"

It seemed as though they would never go. They had to clean the cages and put fresh hay in—lots of fresh hay, much more than usual. We were watching from behind the hydrangea bushes at the corner of the house. "See, they're hiding something in there, behind all that hay," I guessed. Then they had to fill the water pans and get some lettuce leaves from Mama for the rabbits' lunch, and pet each one individually, and clean up the old hay they had spilled on the ground.

But at last the boys started over to Sherry's. As

soon as we saw her let them in the door, we hurried over to the cages.

We could hardly see Brer at all, for the piles of hay they had put in there with him. But I held him, with one hand soothingly on his back, while I scrambled in the hay with the other hand, and Tammy felt around with both hers.

"Feel anything?" I asked.

"Only hay." Tammy sneezed.

"I believe I do!" Yes, it was something that didn't belong in the corner of a rabbit cage. Something hard and heavy, like a rock. Like a cement owl.

"Here it is, Tammy!"

I pulled it out. It looked more like a lump of cement than anything else, but it definitely had golden eyes—the yellow glass marbles—and there were feathered wings outlined with a nail or something before the cement hardened, the way the boys had told us it was made. And you could see the owl-shaped head and curved beak, if you knew what to look for.

Both of us looked eagerly into the golden eyes. How did Miranda put love in its eyes?

As far as we could see, there wasn't any. They were just yellow glass marbles.

Tammy said, "What did she mean, love in its eyes?"

"I don't know. But—" I said slowly, "do you

135

suppose she meant—you know, what's the word
—figuratively speaking? Not actually? Could she
have meant because she loved Miss Judith and
Miss Judith loved her, the owl they made would
have love in its eyes whenever either of them
looked at it?"

"We'll have to ask Miss Judith."

"But we don't want her to see the owl till her
birthday, do we?"

"Well, hide it again, so Sherry won't know we
found it." We tucked it back in the straw, and
then ran over to Alstons'. By that time Sherry and

136

the boys were out in the yard; so we went in to see Miss Judith.

She was in her room, and called to us to come on up. She looked as if she had been crying. Miss Judith is the only lady we know who always looks dignified even after she's been crying.

"We're sorry Dame Pythia was a fraud, Miss Judith," I said. "But you know, we still might find the owl for you. Miranda still might be around. Just because they used some phony stuff trying to fool Dr. Alston doesn't necessarily mean that something real might not have come through from Miranda's spirit anyhow, in spite of them. Maybe the owl was really buried there."

Tammy said, "Miss Judith, please tell us how that owl had love in its eyes? Was it just the kind only you and Miranda could see—the figurative kind—or could anybody see it? Could Lindsey and I see it—if we found the owl?"

"Have you found it?" Miss Judith asked excitedly.

"Not exactly," I said cautiously. "But we need to know about the love in its eyes, in case we should run across a cement owl."

"Well, I'll tell you. Yes, it really was love—the word 'love' was scratched in very small letters with a stylus in the wet cement in each eye socket, and filled in with green paint so the letters would show up, before we put the clear yellow glass marbles in. We put the marbles in very carefully so the letters wouldn't blur, and the paint had dried quicker than the cement. That was still wet; so the marbles stuck all right. It looked wonderful."

I looked at Tammy, and Tammy looked at me. We both said at the same time, "It's the wrong owl!"

11

THE GHOST
RIDES AWAY

"The question is, does Sherry know it's the wrong one?" Tammy said.

"I don't think she does."

"If she does, that means she's putting us on, about Miranda telling her to dig there."

"But if she doesn't know it's the wrong one," I said, "how did she know where to dig at all? For that matter, even if she does know it's the wrong one, how'd she know it was *there?*"

"What are you two talking about?" Miss Judith asked.

"Miss Judith, just trust us," I said earnestly. "All we know is, Sherry dug up the owl that was buried on the bank of the pond. But we think it's the wrong owl. As far as we could tell, it doesn't have love in its eyes. Of course," I said thoughtfully, "we ought to take another look. Not knowing exactly what to look for, we might have missed it. There might have been dirt over the letters or something. Now that we know, we can tell in a minute."

"Where is it?" Miss Judith said. "I could tell at a glance."

"Miranda wanted you to see it on your birthday," I told her. "We thought we might be able to find it and surprise you by showing you where she hid it, on your birthday, and then her Unquiet Spirit could rest. If that's what she wants. Wouldn't you rather wait, in case we do find the real owl?"

Miss Judith surprised us. "No," she said. "If you find the real one, I'd like to have it at once. Because that's not what Miranda wants—if she wants anything. She wants to be recognized, that's all. She wants her father to be proud to say, 'I once had another dear little girl; her name was Miranda.' If you bring me the real owl, I'll put it on the mantel with her picture, and tell everybody that Miranda and I made the owl. It may not have any effect on Miranda's spirit, but I know it'll make me feel a whole lot less guilty."

"But what about Sherry?" I said, and then wished I hadn't.

"What do you mean, child? What about Sherry?"

"Well, we have a theory that maybe Sherry's jealous of Miranda. If somehow she found out—or just guessed—how you loved Miranda, she might think your teaching her to knit isn't as good as teaching Miranda to make a blue rose or a cement owl. Sherry might be feeling sort of left out too." I wasn't saying it very well, but Miss Judith got the message. She looked troubled.

"I see," she murmured, half to herself. "The poor wistful child. I've been unfair to her, too. How could I?"

"Well," Tammy said briskly to me, because it felt awkward to look at Miss Judith right then, the way she was feeling, "let's try to find out how Sherry knew where to dig, and take another look at that owl, and if it's not the real one—I'm pretty sure it's not—then we must find the real one. We've got our work cut out for us."

"Bring me the one Sherry dug up," Miss Judith said.

"We didn't want her to know yet that we found it."

"Why didn't we?" Tammy asked me.

"I don't know exactly," I admitted frankly. "It just seemed like it might be a kind of psychological advantage."

That reminded me of my psychological trick, and I said, "Maybe it'll work on Eddie again—the trap. He might give something away. If we can get him alone—without Sherry, I mean. Good-bye, Miss Judith. We'll let you know what happens."

Luck was with us. Eddie and Kirk were in their room, and Sherry wasn't with them. "Where's Sherry?" I asked.

"She's gone to ask her Dad again to get her a

horse for her birthday. She thinks he might slip up and promise while her mother's away. She'll be back in a few minutes."

We hung around, tickling Kirk and rough-housing with him a little, until Eddie was lying on his stomach on the floor, absorbed in a comic book. I've noticed that when he's doing something like reading a comic book, he sometimes answers a question automatically without thinking exactly what he's saying, but he answers right. It comes out of his subconscious mind, Tammy says. So I asked him, very casually, "Eddie, was it before or after Miranda told her where to dig for the cement owl that Sherry actually found out where it was?"

He answered absent-mindedly, without looking up from Captain Astro, "Before. We didn't know what it was, though, that we saw Mr. Farrar burying there, till Miranda told her."

"You haven't brushed your teeth since lunch," I said, to leave him something else in his subconscious mind to remember that we talked about, and Tammy and I left very quietly, so as not to disturb him. In the hall after we shut the door we hugged each other in silent congratulation, and then rushed down the stairs and outside.

"Mr. Farrar!" I exclaimed. "We might have known. But how—?"

"Remember the day he came by when we were hunting for the owl and the boys told him how it was made?" Tammy said. "He was very much interested in all the details."

"Let's go tell your father," I said. "Even with Dame Pythia out, he'll want to know about Mr. Farrar making a fake owl and burying it."

Dr. Greenfield listened, nodding. "What did it look like? Very old? Or as if it had just been made?"

"Oh, it looked old, all right. It might have been buried for years. All green and moldy, with dirt clinging to it," I said. "Of course, the hole by the pond was pretty muddy—red clay mud."

"That's what he was doing with the copper sulphate," Dr. Greenfield said. "It would give a greenish-blue tinge to the cement, and if he mixed it with red clay or dirt or old green moss and rubbed it in before it was quite dry—yes, it could look old, all right."

"And remember, Tammy, before the séance we saw Mr. Farrar going out the back way toward Alstons' and then coming back the front way. Just before all the people arrived. I bet that was when he went to bury it, knowing the Alstons were already here, and probably thinking Sherry was at our house. But the kids were watching him and went right behind him and dug it up."

"But you say he didn't get the eyes right?" Dr. Greenfield asked.

"That's what we've got to be sure of," Tammy said. "We're going to take another look, now. Of course he didn't know about love in its eyes. And it wasn't in the diary, I suppose. Sherry might or might not have the diary—I guess we'll never know. But anyhow, she doesn't know about the eyes either, whether she has it or not. So she doesn't recognize that it's the wrong owl. And Miranda's ghost never told her where to dig. She must have just told Eddie and Kirk afterward that Miranda said so."

I hated to give up our ghost, though it did sound improbable. "But still, if Sherry doesn't have the diary she must really have been in communication with Miranda about some of those other things. And if by any chance she does turn out to know about the right owl with love in its eyes, then she must have found out from Miranda."

"Let me know," Dr. Greenfield said.

"She does have the diary somewhere," Tammy said with conviction. "She might even be keeping it with her all the time—that's why we can't find it. Sometimes I've seen her putting her hand against her belt—you know, the way you'd do if you were being sure something you had underneath there was secure."

"That would explain it," I admitted. "But we don't know for sure. And she might be smart enough to destroy it, so we never would know."

"Then there's the chance she might find the right owl purely by accident," Tammy said.

We reconnoitered. The coast was clear—the kids weren't at the rabbit cages, but we couldn't spot them anywhere else either. We should have known better than to count on their not seeing us. Just as I pulled the owl out of Brer's cage, and started to rub the dust off its glass eyes, Sherry came tearing around the corner of the house, with the boys panting after her.

"Quick, Tammy!" I said. "Do you see any love?" I held it out and we both looked, but couldn't see anything except cement behind the dingy yellow glass.

Then Sherry swooped in like a whirlwind. "Give me that owl!" she shouted. "Don't you dare take it! I'm the one who's going to give it to Aunt Judith for her birthday, so she'll—" She snatched it out of my hand and ran, and I couldn't tell if she was sobbing or laughing.

Tammy and I ran after her, even though we knew now it was the wrong owl, because you can't let a smaller child think she has gotten the best of you. Especially, you can't let your kid brothers think some younger girl can get the best of their older sister, or you'd never have any control over them again.

Sherry could really run! And when she got to the big old magnolia tree, she proved she could climb, too. She was going up so fast we couldn't catch her, though we're fast climbers, and Tammy and I were afraid she would wiggle onto the roof and into the window of her own room where we'd never get her.

Evidently she didn't think of that. She went right on past her window, on up high, just above the attic window. Even from where we were, the ground seemed so far away that I felt dizzy. I said, "Tammy, what if she should fall? It would be our fault."

"You mean for chasing her? Yes, I guess we'd better not make her go any higher," Tammy agreed, after she looked down too, and tightened her grip around the big trunk of the tree. It was good to have something solid to hold onto. Sometimes where the limbs joined the trunk there were holes you could catch your fingers into—holes that squirrels or woodpeckers had used for nests.

"Look, Sherry," I called, "stop climbing. You're going too high. Stop climbing!"

"You can't make me!" Sherry called back. "This is my tree now. It used to be hers. She climbed as high as she wanted to, and I can go higher than she could. I've been up this high lots of times. So have Eddie and Kirk." I made a mental note to tell Dad about that, though it was probably a big fat lie.

"Why don't you level with us, Sherry?" Tammy said reasonably. "You know you're just pretending about Miranda, but you've got Miss Judith all worried. You don't mean to hurt Miss Judith, do you? She loves you."

There was a silence. Then Sherry said, "Not as much as she loved Miranda."

"Yes, she does," I said. "It's just different. Nobody loves two people exactly the same way. Think it through, Sherry; you don't love your mother exactly the same way you do your father, do you? But you wouldn't say you love one of them the most, would you? You love them differently. That's the way it is with Miss Judith about you and Miranda."

Sherry didn't answer, but I hoped I'd gotten through to her—that she was thinking it over. I went on trying to persuade her. "Come on down, now, before one of us falls and gets hurt. Okay?"

"You won't try to get this owl away from me?"

"No. We don't want that old owl. It's the wrong owl, anyhow—don't you know that?"

She looked down at us suspiciously. She was astride a big leafy limb just above us, as if she were riding Nightmare. The sun made lights and shadows all around us in a sort of shiny-dark-green, black-and-white world. Sherry had the owl in her hand; all that time she had been climbing with one hand, and was still holding on with it, and when I looked down at the ground I shuddered. It really was a terribly tall tree—taller than the two-story-and-attic house.

Now Sherry looked at the owl suspiciously, as if she could see by looking, why it was the wrong one. Then she decided we wouldn't have said it without a good reason, so she went along with what we'd said. "I know it's the wrong one. Miranda told me." She flung it to the ground, and I screamed, "Look out!" in case Eddie or Kirk had happened to be standing there. The owl made a *Chunk* sound as it hit the ground.

"She told me where the right one is, too," Sherry said, in a different sort of voice.

Tammy and I both saw it just as she said that.

There was a squirrel hole almost at Sherry's back, where another limb branched out, but she could see into it when she turned her head. And we could see into it when we looked up at a certain angle. It was simply a round hole, just big enough to form a perfect niche. For a cement owl. With golden eyes.

It was there. I thought for a minute I was imagining it, but no. It was really there. Tammy said, "Look!" in an awed sort of voice. Miranda must have meant for Miss Judith to look out the attic window and see the surprise—Miss Judith could never have climbed that tree, not even thirteen years ago when she was younger.

"Sherry," I said excitedly, "does that one have love in its eyes?"

Did she hesitate a minute? Did she look before she answered? We couldn't tell. But she said, "Yes."

"Then it's the right one."

We stared up at her, and she looked back at us, defying us to touch it. She even let go of the limb and folded her arms and looked down at us with

her chin out, like an arrogant little imp. I wondered how to handle her psychologically.

"Sherry," I said persuasively, "why don't you take that owl, the one Miranda made, and give it to Miss Judith? We don't want it, but Miss Judith does. And she'd love you more than anything in the world if you brought it to her."

"More than she loved Miranda?"

"Differently," I said firmly.

Sherry went back to her fantasy bit. "Miranda wants me to show it to Aunt Judith on her birthday."

"But your Aunt Judith wants it now. She told us so. She doesn't want to wait till her birthday. You can tell her it's an advance birthday present. From you."

Sherry said slowly, "I guess—I will, then."

So we all came down from the tree, and Tammy and I went home, and left Sherry to make up to Miss Judith.

After supper, when we went back over there, Miss Judith had Sherry's picture on one end of the living room mantel and Miranda's on the other, and the owl in the middle. And I thought Dr. Alston looked happier than I'd ever seen him, sitting there holding Mrs. Alston's hand. Instead of the usual lamps, there were lighted candles in the sconces, just like a party.

Miss Judith told us, "Girls, here's the owl my niece Miranda made, with love in its eyes. My dear little niece Sherry found it and gave it to me, for a birthday present." And she smiled at Sherry, and Sherry snuggled up to her, and I could guess who might get a horse for her birthday, if Miss Judith could manage it.

The candlelight left the corners of the room dim, and I felt sort of shivery-happy, as if Miranda had come to the party too. But I couldn't see anything except shadows, hovering around the edges. I was asking silently, Is there—anybody—there? It was no use to listen for *The Dance of the Fireflies* because the piano was right in the room with us, and it was shut.

I wondered why I felt so curiously on the edge of expecting something else to happen, something mysterious and—and about Miranda. But not really sad because she wasn't any longer a girl like us. Just—well, like Shakespeare said, what had happened to Miranda was just *a sea-change into something rich and strange*.

There was nobody else in the house; there couldn't have been. We were all in the livingroom—but I thought I heard something, and felt a little breeze go past me, light and cool.

And it must have blown through the hall, too, because I heard a door softly and finally closing.

And I thought I heard a horse's hoofs, very far off, and then fading out to silence.

But of course it was just my imagination. It had

to be. Tammy said later that she hadn't noticed anything at all.

Miss Judith was waiting for us to admire the owl. So we did. And I winked at Sherry, but she didn't wink back. Then I saw that she was crying.

"Why, what's the matter, Sherry?" Miss Judith said, and she hugged Sherry, with a lot of love in the hug. "What are you crying about?"

"Oh, Aunt Judith," Sherry sniffled, "she's gone away and I'll never see her again. She said so. She rode away on Nightmare and she's never coming back."

The Alstons have gone back to Houston now, and Miss Judith goes to the Garden Club instead of the Psychic Society, and Sherry writes to Eddie once in a while and he answers. The other day when we were all talking, Tammy said, "Well, I think she made it all up, after she found the diary. I don't believe she ever saw Miranda at all."

Eddie said loyally, "I do. I believe she could see Miranda, even if we couldn't."

"Yep," Kirk said.

Tammy said, "What do you think, Lindsey? Was there a ghost next door?"

All I could say was, "I don't know."

Because I really don't.